Greek Society

To my wife, Mandy

Address editorial correspondence to:

D. C. Heath
125 Spring Street
Lexington, MA 02173

Acquisitions Editor: James Miller
Production Editor: Jennifer Brett
Production Coordinator: Chuck Dutton
Photo Researcher: Billie Ingram
Text Permissions Editor: Margaret Roll

Cover photograph: Two girls playing with knucklebones. Terra-cotta, 340–330 B.C. (*Ronald Sheridan's Photo-Library*)
Cover design: Dustin Graphics

Published simultaneously in Canada.

Printed in the United States of America.

International Standard Book Number: 0–669–24499–6

Library of Congress Catalog Number: 90–85302

Preface

The first edition of *Greek Society* appeared twenty years ago. Rather than feeling personally flattered by the book's longevity, I attribute its continuing popularity primarily to the subject matter: the eternally fascinating society and culture of the Greek people during the approximately twenty centuries from the Bronze Age to the fall of the Roman Empire in the West. It is the Greeks' achievement that will keep drawing students back to the story of Greek origins, Greek history, and eventual Greek cultural domination of the ancient Mediterranean world.

When I wrote the preface to the first edition of this book I felt compelled to explain, almost apologetically, that I did not intend to write just one more political and military chronicle of Greek history. Instead, I wished to describe the lives of the ordinary Greek people in their cities and farms; and, with a few exceptions, I kept to this plan, sketching the environment, explaining typical Greek attitudes and behavior through anecdotes, trying to make the reader feel like a spectator of events in an exciting and creative society. Since that time, most college textbooks have increased their emphasis on social and cultural developments in all periods of history. I no longer feel that I have to explain why I follow the career of the Greek people far down into Roman times or why I pass over most military history in silence. (Actually, in this edition I have relented to the extent of adding a section on the conquests of Alexander the Great.)

I have kept intact the chapters in which, instead of dealing with Greeks en masse, I take certain interesting and representative individuals and show them at work (or play). The career of one person often brings the whole history of the age into more dramatic relief, and such treatment is more in accord with the philosophy of the Greeks themselves, who have always clung stubbornly to the belief that the individual is more important than any abstract concept of the state.

Greek Society continues to be based, for the most part, on study of the primary sources: Greek and Latin writers and evidence uncovered by archaeology. At the end of each chapter I have indicated briefly which ancient and modern writers contribute most to an understanding of the period or subject in question. I have been both selective and arbitrary in listing the works of modern scholars; the titles that appear have either been very helpful to me or will provide both comprehensive treatment and full bibliographical references to anyone who wishes to investigate further.

One recent work I mention here if only to dispose of it. In *Black Athena* (Rutgers University Press, 1987), Martin Bernal has claimed that modern scholars have overemphasized the "European model" (i.e., the white and "Aryan" aspects) of Greek culture at the expense of the Semitic and Egyptian influences that shaped that culture. But the controversy Bernal attempts to create is irrelevant. The Greeks insisted on being influenced by every culture with which they came in contact. What they created from all these influences, however, was an entirely *Greek* culture—not "European" or "Afroasian" or anything else. I urge readers to examine closely the argument of *Black Athena*, together with the picture of Greek society I have tried to draw, and make up their own minds.

Since the third edition of this book appeared in 1987, I have continued to invite suggestions from colleagues, friends, and the ultimate critics—my students—as to how the work might be improved, expanded, or in some cases corrected to remove misleading or inaccurate impressions. In this edition I have adopted most of these suggestions and have also revised some sections simply because archaeology in the Greek world continues every day to modify our picture of the development of Greek society, particularly in the earlier periods.

I am grateful to D. C. Heath for this opportunity to revise and improve *Greek Society*. Many thanks to the reviewers of the manuscript—A. R. Littlewood, University of Western Ontario; Charles Murison, University of Western Ontario; and Josiah Ober, Princeton University—for their suggestions and corrections.

F. J. F.

Contents

Chronology

Date	Historical Developments	Cultural and Intellectual Landmarks
ca. 1700–1100 B.C.	Mycenaean civilization arose on the Greek mainland, spreading to Crete and Asia Minor.	Palace architecture, cultural and economic uniformity. An early form of the Greek language was used for keeping records.
ca. 1225	The Trojan War.	
ca. 1100–800	Mycenaean civilization disappeared. The Greek communities were reduced to scattered and isolated rural settlements.	Protogeometric pottery ca. 1025–900. The first iron tools and weapons appeared.
ca. 800–700	Overseas trade revived. The first colonies were established in Sicily and south Italy.	Geometric pottery ca. 900–700. Literacy was rediscovered. Homer and Hesiod composed their poems.
ca. 700–550	The great age of colonization also saw the beginnings of organized governments, law codes, constitutions.	Orientalizing (Corinthian) pottery. Lyric poets flourished. Philosophers began to speculate about the nature of the universe.
550–500	The Persian Empire expanded to dominate the Greeks of Asia Minor. Athens grew to prominence while Sparta was dominant in the Peloponnesus.	Athenian black figure pottery rivaled Corinthian. Temple architecture and sculpture advanced rapidly all over the Greek world.
490–479	The Persians attacked the Greeks, who won great victories at Marathon (490), Salamis (480), and Plataea (479).	Aeschylus began to produce tragedies. Athenian red figure pottery became standard.
476–431	The Athenians created an empire which was resented by other Greeks. Pericles was politically dominant at Athens ca. 454–429.	Tragic drama was produced by Sophocles and Euripides. The Sophists began to teach. The Parthenon and other buildings were built.
431–405	The Peloponnesian War between Athens, Sparta and their allies led to total defeat of Athens and installation of a pro-Spartan tyranny.	Socrates began to teach. Aristophanes produced comedies. Histories were written by Herodotus (ca. 425) and Thucydides (ca. 404).
403	The Athenian democracy was restored.	
396–356	Athens, Sparta, and Thebes competed for leadership unsuccessfully while Persia recovered the Greek cities of Asia Minor.	Plato founded the Academy, taught the Socratic path to virtue. Xenophon wrote his history, the Hellenica. Political rhetoric became a fine art.
356–338	King Philip of Macedon rose to power in the North and eventually defeated Athens and Thebes at the battle of Chaeronea (338).	Aristotle left the Academy to found his own school, then was hired by Philip to tutor the young Alexander.

336–323	Philip was assassinated. Alexander (356–323) invaded Persia (battle of Gaugamela, 331) and conquered the East as far as northwest India before dying in Babylon.	Alexandria was founded. Aristotle and Demosthenes both died in 322.
322–272	Alexander's generals fought over his empire, finally creating the three Hellenistic kingdoms of Egypt, Syria, and Macedon.	The Alexandrian Library was founded. Zeno and Epicurus created the Stoic and Epicurean philosophies. Many Greeks emigrated to Egypt and the Middle East.
272–146	The zenith of Hellenistic civilization. The Aetolian and Achaean leagues rose. Cleomenes led the Spartans to revolution 229–222. The Romans began to intervene in 200, finally conquering Greece and Macedon in 146.	Great age of scientific research in Alexandria and elsewhere saw Euclid's geometry, Archimedes' inventions; Eratosthenes measured the circumference of the earth. Polybius wrote his *History*, tracing the rise of Rome and decline of Greek independence.
146–30	The Romans completed the conquest of the Hellenistic world, converting it all to Roman provinces.	Greek philosophy and culture began to dominate Rome.
31 B.C.–A.D. 181	The PAX ROMANA. Zenith of Graeco-Roman culture.	
330–1453	Survival of the Eastern Roman, or Byzantine Empire, ended with the capture of Constantinople by the Turks.	Much classical Greek literature was preserved and copied in monasteries.
1453–1821	The Greek world languished under Turkish rule.	The Western world rediscovered Greek literature during the Italian Renaissance.
1821–1831	The Greek War of Independence expelled the hated Turks.	

1 The Mycenaean Prologue

ABOUT 2,000 years before the Christian era, wandering tribes began to descend into the southern part of the Balkan Peninsula. There they found an indigenous population the origins and antiquity of which is impossible to guess. It would be misleading to call the invaders Greeks because we know nothing about their language or culture. One can only say that over the next four centuries their relationship with the local inhabitants produced a stable mixture of peoples with a language and a culture that would one day be Greek. By the beginning of the seventeenth century B.C., we can trace the rise of the first great civilization that can properly be identified as Greek, although it was called Achaean by Homer and Mycenaean by modern convention: a network of princely citadels surrounded by the fields and villages of farmers and craftsmen.

About 1600 B.C. or so, the Mycenaean power expanded to include the island of Crete, where the non-Greek Minoans had created an elegant and wealthy civilization. The Mycenaeans evidently destroyed the Minoan capital of Knossos, occupied and rebuilt it, and remained as stewards of the surrounding area for the next four centuries. By 1300, Mycenaean culture had spread to the shores of Asia Minor and westward to Italy. But a major war against Troy, about 1200 or earlier, dangerously drained the power of the Mycenaeans. A century later that civilization lay in ruins, while a far more primitive population of Greeks took over the fields and flocks, but not the palaces. There, only the wind moaned in the ruined battlements, lizards scampered in the great audience halls, and in the counting rooms spiders wove their webs. It would be another three centuries before an urban society of any complexity reappeared on the shores of the Aegean Sea.

The evidence for Mycenaean society is threefold: the ancient legends, archaeological excavation, and actual written records. The traditional tales were never forgotten and were preserved by Homer, the poets, and later compilers of mythology. These legends describe the founding of the great Mycenaean states by sons and grandsons of the gods, the great deeds of these heroes, and finally, the culmination of Mycenaean military adventures in the grand, tragic war of the Greeks against the Trojans. But legends preserved by oral tradition and folk memory can be confusing and contradictory. An inevitable element of the supernatural and the miraculous in every legend also makes it easy for the skeptical to condemn the entire tradition. Therefore, as little as a hundred years ago, in an era when scientific method was beginning to be demanded of history, classical scholars treated the Greek myths only as a contribution to world folk literature.

One person went to the opposite extreme. Heinrich Schliemann (1822–1890), a brilliant and wealthy German merchant, had been so captivated in his youth by Homer's account of the Trojan War that he resolved to find the actual site of Troy, long forgotten to the world. In 1870, believing that every word of Homer could be taken literally, Schliemann started to dig at Hissarlik, in the northwestern corner of Turkey. Almost immediately, he came upon massive fortifications, one level of which had been destroyed in a vast conflagration. Despite Schliemann's crude methods and overly romantic interpretation of the evidence uncovered, when he left Troy three years later he had laid the groundwork for Greek archaeology. Few scholars would now deny that there was a Troy and that Schliemann had found it.

Crossing to the Greek mainland, Heinrich Schliemann began to excavate the great Mycenaean palaces, most of which were far better preserved than the city of the Trojans. His work, carried on by generation after generation of modern archaeologists, has demonstrated to the world that the Greek legends contain a considerable nucleus of accurate historical data. Some of the palaces of the Achaeans (as Homer called them) are where Homer said they were. Mycenaean cemeteries proved to contain a race of warrior nobles such as those described in the Greek epic tradition. And the uniformity of the pottery and other hardware found in graves and in the ruins of the citadels showed conclusively that Mycenaean society was the product of a civilization unified culturally and economically, as the tradition suggested.

By the 1930s, archaeology had revealed a whole new world to historians of ancient Greece, who had once been content to scoff at myths and confine their research to libraries whole continents away from the shores of the Aegean. One thing only was lacking to provide better understanding of Mycenaean society and to confirm for once and for all that the Mycenaeans were the real ancestors of the Greeks: literary documents of some kind.

In 1939, the American archaeologist Carl Blegen located the ruined and forgotten palace of King Nestor of Pylos, known to all readers of the *Iliad* for his wise (and often lengthy) counsel. Almost the first day of work, the excavators came across thousands of clay tablets inscribed with a peculiar syllabic script and baked in the conflagration that had destroyed the palace. Similar tablets had been found many years previously in the great Minoan palace at Knossos, and it had been taken for granted that they were written in the unknown Minoan language. Now here was a far greater number, preserved in the archive rooms of a society that Blegen, for one, was convinced was Greek. The Second World War intervened to delay publication and study of the tablets, but in 1953, a brilliant young English architect named Michael Ventris deciphered the script and demonstrated to the world that the language was in fact an archaic form of Greek, written in a script borrowed from the Minoans (as the Greeks were later to borrow the Phoenician alphabet).

The tablets are records from the Mycenaean archives, and similar ones have subsequently been found at Mycenae and Thebes. Because of their nature they are often difficult to interpret, being no more than the accounts and receipts of royal accountants. But despite the difficulties and sometimes bitter controversy that surrounds the tablets and their use, they have provided a vitally important link in the network of evidence for the workings of Mycenaean society.

The Mycenaean Environment

In the so-called Catalogue of Ships, in the second book of the *Iliad*, epic tradition has preserved the names of all the cities and towns that sent troops and ships to the Trojan War. The reader might assume the task of the archaeologist to be a simple one: locate these towns and start digging. But discovery is not that easy; a great deal of effort has been expended in finding even some of the most famous of the Mycenaean citadels. The Catalogue, therefore, has proved most useful only in indicating the main regions of Mycenaean settlement and in suggesting the relative population of these areas.

The region of Thessaly was the land of Jason, Achilles, and many another hero, but so far, only the citadel at Iolchos has been identified with certainty, on the Gulf of Pagasae in central Greece. It was evidently from this secure harbor that Mycenaean influence spread northward into the broad plains of Thessaly, rich in wild grasses and famed later on for superb cavalry. But exploration and excavation have hardly begun in Thessaly. Much more solid archaeological evidence is needed before scholars can even start to test the rich body of tradition about this wild land on the northern borders of the Mycenaean world.

South of Thessaly is the broad and fertile valley of Boeotia, ringed with mountains and dominated by the citadels of Orchomenos, Gla, and Thebes, home of the unfortunate Oedipus and his unhappy family. Excavation and surface exploration have proved what the numbers and names from the Catalogue would seem to indicate: that the well-watered

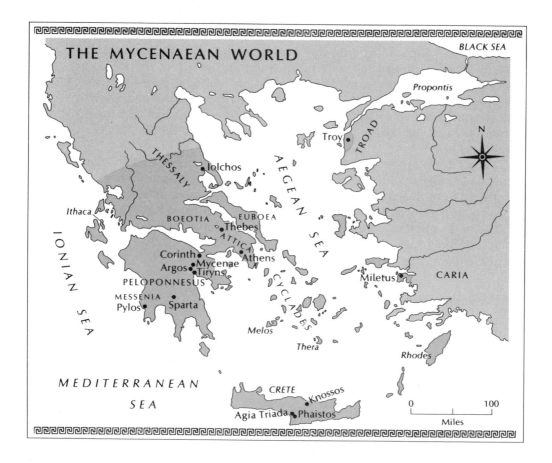

fields around Lake Copais satisfied the needs of a large population residing in many small settlements surrounding the fortified centers.

"Boeotian swine and Attic salt" was an old saying that contrasted the rich farmland of Boeotia with the parched and rocky profile of the peninsula of Attica (it also contrasted the reputed sluggishness of the Boeotian peasant with the wit of the Athenian mariner). But there are many pleasant districts in Attica. The acropolis of Athens invited occupation from earliest times, and the rulers of the Mycenaean citadel here may have commanded the obedience, if not the loyalty, of the many settlements scattered about the Attic countryside.

The political and perhaps military center of gravity of the Mycenaean world was the plain of Argos, located in the eastern Peloponnesus, where Agamemnon's palace, the citadel of Mycenae, crowns a low hill and even today gives mute evidence of the warrior breed that made this plain such a military power. This is a bleak countryside. The mountains are stark and unforested; the bones of the earth lie close to the surface here; and there is often more rock than soil in the fields. Modern irrigation techniques have produced endless citrus orchards, but in ancient times rainfall was meager in this part of Greece. The plain supported only a limited amount of grain farming, and the thistles and weeds of the hillsides nourished few flocks. It is easy to imagine this harsh land giving birth to generations of robber barons—and the Mycenaean code, all heroics aside, was basically that of the robber baron. To topple city walls, to slaughter the defending champions, to drive away fat cattle, to seize gold and silver, and to carry away prisoners for ransom and maidens for pleasure—these were the finest accomplishments of the Mycenaean gentleman, idealized by Homer and imitated all too often in later centuries. The tombs of Mycenae's rulers were stocked with treasures; only an idealist would argue that all these goods arrived through the normal avenues of peaceful trade. One has only to look at the walls of Mycenae, or her neighbor Tiryns (where some stretches are forty feet thick). These fortifications are so ponderously strong that later generations of Greeks believed them built by a race of giants. They are living testimony to the fact that Mycenae's primacy was won by the sword.

Across the central mountains of the Peloponnesus, in its southwest corner, lies a softer land. This is Messenia, home of King Nestor. The first clues to the way of life in Nestor's principality come from the palace: it was virtually unfortified, and in one storeroom were found over 2,400 drinking cups. Maybe Nestor had gone soft. Or perhaps he relied on the combination of a strong navy (he sent ninety ships to Troy) and two more strongly fortified bastions on his northern borders. Whatever the answer, the surrounding countryside is far more congenial than the plain of Argos. The hills are lower and covered with trees, the

The martial values of Mycenaean society are illustrated by this file of soldiers on the so-called Warrior Vase. (*National Archaeological Museum, Athens*)

meadows are deep and fertile, and the valleys are rich with springs and small brooks. As one might expect, a survey team recently discovered enough evidence to show that Messenia was probably the most heavily populated region in the Mycenaean world.

In contrast to its neighbors, the rich province of Messenia was poor in heroes, according to the traditions remembered by later generations. Although King Nestor admits in the *Iliad* that he had stolen cattle once or twice in his youth, his domain, unlike Mycenae, never seems to have produced more epic deeds than could be consumed locally.

These are the principal regions of Mycenaean occupation on the mainland, but the mainland was by no means the limit for Mycenaean ambitions. This first Greek society seems to have had the same irresistible drive to expand overseas that possessed every succeeding generation of Greeks. Although Homer's Catalogue mentions no provinces west of the island empire of Odysseus in the Ionian Sea, Mycenaean settlements in Sicily and southern Italy are well attested. As for the Aegean, the conquest of Crete was only one part of a wave of expansion that saw Mycenaean trading posts established on the islands and along the coast of Asia Minor, where Hittite records indicate they had become a force to be reckoned with.

Mycenaean Social Organization

> Then all the rest of the Achaeans shouted approval
> But it did not please the soul of Agamemnon, Atreus' son.
>
> Homer *Iliad* 1. 22, 24

According to Homeric tradition, Agamemnon was the Great King; his authority was imposed on all the lesser kings and barons who followed him to Troy. But he was never the absolute despot. He was only acknowledged first among equals. When decisions needed to be made, he sat in council with his peers and listened first to one argument, then to the other, while the assembly indicated approval or dissent by shouts and applause. He did not always have to follow the will of the majority, but if the issue were a continuing and aggravating one, pressure could mount until he was forced to change his mind.

The Mycenaean tablets confirm that there were kings in the Bronze Age Greek world. Unfortunately, we cannot rely on the Homeric poems to tell us how that kingship functioned. Neither does archaeological excavation expand our knowledge of the Mycenaean monarchs because the art of writing was not used (as in the Near East and Egypt) to record the deeds or even the names of kings. But it does show that Mycenaean society was unswervingly aristocratic. The major districts of the king's territory were ruled by the great nobles. This is the class that fills all the roles in the Homeric epics; these are the bodies that have been found in the Mycenaean grave circles and in the magnificent tholos tombs, surrounded by choice pottery, implements of war, gold jewelry, and death masks. One assumes the nobles held their land from the king in some sort of feudal relationship. At least this is what the epic tradition implies. One could wish that tradition gave as good a picture of a noble's daily life at home as it does of his martial deeds abroad. But it is precisely at those points where Homer describes peaceful pursuits that scholars suspect the most contamination of the legends by the conditions of Homer's own day, four centuries later.

Social distinctions are not as easy to make beneath the aristocratic upper caste. The tablets frequently mention a class called *telestai*, who were allotted land by the king and in turn owed him service: a share of crops or livestock, or participation in military ventures. The remainder of the land belonged to the *Damos* (this being the Mycenaean dialect form of the later Greek word *Demos*), which seems to mean that it was held in common, perhaps by a population of free peasants. The only member of these lower classes mentioned by Homer is Thersites, who had the effrontery to offer his opinion at a council of noble heroes and was quickly silenced for his presumption. But the vast majority of the Mycenaean population would have been from the class represented by Thersites or even lower. Relatively few citadels have been located, but scores of settlements of modest dwellings dot the Mycenaean landscape. Archaeology was once preoccupied with the palaces, but in recent years, the villages have received their share of attention. They can be found anywhere one cares to look—including under the sea.

Slaves occupied the lowest class, and the tablets show that their numbers also were large. In these archives they are dealt with simply as property, like other livestock, although we must assume that their numbers included many skilled craftsmen. Indeed, it is often suggested that the scribes who maintained the archives, and who were probably the only literate class in Greece, were themselves slaves. For it is exactly in this type of society—a feudalistic warrior aristocracy—that the possession of certain skills bears with it the stigma of social inferiority.

Archaeology and the tablets show that by the thirteenth century B.C., the rural farming population had been joined by an urban society of some complexity. The artisans included weavers, tanners, and metalworkers. A mercantile class assumed the responsibility for distributing the products of their labor and the agricultural surplus. At Mycenae in particular, excavation seems to show that certain kinds of labor and the merchandising of certain products were royal enterprises, run by the king from his palace.

The Minoan syllabic script was adopted by the Mycenaeans sometime after their conquest of Crete. This tablet from Knossos was preserved by baking in the great fire that destroyed the palace of the Mycenaean overlords in about 1200 B.C. (*Ronald Sheridan's Photo-Library*)

Naturally enough, the moment that social and economic organization becomes complex, accountants must be trained to keep track of personnel and accounts. It has been proposed that in the early days of Mycenaean civilization, visitors or perhaps ambassadors to Minoan Crete were impressed by the efficiency of Minoan accounting procedures. The clay tablets and the Linear B script are obvious adaptations of the methods used in the great Minoan palaces at Knossos, Phaistos, Agia Triada, and elsewhere on the island of Crete. Even the small number of tablets preserved today indicates the enormous labors of the Mycenaean bureaucrats in keeping track of every transaction, no matter how minor. Because the tablets were just sun-dried, the only surviving ones are those that were accidentally baked in the fires that destroyed the palaces. Consequently, the 3,000 or so tablets from Pylos, for instance, must represent the accounts from the *last weeks only* in the lifetime of Nestor's palace. If we project this number, we may imagine the staggering amounts of "paperwork" performed annually by palace scribes and clerks.

In every primitive society, every able-bodied man is a warrior. One mark of civilization is the gradual exemption of portions of the population from permanent military readiness. Homeric tradition and archaeology both seem to agree that warfare in the Mycenaean world was the exclusive province of the upper classes. The *Iliad* shows us war as a series of individual clashes between heroes who ride to the battlefront in chariots and dismount to fight. The rest of the army is composed of attendants of various sorts. They are cooks and grooms; they dress the champion, haul away the booty or the prisoners he has taken, or try to save his body for burial if he gets in the way of a spear. Archaeological evidence shows that military equipment was simply too elaborate and expensive for the lower classes to afford. Horses, chariots, oxhide shields, bronze armor, and weapons—these were the possessions of the wealthy aristocrats. The commoners who went to war probably carried wooden clubs and no more. In this respect, as well as in many others, a gulf separated master and servant in the Mycenaean world.

The Mycenaean Economy

In a common enterprise, most notably the Trojan War, all the kings of the various areas of the Mycenaean world came under the authority of the Great King. How such authority was maintained is unknown; we assume it to have been a wobbly business at best, considering the savage pride and easily bruised feelings of these warrior-children, as they are pictured for us by Homer. In fact, many scholars today deny any effective political unity within the Mycenaean world. There is really very little evidence either for or against the empire concept.

The so-called mask of Agamemnon, a gold death mask found at Mycenae and now located in the National Archaeological Museum, Athens. (*Hirmer Fotoarchiv*)

But there can be no doubt of the economic and cultural unification of the various areas of Mycenaean civilization. Whether at Knossos on Crete, Mycenae, Pylos, or the various outposts on the coast of Asia Minor, Mycenaean craftsmen turned out the same styles in pottery, weapons, personal dress, and other artifacts. In fact, only recently have scientific tests been developed that enable one to tell whether Mycenaean pottery found in foreign lands was made at Mycenae, or Knossos, or some other mainland town. By contrast, the ceramic wares of the later classical Greek cities are immediately distinguishable by style alone.

Moreover, Mycenaeans buried their dead the same way, whether in the southwestern Peloponnesus or in the northern Greek mainland or on the island of Rhodes. And the bereaved placed the same articles in the graves of the departed. Finally, the archives from Knossos, Pylos, and Mycenae seem to show that all these states kept their accounts in the same way, based on the same division of labor. Despite a tradition of internal warfare from time to time, Mycenaean culture was common to all the centers and must have been a product of common efforts over the centuries. Only in this way could Mycenaean prosperity have been achieved.

The Mycenaean civilization at its zenith was a wealthy one. Many graves seem to flaunt the expensive tastes of their occupants: gold death masks, cups, and jewelry are familiar to all students of Bronze Age Greek art. The Mycenaean world also abounded in costly imports of which the most common was bronze, essential to any warrior society. There are no deposits of either copper or tin on the Greek mainland, and gold and silver mines were not exploited until the classical era. The question is inevitable: since Greece had no mineral resources to speak of, and since her narrow plains produced food barely sufficient for domestic needs, how could any Greek society have achieved material prosperity and commercial expansion?

The answer seems to be that anyone who wished to live in a poor land like Greece and still enjoy the good things of life had to develop military aggressiveness, naval dominion, and mastery in international commerce. To put it bluntly, the Mycenaeans acquired their venture capital by piracy and conquest; subsequently, they used this capital to acquire a position of near dominance in trade with cities that could protect themselves, while continuing to take what they pleased from cities that could not.

Sometime around 1600 B.C., the Mycenaean sea raiders took over Knossos, the largest and most prosperous Minoan center on the island of Crete. Mycenaean products had already begun to replace Minoan ones in the marts of the Near East and Egypt, but from this time on we see a dramatic and sudden change in Mycenaean fortunes, accompanied by an almost total eclipse of Minoan commerce. This is revealed by the prevalence of Mycenaean trade goods found in the excavation of foreign sites. At the same time, pottery and other articles produced at home begin to show foreign influence, both Syrian and Egyptian.

Mycenaean ships sailed the coasts of the eastern Mediterranean, dealing in copper from Cyprus and choice pottery from mainland workshops. Mycenaean products found their way up the amber routes into northern Europe, and it is possible that Mycenaean ships competed with Phoenicians in bringing tin from Spain. With the exception of pottery, the principal items of exchange in Mycenaean trade are still in doubt. It is usually assumed that olive oil and wine were two of the most common exports of Greece, as they were to be later. Oil in particular was in demand, not only for cooking purposes but also as an all-purpose unguent and perfume base. Evidence from Mycenae shows that in a local factory, various herbs and spices were steeped in olive oil to give the oil a pleasant fragrance, or perhaps a suppositious medicinal value. Otherwise, besides a few crafted products like carved gemstones, gold cups, and inlaid metalwork or raw materials like the prized green porphyry building stone from Sparta, it is difficult to describe exactly what cargoes the Mycenaeans carried to foreign shores.

In 1300 B.C., Mycenae was one of the three great civilizations of the Mediterranean, rivaled only by the Hittite masters of Asia Minor and Syria, and the flourishing New Kingdom of Egypt. Two centuries later, Egypt had been reduced to the status of a survivor, hanging on grimly—but the empires of the Hittites and Mycenaeans lay in ruins.

The End of the Mycenaean World

> The return of the Greeks from Troy after such a long time caused
> many changes; in general, there was civil strife in the cities, and exiles
> from these founded other cities. . . . And eighty years after the War,
> the Dorians occupied the Peloponnesus with the Sons of Heracles.
>
> Thucydides 1. 12

Thus the historian Thucydides described the end of the Mycenaean
world, but his brief words do little to describe the true picture: nearly
every Mycenaean citadel and settlement destroyed or abandoned, an
almost complete end to overseas trade, and the disappearance of a
sophisticated town economy. There followed a 300-year period that
may with every justification be called the "Dark Age" of Greece.

Anyone interested in a given society must also be concerned with
the reasons for the disintegration of that society. There is still disagree-
ment about the end of the Mycenaean world; epic tradition and archaeology combined can only hint at the great disturbances that seem
to have overtaken the entire eastern Mediterranean in the twelfth century B.C. For many years, scholars were content to assume that the great
palaces were destroyed and the surrounding lands taken over by the
Dorians, as tradition suggested. There can be no doubt that the Dorians
occupied lands once ruled by the Mycenaeans, because in classical
times, the people of these areas spoke Doric and related dialects and
were proud of their tribal heritage. The difficulty comes from analyzing
the archaeological evidence, which indicates only that the old society
had broken down. There was no replacement of Mycenaean hardware
with Dorian counterparts.

Today many scholars concentrate on the first part of Thucydides'
statement, which focuses attention on internal strife. There is wide-
spread literary tradition to support this theory because even before the
war, Thebes had been destroyed by returning exiles. Furthermore, all
the heroes who returned from Troy found unrest at home. Agamemnon
was butchered in his bathtub; Odysseus survived only by the skin of
his teeth through a bloody massacre of his rivals. In city after city new
dynasties had taken over, and refugees filled the eastern Mediterranean.
In 1191 B.C., Rameses III repelled a great invasion of "sea peoples" from
the coasts of Egypt, and it is often assumed that these marauders were
a product of the contemporary disturbances in Greece. We are told by
tradition that only Nestor returned to safety and prosperity at Pylos.
Unfortunately, the archaeological record challenges tradition at this
point, showing that the palace at Pylos was one of the first to be destroyed and its destruction was awful and complete.

Civil war, therefore, may have been responsible for the destruction
of many citadels, for depopulation and abandonment of other sites, and
finally, for a breakdown in the Mycenaean economy. Such an elaborate

An engraved bronze blade depicting a lion hunt. (*National Archaeological Museum, Athens*)

social and economic structure must always depend for survival on relatively peaceful conditions: the crops must be sown and harvested at the right times, goods must exchange hands, ships must arrive at their destinations, taxes must be paid, and clerks must keep records. A generation of war can easily upset the delicate balance of such an economy. Once foreign trade ends, domestic prosperity begins to decline. Towns become isolated, driving artisans and merchants who have no more markets back to the soil as farmers—for farmers at least eat during hard times.

The archaeological evidence can only show that a great civilization fell. In the absence of a "smoking gun," it cannot indicate who was responsible for the disaster. Tradition claimed that the Dorians came rampaging out of the north. But in recent years scholars have begun to question the legends of a Dorian invasion because of the lack of archaeological evidence; instead, some scholars propose that the Dorians were in Greece all the time as a class of peasants and herders subject to the warrior aristocracy. When Mycenaean civilization weakened, the Dorians may have risen to complete the downfall of their rulers. If this theory is correct, one can see why they chose Heracles as their heroic ancestor: Heracles, in Greek mythology, was a man of the people—he fought with a club, mastered all problems with primitive violence, and was continually running afoul of civilized niceties. Unfortunately, evidence to resolve the controversy one way or another does not exist at the present time. It is quite possible that some archaeologist will uncover a piece of evidence tomorrow that will indicate a totally new approach to the problem. All we can say with certainty is that the Dorians became dominant in much of southern Greece, in Crete, and in the southeastern Aegean. Elsewhere, in Athens, and in the rest of the Aegean, the civilized arts underwent a decline, but there is no evidence of an occupation by newcomers.

Mycenaean Civilization in Retrospect

Although the civilization of Bronze Age Greece fell abruptly and disastrously, it left an important and lasting heritage for each subsequent Greek society.

The first legacy was a common historical tradition. All later Greek cities, families, and individuals of any importance found it absolutely necessary to trace their descent from the semidivine heroes who created and ruled the Mycenaean world. It was probably sometime in the eighth century B.C. that the epics of Homer began to stimulate and focus the natural desire of every Greek to find some connection with the glorious past. A poem entitled the *Catalogue of Women*, compiled in the sixth century B.C.,[1] listed the offspring of various legendary women by both mortal and divine fathers and may have been produced to assist aristocrats in the twofold task of proving divine ancestry and justifying their current social status. Even more concrete evidence of heroic ancestors had emerged in the centuries after the collapse of Bronze Age Greek civilization when Greeks began to discover the impressive beehive-shaped tombs of their Mycenaean forebears. Oracles, or priestly ingenuity, could supply the name of the great hero who had supposedly occupied the tomb, and the local population would establish a cult center dedicated to the hero, cults that were often still thriving a thousand years later.

Folk memory of the heroic age provided more than religious heritage: it had political significance as well. Sixth-century Athens pushed its claim to the island of Salamis by entering as evidence a line from the *Iliad*. Alexander the Great proved that he (if not the rest of the Macedonians) was a Greek by tracing his ancestry back to Achilles and Heracles. And King Agesilaus of Sparta sought to sanctify his fourth-century invasion of Asia by leaving from the same port used by Agamemnon on his way to Troy.

One of the strongest surviving elements from the Mycenaean period was the code of conduct of the Homeric warrior, which unfortunately persisted long after any need for it had passed. The Greeks never forgot that their ancestors were heroes in the purely physical sense. If we take a simplistic view of the legends, we must admit that almost all of them are about crude supermen breaking other people's heads, destroying cities, and in general crashing through life with the maximum noise and inconvenience to others. But these are the stories the Greeks enjoyed the most; perhaps they took a vicarious delight in heroic violence (as modern society does in television brutality and contact sports). A great deal of the Homeric code involved an exaggerated sense of per-

---

[1] Ancient writers attributed this poem to Hesiod, who had lived more than a century earlier (see pp. 119–123), but modern editors date it no earlier than the sixth century B.C.

sonal honor and pride. The entire plot of the *Iliad* is motivated by the injured feelings of one man—Achilles. There is little noticeable diminution in Achillean pride in later generations of Greeks, right down to the present day.

The exciting exploits of the heroes left little room in the tradition for descriptions of commercial ventures, but archaeology leaves no doubt that the Mycenaeans were master traders, and their instinct for commerce seems to have passed on to later generations of Greeks with renewed vigor after a brief hiatus during the Dark Age. In fact, long before the Greeks learned to write again, long before their cities approached the old Mycenaean centers in size or complexity, the pottery of the so-called Geometric period began to appear in the marketplaces of the Near East. No catastrophe was great enough to halt for very long the typical Greek love of visiting far places, bringing goods that could be exchanged.

A final and most important heritage is that of the Greek language. It started out, many assume, as a mere dialect of a wandering Indo-European tribe, but by the twelfth century B.C., it had become a magnificent instrument of communication. By that time, it had incorporated some of the vocabulary of the pre-Greek population and of other intrusive elements, but its basic structure remained the same and has remained the same ever since, undoubtedly owing its persistence to the vigor and precision with which ideas could be exchanged.

In one respect, the Mycenaean civilization was a false start. No one reading the epic tradition, no one who evaluates the archaeological evidence can escape the impression that there are actually two societies coexisting within Bronze Age Greece: masters and servants. If we can ignore the majesty of the tradition, which all too often obliterates perspective, we shall have to admit that the mass of the population consisted of Neolithic farmers living in very much the same condition as Stone Age farmers all over the rest of High Barbarian Europe. Bronze Age is actually a misnomer; Mycenaean peasants had no bronze. They plowed with a sharpened stick and their hardware was made of wood, bone, or stone; they fought, when they had to, with a club or fire-hardened stake. The glorious Mycenaean palaces and their occupants were really only a veneer—an elite warrior caste.

Rarely again in Greek history do we see such discrepancy between social classes. In fact, it is possibly because of the domination of the Mycenaean barons that one of the most deeply ingrained and intuitive Greek prejudices developed. The Greeks have never been so idealistic as to expect people to be equal, but in every Greek society the greatest indignation and violent reaction is reserved for Greeks who seek to set themselves too far above their fellows. Through the centuries, Greeks have acquiesced from time to time to being ruled by outsiders, but any fellow Greek who presumes to play the master must accept the consequences.

SUGGESTIONS FOR FURTHER READING

The only surviving literary evidence for Mycenaean history is the thousands of clay tablets inscribed in the Linear B script. John Chadwick, in *The Decipherment of Linear B* (New York: Cambridge University Press, 1960), describes the brilliant achievement of Michael Ventris; Chadwick's *Mycenaean World* (New York: Cambridge University Press, 1976) discusses the world of the tablets. Homer's *Iliad* provides limited evidence for Mycenaean history and institutions but is full of anachronisms and must be used with care. Michael Wood's *In Search of the Trojan War* (New York and Oxford: Facts on File, 1985) is a fascinating journalistic treatment of all the problems of late Bronze Age Greece. A century of Mycenaean archaeology and scholarship is illuminated by William A. McDonald and C. G. Thomas, *Progress into the Past: The Rediscovery of Mycenaean Civilization*, 2nd ed. (New York: Macmillan, 1990).

2 The Dark Age and the Archaic Age

THE DISRUPTION of Mycenaean civilization started a round of migrations that lasted three or more generations, roughly 1100–975 B.C. Both refugees from the Greek mainland and groups of Dorians drifted east across the Aegean Sea to find new homes on the coast of Asia Minor. During their flight and dispersion, memory of recent and violent historical events was almost entirely lost, making it difficult for the modern historian to interpret traditions. To the wanderers, it evidently seemed more important to preserve a memory of their tribal identity and origins. As so often in history, it is this type of folk memory that lends comfort, courage, and cohesion in a strange land. It was on this shore, looking westward to the sunset and old Greece, that the epics of the heroic age were most sung. But legends went back still further: later generations on this coastline claimed to be descended from one or another of the mythical heros, Aeolus, Ion, or Dorus, and use of the Aeolic, Ionic, or Doric dialects continued to be distinguishing features of the Greeks in Asia Minor right down into the period of the Roman Empire.

A glance at the accompanying map will show that the west coast of Asia Minor can be roughly divided into three areas. Emigrants from Thessaly and northern Greece traveled directly across the Aegean and settled on the northern part of the seaboard and on the island of Lesbos. Here the Aeolic dialect was spoken by descendants of the first immigrants, a form best represented in Greek literature by the poems of Sappho and Alcaeus.

According to tradition, the refugees from King Nestor's Pylos wandered first to Athens, where they were welcomed and given protection from the Dorians, who were never able to gain a foothold in Attica. A generation or two later, about 1025 B.C., the Pylians set forth once more, this time joined by many Athenian families, and established numerous settlements on the central coast of Asia Minor and the islands of the Aegean. Their descendants preserved the Ionic dialect, and the Ionians played such a predominant role in later Greek history that the entire west coast of Asia Minor is often referred to simply as Ionia.

GREEK DIALECTS AND THE PATTERN OF POST-MYCENAEAN SETTLEMENT

THESSALY
AEOLIA
Lesbos
NORTHWEST GREEK DIALECT
Chios
Athens
IONIA
Corinth
Samos
ARCADIAN DIALECT
Sparta
IONIAN SEA
AEGEAN SEA
DORIS
Cos
Rhodes

Migration of Aeolic dialect populations
Migration of Ionic dialect populations
Migration of Doric dialect populations

CRETE

0   100
Miles

Once the Dorians had become masters of the Peloponnesus, their momentum carried them across the southern Aegean to Crete and, perhaps a few generations later, eastward again to the islands of Rhodes, Cos, and the mainland opposite. Once more, the immigrants retained their original dialect with the same sort of personal attachment that all Greeks seemed to feel toward ancestral usage.

The Greek mainland itself, with the exception of Attica and the mountainous region of Arcadia in the central Peloponnesus, was settled by the Dorians and related tribes moving down from the north. But every community of Greeks that emerged from the ruins of the Mycenaean collapse suffered from the results of that collapse. The two most important consequences were geographical isolation and the return to a simple agrarian economy. It has been pointed out that much of the Greek world is poor in resources. Mycenaean prosperity was based on a complex economy and a commercial vigor that broke down the isolation imposed by geography. But when this economy was destroyed, the specialization of labor and the bustle of urban life vanished with it. There was little left for Greeks to do except go back to farming for their living.

Historians call the ensuing period a "Dark Age" because farmers leave few traces to illuminate the historical record. Because most farmers produced only enough food for their own families, the agriculture of the Dark Age could never begin to support the sort of population once seen during Mycenaean times. Dark Age cemeteries have been analyzed to show that an average settlement had as few as one hundred inhabitants.

The lands surrounding the Aegean Sea are mountainous and deeply indented by gulfs, bays, and inlets. Therefore, the usual Greek community, whether on the mainland, the Ionian coast, or on one of the numerous Aegean islands, was situated on a peninsula or in a valley protected by mountains on one side and the sea on the other. Such an environment bred isolation, and isolation in turn helped to create the strong bonds of loyalty and instinct for common action that were so typical of the later city-states. This environment must be kept in mind as we explore three aspects of the developing archaic Greek states: the farm, the town, and the shore.

The Farm

The climate of Greece is characterized by hot, dry summers, a pleasant spring and autumn, and mild winters during which most of the annual rainfall occurs. Much of the Aegean basin is rocky and mountainous; but where soil has accumulated in valleys and plains a variety of crops can be grown, providing a reasonably secure source of food for farmers willing to invest time and labor in clearing land and preparing the soil.

All Greek communities realized that the natural balance was precarious and that powers beyond their knowing could send either rain or drought, warming sun or killer frosts. Because this fundamental relationship with the life-giving earth had such an impact on Greek religion, social organization, law, and government, it is necessary to understand the essentials of agriculture in the Greek world.

Wheat and barley were the all-important staples serving as the mainstay of the Greek diet; therefore, the best bottom land was reserved for their cultivation. Fields were plowed in the fall after the first rainfall of the season to prepare the soil for planting. When it was obvious that the rainy season had really started, Greek farmers sowed their precious seed grain. All winter the grain lay in the ground, absorbing moisture and slowly germinating. In late winter, as the days grew warmer, the grain began to sprout. Early spring was a crucial time. If enough rain continued to fall, the grain crop would be large and farming families would be relieved of the annual anxiety. In May and early June the grain turned golden as the weather became dry and warm. Then farmers harvested the grain and left it piled in the fields to dry. Later it was threshed and winnowed to separate the kernels of grain from chaff and the grain was stored for another year. Grain was eaten as porridge, bread, and barley cake; this was the main diet of most Greeks. Other foods supplemented this diet but could never really replace it. Chickpeas and beans provided variety (and protein) and could survive long periods of storage. A few leafy vegetables, gourds, root vegetables like turnips, onions, and garlic helped to enliven the menu.

In the fall came the second harvest of the year. A number of orchard crops thrived in the Aegean climate and the Greeks have thoroughly

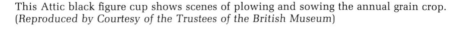

This Attic black figure cup shows scenes of plowing and sowing the annual grain crop. (*Reproduced by Courtesy of the Trustees of the British Museum*)

exploited these since earliest times. Most important, of course, was the olive. Once cured, olives could be eaten plain. But most olives were used to produce oil, serving not only as an essential food in a relatively fat-free diet but as fuel for lamps and as a universal base for perfumes, salves, and ointments. Nearly as important were grapevines. Most of their produce was converted to wine—consumed daily by almost every Greek man, woman, and child—but some grapes were converted by drying into raisins and currants, which also stored well for the winter.

Greek farmers also kept numbers of domestic animals. Most numerous were sheep and goats, which provided not only milk to be turned into cheese but also wool for clothing and bedding. A few hens would produce occasional eggs and farmers considered themselves fortunate if they could keep a small herd of pigs going. Nevertheless, meat in the diet was comparatively rare. Because the arid Greek countryside does not produce enough natural fodder to support large flocks, these are kept at manageable levels by slaughtering excess males and sickly or inferior females every year. Early spring is the most suitable time for cutting down the flocks, so it is no coincidence that both ancient festivals and modern Easter feasts take place at this time. But during the rest of the year Greek farmers found their animals too valuable for other products to butcher them for meat. Only when a farm animal became unproductive or was injured or sick could the Greek family look forward to meat on the table joining the usual diet of bread, cheese, olives, and vegetables.

The fundamental social unit of agrarian Greece was the *oikos*, or household,[1] meaning the lands and buildings owned by one man—the patriarch of a family—and including his tenants, slaves, and livestock. But unlike modern farmers living in isolation, Greek farmers lived together in small communities and went out to their fields during the day. Whether the holding was large or small, the ideal pursued was *autarkeia*, or self-sufficiency, meaning that each family hoped to raise its own grain, olives, and vines, and have enough livestock and a kitchen garden to provide all the nourishment required every year.

Both the monarchy and the exalted nobility of the Mycenaean world seem to have died out with the gutting of the palaces. In rustic, archaic Greece the social spectrum was not so broad: it ranged from the slave and other persons of dependent status, to the small free farmer with a few stony acres on a hillside, to the lord of a large estate down in the more fertile valley, a man who could prove descent from a legendary hero. Distinctions between nobles and commons were slight compared to the awesome elevations of the Mycenaean caste system. An aristocrat might own a third of the land in the valley of his com-

---

[1] *Oikonomia* in Greek means the management of such a household; from this word we derive the English word "economy."

munity, but he lived in a house only slightly more splendid than that of his tenant farmers. He may have been a leader in wartime, a priest of Apollo, and a statesman to whom all turned during council meetings; but he was still primarily a farmer and he got his hands dirty just like any farmer. He personally supervised the work that went on throughout his lands; he knew how to till fields, graft olives, shear sheep, and deliver foals.

The domestic scenes from Homer's *Odyssey* are generally agreed to represent conditions more from Homer's own day than from the Mycenaean period, and Odysseus was a noble of this type. He was on easy terms with his inferiors, even his slaves. His swineherd entered his house and passed the time of day with Queen Penelope. Odysseus himself knew how to plow a straight furrow; he described how he built his own house and constructed his great bed with his own hands.

The center of the aristocratic *oikos* was the house itself, a large building divided into private quarters for women, servants, and other residents, and public areas—courtyard, banquet, and audience halls. This was a busy place, night and day. A large household staff composed primarily of female slaves prepared food, wove rugs or bedding, kept an eye on children, and did its best to keep a rude dwelling as clean as possible, for a passion for cleanliness has always existed among the Greeks.

There was a constant flow of visitors. The lord's own shepherds and farmers brought in livestock or produce for the larder, wine and oil were delivered, smiths and potters called to take orders for merchandise or to barter completed articles. The lord or his wife (who was not a pampered creature in oriental seclusion but an autocrat in her own right) was in constant attendance to give orders, assign tasks, supervise the stream of products continually going in and out of the courtyard, or to sit in judgment when a dispute arose between two or more persons for whom the lord was responsible. And we may imagine that many of the visitors had no business at all. For Greeks are and have always been among the most sociable people in the world. They love company and talk, and noise and bustle. People from all stations in life would have dropped by the courtyard of the great lord's house to gossip with the help, or exchange news with other visitors, or to give helpful advice to anyone and everyone, or to see if the lord or his lady was in the mood for a handout. And anyone who happened by at mealtime was asked to stay, for another constant trait of the Greeks has been their delight in being able to give food and drink to company, from the grandest neighboring baron to the humblest beggar.

Clustered near the household of the lord were the small houses of his tenant farmers. They turned the bulk of their produce over to their landlord and in turn were allowed to keep a certain percentage. In addition, the lord was responsible for his tenants; he protected them from injury at the hands of others and settled their disputes. During

The valley of the Eurotas River, heartland of the Spartan domains, provided ideal farming conditions: land for cereal crops, orchards, and grazing; and a river that flowed all year round. (*The J. Allen Cash Photolibrary*)

hard times he may have opened his storerooms to them to prevent starvation. He may even have helped a new tenant to build his house.

The lord's lands reached up into the hills as well. Here his herdsmen watched over flocks of sheep, goats, and pigs. Odysseus' faithful swineherd was a slave but nevertheless a person of substance and responsibility. He actually had free men working under him and had acquired enough wealth to buy himself a slave. The herder was as important as the steward of the lord's household down in the valley, for a man's herds were part of his fluid wealth in an age without currency. On sunny southern slopes there would have been vineyards. Just as inevitable was a grove of olive trees somewhere on the property. To live without wine and oil is unthinkable in Greece, past and present.

All these lands and all these people constituted the *oikos* of the lord. But there were also smaller farmers with an *oikos* of perhaps only a few acres. They too would have had a slave or two, if they could afford it, and would have wrung the last grain of wheat from the land. For the most part, they worked the poorer fields on the hillsides where the soil is rocky and terraces are required for planting. And from time to time, they had to borrow seed from their richer neighbors, for which their own land became surety.

In this pastoral and agrarian society, almost no social or economic mobility existed. Because everyone had his place and his property, the most wretched and despised soul was not the slave, but the free man with no place—forced to wander the land taking what employment, generosity, or abuse anyone wished to give him. Small farmers, even if their wealth increased, could not buy land; generally law and custom prevented the free exchange of real estate, which changed hands only during marriage settlements or in division among heirs. But they could lose their land, if they were unlucky enough to accumulate debt after debt until they had to default and become a tenant to their creditor. Land division among heirs could also be a source of anxiety. Greeks did not leave property to the eldest son; ancient custom demanded equal division among all male heirs. Therefore, if each generation of a family produced three or more sons over the course of several generations, a large, prosperous estate could be fragmented into many small and marginal ones, where heirs would struggle to eke out a living.

Change is slow in the agricultural community. The farm households just described were pictured by Homer and Hesiod and illustrate conditions in perhaps the tenth to eighth centuries B.C.[2] But conditions never really changed in the rural countryside. The rich landowner in the age of Pericles kept the same sort of household out in the plains of Attica. While he was in the city of Athens, no one called him master, and in court or in the assembly the poorest landless citizen was his equal. But back on his lands he was still a lord, both disciplinarian and benefactor to tenants, slaves, and hired hands. And we can assume that conditions were still much the same on the estate in Boeotia where Plutarch grew up in the first century A.D. Country life was conservative. Change and social and economic mobility were to come from another quarter of the archaic Greek state.

The Town

Almost every early community in the Greek world had a high place of refuge—a hill or crag that could be used for shelter or as a rallying point in time of danger. The word *polis* was first used to describe this sort of defensible high ground. Later on the polis came to mean the urban center surrounding the hill, and the height itself was distinguished as the *acropolis*. And finally, in its best known and classical sense, polis meant the entire city-state: all the territory, fields, and villages that were ruled, protected, and administered by the urban center under the acropolis. This was the physical concept of the polis. But in the spiritual sense, the polis had its origin in the first public building of any community, and this structure was almost without exception religious.

---

[2] See a sketch of Hesiod and life on the small farm, pp. 119–123.

Like all other peoples of the ancient world, the Greeks believed that their lives were governed by powers beyond their control. The gods and goddesses who lived on Mount Olympus made a prominent appearance at the very beginning of written Greek literature. In the *Theogony*, the poet Hesiod handed down the creation story, as the Greeks knew it, and described the origin and activities of Zeus, Hera, Apollo, Athena and their relatives and offspring who made up the colorful Greek pantheon. Gods and goddesses dominate Homer's *Iliad* and, to a lesser extent, the *Odyssey*. The stories we see in earliest literature are evidence of a well developed, centuries-old theology. If these deities seem to be portrayed too familiarly and irreverently, if they seem to be subject to all the human failings and weaknesses of greed, jealousy, rage, and sexual infidelity, the reason is that the Olympians were, after all, first and foremost the ancestors of the human race. They were blessed with immortality and gifted with superhuman strength and wisdom, but other than that they were unabashedly human in their virtues, vices, and emotions.

As parents and guardians of the Greek race, the Olympian deities were credited in the traditional tales with assistance of various kinds to their children in time of need. They all had well-known attributes and functions that were available to the suppliant. All over the Greek world there were sacred precincts where these particular attributes had first been recognized centuries before and where mortals could appeal to the deities for help. One thinks first of Delphi, where Apollo helped humankind with his gift of foresight, explained to pilgrims by his priestess in verse oracles, or Epidaurus, where Apollo's son Asclepius healed the sick by divine intervention. But these were only among the most famous. Greeks had an endless inventory of deities offering various services, from Artemis, who helps in childbirth, to Hermes, patron of merchants (and thieves), and above all, Zeus, who could be asked to bring good luck, to avenge murder, or simply to drive away flies—an important function in the heat of midsummer. These services were paid for at each shrine by certain prayers and sacrifices. The price of the sacrificial animal was generally proportional to the importance of the service to be performed.

But all humankind is prey to nameless fears, anxiety, and guilt that can hardly be placated by this sort of businesslike transaction with a god of human form. The Greeks had a very different set of deities to whom they turned for a more spiritual and mystical relationship, for cleansing of guilt, forgiveness of sins, and promise of salvation. While it is obvious that the Olympians were gods of the sky (as their home on Mount Olympus demonstrated), the most casual investigation of Greek religion shows that they were secondary as objects of worship to the spirits of the earth, or *chthonic* deities (Greek: *chthon* means earth). The Olympians performed valuable services, but the earth sup-

"We build our churches where the people are. The Greeks built theirs where the gods are" (H. D. F. Kitto). The temple of Apollo at Bassai rests in solitude on a remote mountain in the southwest Peloponnese.

ported life itself. Every Greek community had solemn rites celebrating the birth and death each year of life-giving crops. The cult figure symbolizing this cycle of vegetation had many names, like Demeter (Greek: Earth Mother), or remained nameless, for instance, Great Goddess, or Great Mother. These rites were called mysteries because they were secret, revealed only to initiates. They offered to worshipers a mystical communion with the cult figure and promised purification from guilt and, therefore, the favor of the gods. While individuals sought a one-to-one relationship with the Olympian deities, the whole community worshiped the chthonic spirits, for the very life of the community depended on the continued fertility of the earth.

Both sets of deities were honored in many ways in the Greek world, but each community also had a particular god or goddess as its own private guardian and benefactor. Some settlers had brought their old gods with them, as in the case of the Dorians or the Ionian colonists of Asia Minor; or inhabitants of a certain district would begin to have a community consciousness and cast about for a divine protector. The founding legends often give the details of how communities discovered their particular god or goddess. An oracle may have informed them, or a local notable may have been instructed in a dream that a temple to a certain deity must be built. In any case, the first act of incorporation of the earliest Greek states was constructing a temple and reserving a precinct for the local god or goddess. In these communities, the precinct was on, or more commonly just below, the hill of the polis; this area was the only public land—the only land not actually owned and farmed by some citizen. Here throughout the year, nobles holding priestly of-

Graves of community leaders were adorned with massive funerary vases in "geometric" style. The small figures on the pyre seem to represent a sacrifice of living humans; this supposition may be borne out by the recent excavation of a great noble's grave on the island of Euboea—the corpse of a young woman was found in his grave, along with his horses. (*The Metropolitan Museum of Art*)

fices conducted the various ceremonies and sacrifices necessary to keep the patron spirit in a good mood. And almost as soon as the land was set aside, we can assume that some area nearby began to be used as an *agora*—originally meaning an assembly or place of assembly for the people to hear discussion of common problems or to observe the settlement of disputes. This sort of folk assembly seems to have been an intuitive response of all Greeks, wherever they lived, to any problem, large or small. It was taken for granted that open discussion would produce a greater sum of wisdom than that available to any one man, no matter how gifted he might be in good counsel. Only later did *agora* also come to mean a place where things were bought and sold, that is, a marketplace. This shows that the institution of the folk assembly in early Iron Age Greece was even older than the first stirrings of commerce.

The towns also saw other beginnings of organized government, such as it was, for there was actually little need for government in the archaic community. Some sort of leadership was required to keep proper relations with the gods, to guard the frontiers, and to settle disputes between members of the community. Originally, we are told,

Greek cities had kings, and kings had served as chief priests, as leaders in wartime, and as judges. Later the institution of monarchy died out almost everywhere in the Greek world. No one can say why with certainty, but it is possible that the principle of hereditary succession to the monarchy was subject to the consent of the king's most powerful relatives and companions (as we see later in Macedonia) and that at some point they refused to accept a weak, ineffective, or immature aspirant to the throne and simply distributed his functions among themselves.

In practice, the largest local landowner exercised some sort of authority in his neighborhood. He served as priest because he could trace his ancestry back to a god or goddess. He could round up the fighting-age men of the locality and lead them in defending their fields (or in raiding those across the frontiers). Small farmers would intuitively turn to him to settle disputes over property or inheritance. But as urban centers developed, there was a trend to a more organized system of authority. Although the beginnings of government are obscure in the Greek world, we assume that various positions of authority and leadership gradually became traditional, were recognized by the whole community, and were competed for by the land-owning aristocracy because they symbolized power and honor.

Temple and agora—this complex was the axis of the future city, and it was here that urban life (considered by later generations of Greeks as the only kind of life worth living) had its start. In an agrarian society, where every person has a place and is tied to the land either as proprietor or tenant, a class of permanent city dwellers grows slowly at first. Perhaps we are to think of uncommonly fine craftsmen, who spend more and more time making and bartering their wares, and finally move permanently to shops in town. Surely one of the first such professionals was the local blacksmith; he was joined by potters, weavers, tanners, and of course tavern owners—for nowhere in Greece, at any time, can four or more persons congregate for any purpose for very long without needing some place to go where they can sit in the shade, or by the fire, and eat and drink and entertain themselves with fine talk. Furthermore, in the city there is a chance to escape the rigid confines and the monotony of an agrarian society and economy. Here a person's talents are worth more than extensive lands or glamorous ancestry. And here, in the first urban communities, we can see the rebirth of a market economy and foreign trade.

The Shore

No place in Greece is very far from the ocean. The original center of most city-states was located a few miles inland to make things a little more difficult for sea-going marauders who might chance by looking for an easy slave haul. But if the state developed lively commercial interests, or if fishing provided a share of the community livelihood, a second population center might have grown up on the coast near some broad sandy beach on which ships could be drawn up.

It can be said that the normal posture of a Greek was with back to the land, looking out to sea, and in fact, it is impossible to exaggerate the importance of this broad and convenient avenue at the doorstep of almost every Greek state. Navigating the Aegean Sea can be exasperating because there is often either too much wind or not enough, but there are compensating features. The Aegean has neither tides nor currents, and a minimum of surf. During the sailing season, from April through November, strong winds usually come from the north, making at least one aspect of a voyage predictable. For most of the year the skies are clear, permitting line-of-sight navigation. In moderate winds, a small boat could sail from Athens to Miletus in Ionia in two or three days, steering from island to island. And a boat leaving Athens in the morning would be in the harbor of Corinth before nightfall; the same trip by land was a two- or three-day affair along miserable roads infested by brigands. It was the sea that made all Greeks neighbors.

The first coastal communities consisted of a few fishermen and their families living off the slender produce of the sea; Greek waters have never been particularly rich in fish. A collection of huts and small boats on the shore indicated a larger population center farther inland to passing ships, which landed from time to time in the hope of trading part of their cargo—metal wares, wine from the islands, or perhaps curios picked up in Near Eastern ports. In turn, they hoped to replenish their supplies of food and fresh water. The historian Thucydides described encounters of earlier times between land dwellers and strangers from visiting ships: both parties were cautious at first, with the people on shore politely inquiring whether the visitors were there in the way of trade or as pirates, no doubt keeping their weapons close to hand and their women out of sight.

If a state began to produce an agricultural surplus—olive oil, for instance—it became a regular stopping place for Greek and Phoenician trading vessels. In time, urban centers grew up right on the shore and local entrepreneurs themselves built ships. Athens and Corinth are good illustrations of such development. In both places the actual city is some distance inland, dominated and protected by a fortified hilltop. At Athens, the first maritime settlements grew up on the wide, open beach of the bay of Phaleron. Situated on an isthmus, Corinth eventually possessed two harbors, one on the Saronic Gulf and the other on the Gulf of Corinth.

The commercial instincts of the Greeks were only briefly interrupted by the fall of the Mycenaean civilization. By the ninth century B.C., the remains of the characteristic Geometric style pottery could be found all over the Greek world, indicating that communication existed between major centers and that cultural unity of a sort was being pre-

served by travel and trade. The farmlands of Greece had provided continuity and stability in a time of troubles, but it was the city and the
sea that combined to make possible a rebirth of Greek society. In the
coming centuries there was to be a phenomenal expansion of Greek
horizons, both physical and intellectual.

The Age of Colonization

About the beginning of the eighth century, the Greek world once more
began to have a history. There is one precise, if symbolic, date that may
be recorded: 776 B.C., the year of the first Olympic Games. Whether
this date is correct or not, archaeology can show that this approximate
period saw the flowering of great Panhellenic sanctuaries at Olympia,
Delphi, and Delos. The revival of these cults was just one of the remarkable developments contributing to what has been called the Greek
renaissance of the eighth century B.C. Others are the rapid spread of
Homeric epic from Ionia to the rest of the Greek world, the rediscovery
of literacy, and a sudden increase in population which helped cause a
wave of expansion and colonization from about 750 to 550 B.C.—an
amazing explosion that eventually saw as many as two hundred Greek
colonies established from the straits of Gibraltar to the Crimea.

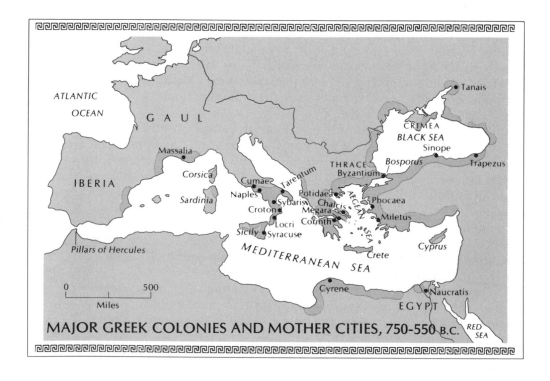

MAJOR GREEK COLONIES AND MOTHER CITIES, 750-550 B.C.

Another important reason for colonization was lack of opportunity at home. Some leaders of the colonies were sons of aristocratic families whose share of inherited land was insufficient to support them in style. Others were noble bastards, born to concubines or serving women; these young men inherited aristocratic status from their fathers, but could not normally inherit land. The leaders of colonies collected other land-hungry and adventurous spirits and struck out for less heavily populated areas with the blessing of their mother city and with an oracle to guide them.

All colonies had common features, whether located on the coasts of the Black Sea, Sicily, Italy, North Africa, or southern France. The colonists came prepared to use force to seize the land and were often compelled to do so by a hostile indigenous population. Once settled, the colonies became self-governing city-states; giving up all political ties with their mother city, they retained only shared religious traditions and other ancestral institutions. The most important person during the early days of a colony was the *oikistes,* or founder, a man appointed by the mother city to lead the colony to its new home, designate sacred ground for cults, and apportion the new lands among the settlers. His authority was absolute during this crucial period, but once the foundation was complete, the colonists were free to hold assemblies and elect leaders and councils as they may have done in the mother city.

Because land hunger was the driving force behind most colonies, it is not surprising that they began as agricultural communities. But foreign lands, new products, and sometimes new neighbors with long traditions of trade stimulated mercantile activity. The communities of old Greece would eventually have developed commercial economies again but there is no doubt that the colonial movement hastened the process and led to an increase of markets, commodities, and avenues of trade throughout the Mediterranean.

Interaction with native peoples was not always hostile. In many cases there was both intermarriage and cultural exchange, which broadened Greek intellectual horizons. Most important of all, at the very beginning of this period the Greeks learned once more how to read and write their language. The Mycenaeans had borrowed their syllabic script from the Minoans in order to keep accounts. It is often assumed that the later Greeks adopted the Phoenician alphabet for the same purpose. The vast difference between the two scripts is that the alphabet can be immediately adapted to uses outside commerce. The twenty-four letters are quickly learned and pronunciation is phonetic.[3] The Greek love of conversation extends to communication of all kinds; so

---

[3] The name Klytaimnestra, for instance, is pronounced the way it is spelled; in the Mycenaean syllabic script, on the other hand, the grotesque result would be Ku-ru-ta-i-me-ne-ta-ra.

once an easy method of preserving words and thoughts became available, literacy spread rapidly and was never again limited to a class of professional scribes. The longest eighth-century inscription is on a cup from a grave at Pithekoussai on the Italian island of Ischia. It is written from right to left, like Phoenician, and reads, "I am the cup of Nestor, fine to drink from. But whoever drinks from this cup will be seized straightway by desire of fair-crowned Aphrodite." Perhaps a hundred and fifty years later a group of Greek mercenaries in Egyptian service far up the Nile River paused in wonder before the colossal statue of Rameses II at Abu Simbel, and like tourists since the world began, they cut their names into the monument. Between these two inscriptions the Greek world witnessed an unprecedented outburst of poetic creativity. Whereas the works of Homer are epics of a whole people with no hint of the author's personality, the adoption of a written language brought about personal literature. The seventh century B.C. saw the emergence of a literature of intensely personal expression in which we see the characteristic Greek yearning to expose one's innermost feelings to the world.

The Lyric Age: Poets and Philosophers

The first European to speak to us in his own voice is a boisterous, brawling rakehell named Archilochus—poet, fighter, and lover, a Greek renaissance man. The sudden contrast with the impersonal dignity of Homer is startling. It is as if stately music coming from a darkened stage were suddenly replaced by glaring light and the deafening appearance of a rock star in full throat. And in many ways, the first great lyric poet exemplifies the entire archaic period (approximately 750–550 B.C.)—those two centuries of brilliant and disorderly energy that preceded the more settled era of the polis.

Archilochus was born on the Aegean island of Paros in about 720 B.C. He was the son of an aristocrat by a slave woman and therefore had noble status but no rights of inheritance. Like other young men in similar straits, he joined a colony: in this case, an expedition to the rugged, lonely isle of Thasos in the far northern Aegean, where land was to be had only by driving off savage Thracian tribesmen. But on Thasos he was disappointed in love and disillusioned with the harsh landscape, so he left the island to enter service as a mercenary soldier. Archilochus wandered the Aegean during his lifetime, fighting, wenching, and pausing from time to time to fill his gut with wine.

> Drain the red wine to the dregs,
> For we'll never stay sober on this watch.

There is little of the Homeric hero in Archilochus. He admitted himself to be an adulterer and a lecher:

> An eager workman . . .
> Belly to belly and thigh to thigh.

And sometimes less than stalwart in battle:

> Some Thracian now enjoys my blameless shield
> Which I unwilling left beside a bush.
> But I was saved—what do I care about that shield.
> Let it go, I'll get another no worse.

For admissions such as this, the Spartan government forbade the reading of Archilochus' poems, fearing the young would be corrupted by such an example.

The poet-adventurer finally returned to the island of his birth, and there he was killed in a battle with the neighboring islanders of Naxos.

If the maxim "nothing in excess" represented the Greek ideal, Archilochus represented the reality—a sublime neglect of such admonitions. He sang of the joys of unrestrained life and love, fierce battle and festive victory. He never hesitated to complain of days when things went wrong, of hard times on Thasos, of sluts who take on all comers, of unrequited love, or of a thankless friend. And he could gloat horribly over the fate of an enemy doomed to a life of slavery in a savage land.

In the seventh century, much of the Aegean was still a frontier, and Archilochus was as much a rough-hewn frontier hero as any legendary figure from the American West. Such a world was tolerant of unorthodox people because values and traditions had not yet become established and solidified into canons of behavior. Nor had this Aegean world changed much fifty years or so later when the Greeks first heard from Sappho of Lesbos.

Mytilene, the largest city of the island of Lesbos, was still ruled in the seventh century by an aristocracy that prided itself on descent from Orestes, son of Agamemnon. These nobles were merchant princes; they had joined with other Ionian cities in building the commercial depot of Naucratis on the Nile River Delta, and their ships traded from Syria to southern France. Warrior poets lived in Mytilene too, like the great Alcaeus, or his brother, who served as a mercenary under the king of Babylon.

Sappho was of good family; like other girls of quality she was married off to a suitable husband, and we are told that a daughter was born to the couple. So much is unremarkable. But after her husband's early death, Sappho's career suddenly became startling and unique in two different ways. First of all, the parade of notables in Greek history from beginning to end is almost unrelievedly masculine: Sappho was one of the few Greek females to break through what seems to be the prejudice that women should be neither seen nor heard. Second, Sappho spent her life attracting girls from all over the Greek world to come and join her circle; and in her poems she is quite frank about the sensual love she felt for many of these girls:

The poets Alcaeus and Sappho are depicted by an imaginative vase painter. (*Courtesy, Staatliche Antikensammlungen und Glyptothek, Munich*)

> Like the Gods he seems to me—
> The man who sits facing you
> And hears your sweet voice near him,
> And loving laughter
> Which once made my heart leap
> In my breast . . .

In one of the most famous Greek love poems, she begs Aphrodite for aid in recovering a lost lover, and the goddess answers:

> Who has wronged you, Sappho?
> For if she flees, she will soon pursue—
> And if she will not accept, soon she will give—
> And if she loves you not, soon she will love,
> Willing or not.

The girl in question may have been the lovely Atthis, who seems to have left Sappho's circle for the company of another woman:

> Eros arouses me, loosens my limbs,
> That bittersweet implacable serpent—
> Atthis! You've come to hate the sight of me
> And fly to the side of Andromeda.

Later Greeks were of two minds about Sappho. Even Plato, who was normally indifferent to the accomplishments of women, eagerly joined the ranks of those who applauded the genius of her poetry. And the scholars of the great library at Alexandria made her one of the Nine Lyric Poets.[4]

But there was also a sense of shock and scandal. Later ages were quite tolerant of male homosexuality; but they were not quite so willing to grant women the same freedom, and were perhaps even a little offended that Sappho should be so innocent, so utterly lacking in shame. The censors of the early Christian church saw in Sappho just another example of pagan depravity and were hostile to her poetry. For this and other reasons, we possess today only a few quotations of Sappho's verse in the works of later Greek writers.

Sappho's world was a world in flux, a world of changing values. Horizons were expanding, and minds were being stretched not only in artistic expression but also in speculation about the nature of the universe. We have seen what a great influence the legends of ancient Greece had upon later generations. For centuries, no Greek of sound mind had questioned the fact that the same gods who created mortals and dominated the age of heroes continued to exert influence on people of every succeeding generation. It was simple to believe that the sun was Apollo's fiery chariot, that Poseidon the Earthshaker rattled the world and threw down buildings from time to time, and that thunder and lightning were the results of the rage of Zeus.

But during the seventh century, on the outskirts of the Greek world where Greeks came in contact with the age-old science and mathematics of the Near East, some individuals began to seek rational explanations for natural phenomena and for the nature of the universe. One of the first we know by name was Thales, and his city, Miletus, was to be the home of the most famous school of early Greek philosophy.

The first Greek philosophers were more interested in physics than in ethics. Although later thinkers would take up the question of how people ought to act, the first inquirers wanted to know what kind of world they were living in. Thales was born about 625 B.C., probably to a distinguished family of Miletus. Little more than anecdotes have been preserved about his life, career, and teaching. We are told that he studied "nature." This undoubtedly included the Chaldean science of astronomy, which was centuries old and recognized the regular movements of the primary visible heavenly bodies. The most famous event in Thales' life was the solar eclipse of 585 B.C., which he supposedly predicted and explained, but he also contributed theories about the size and orbits of the sun and moon. We are told that he studied

---

[4] These self-appointed critics kept themselves busy compiling lists of the "best" writers of every genre: the Ten Attic Orators, the Three Historians, and so on.

for a while with the priests in Egypt—probably learning Egyptian geometry and engineering methods: he determined the height of the pyramids by measuring the length of their shadow at the time of day when a person's shadow equaled his height.

Thales divided the universe into material objects, all of which had their origin in water, and animate spirits, which he had detected in the mysterious attractive properties of magnets and amber. Some stories make him a typical absent-minded professor who once fell into a ditch because he was staring so intently at the stars. But the most famous story was used throughout antiquity to show that philosophers could be practical when they wanted to be. Someone made the age-old jibe: If you're so smart, why aren't you rich? This irritated Thales; during the winter, when there were no other bidders, he made a small deposit to secure an option on every olive press in Miletus. The next year during the olive harvest, it was discovered that he had a complete monopoly on olive pressing and could charge whatever he wanted.

Thales and his successors are often referred to collectively as the Milesian school. In general, they defined the world as tangible, finite, and knowable. On the opposite side of the Greek world, in Sicily and southern Italy, other philosophers held that the world was infinite and unknowable. And some of the early thinkers ventured into metaphysics so arcane it resembles mysticism more than science. What they all had in common, of course, was their dissatisfaction with Homeric theology and theological interpretations of the universe. This demand for rational answers came to typify the Greek spirit of inquiry in centuries to come. The only drawback in their investigation was the tendency of Greek inquirers to accept the first and most obvious answer.

Contributions of the Archaic Age

The word "archaic" comes from the Greek word *arche*, meaning "beginning," and it was truly during the centuries between Homer and Thales that we can see the beginnings of the Greek culture that was to mature following the sixth century B.C. During this period the Greeks first took a good look at themselves and the world around them and were pleased with what they saw. To be pleased with oneself is a very common Greek mood—an egotism in the best sense, expressed by good humor, laughter, and song, rather than by arrogance or snobbery. This was an age of conflicting moods, however, because the Greek who faced a world of change cocksure of himself and eager to tell the world of his accomplishments could suddenly turn into a naïve and marveling child, awestruck by the beauty of a sunset, or the savagery of a storm, or by the intensity of his own emotions. The swashbuckling adventurers of the archaic period—the merchant princes, the colonists, the poets, and the scientists—must remain some of our favorite people, for as individuals and individualists they could face any environment with confidence, and yet never lose their marvelous capacity for wonder.

The Greeks of the archaic period ventured from one end of the Mediterranean to the other. Seven hundred years later, Julius Caesar found the Gauls writing their language in the Greek alphabet, taught to them by the Greeks of Massalia on the coast of southern France. And on the remote shores of the Black Sea, in what is now the Ukraine, Greek colonists reported to travelers that in the gloomy interior of their country, snow fell for half the year. In Babylon, and Naucratis on the Nile delta, Greek visitors sat down with scholars of older and wiser races and eagerly picked their brains: How do you build a pyramid? How do you predict the orbit of the moon? Why does the Nile flood? and so forth. Meanwhile, other tourists reported that to the south of Egypt, where the sun went during the winter, the climate was so hot that human habitation was impossible.

Thus did the Greeks explore their physical and intellectual surroundings. In probing the limits of their physical environment and in learning the strange and varied customs of the human tribes, they gradually discovered their own identity as Greeks. One sort of quest had ended. But in their exploration of the mind, they found there were no limits. A whole new world lay before them, and in coming centuries they could devote themselves to new questions: What is man and what is the proper society of man? What is truth and how is truth recognized? What is virtue, and how can one acquire it?

SUGGESTIONS FOR FURTHER READING

Homer's *Odyssey* is generally thought to reflect conditions of Dark Age Greece, that is, from the tenth to the eighth centuries B.C. A useful companion volume is M. I. Finley, *The World of Odysseus* (New York: Penguin, 1979). The gloomy outlook of an Iron Age farmer is presented in Hesiod's *Work and Days*. Hesiod's *Theogony* and the "Homeric" *Hymns* are the earliest statements of Greek mythology. There are good translations of Hesiod and of the *Hymns* by my colleague Apostolos Athanassakis, published by Johns Hopkins University Press. There are numerous translations of the Greek lyric poets. A. R. Burn's *The Lyric Age of Greece* (New York: St. Martin's, 1960) is a lively commentary on the whole period. Two books by Chester G. Starr furnish valuable perspective: *The Economic and Social Growth of Early Greece* (New York: Oxford University Press, 1977) and *The Rise of the Polis* (New York: Oxford University Press, 1986). Two good surveys of the period are Oswyn Murray, *Early Greece* (Stanford University Press, 1983), and Anthony Snodgrass, *Archaic Greece* (Berkeley and Los Angeles: University of California Press, 1980). Important aspects of the period are treated by Antony Andrewes, *The Greek Tyrants* (New York: Harper and Row, 1963), and A. J. Graham, *Colony and Mother City in Ancient Greece* (Chicago: Ares, 1983). Finally, the importance of the rural countryside for all periods of Greek history is emphasized by Robin Osborne's fine survey, *Classical Landscape with Figures* (Dobbs Ferry: Sheridan House, 1987).

3 The World of the Greek Polis

Historical Background, 550–336 B.C.

THE MIDDLE of the sixth century before Christ marks a turning point in Greek history. From our perspective, it is possible to recognize the end of one era and the beginning of another. The energy and vigor of the archaic period had carved out a new world for Greeks to live in; the succeeding age, which is conventionally called the classical period, was one of consolidation and a search for stability and harmony.

In spite of these ideals, the history of the classical age is largely a history of war—a tragic paradox that was apparent to contemporaries as well as to later generations. The course of Western civilization has always been determined to a large degree by the fortunes of its most serious enemies—traditionally those lying to the east. In the case of the Greeks it was the Persian Empire that profoundly influenced the direction Greek history was to take, from the emergence of its ruler

Cyrus the Great in mid-sixth century to the final conquest of that empire by Alexander the Great. The period opened with the Persians expanding westward to dominate the Greeks of the Ionian coast. Finally, in 499 B.C., the Ionians raised the banner of rebellion against their Asiatic overlords, characteristically not for any burning desire for liberty, but because of the intrigues and bungled plans of Ionian leaders. Mainland Greece was brought into the affair and thus attracted the wrath of two Persian monarchs, Darius the Great and his son and successor Xerxes. Two Persian expeditions were hurled against Greece in 490 and 480. The last invasion was so massive that almost everyone involved despaired for the future of the Hellenic race. From the councils of supposedly fearless Spartan generals to Apollo's own oracle at Delphi, defeatism was rampant.

Only a handful of Athenian statesmen and soldiers kept their nerve, persuaded their allies to remain firm, and finally exposed the Persian colossus for what it really was: a handful of superb Iranian cavalry

CLASSICAL GREECE

surrounded by worthless masses of unwilling and unmotivated Asiatic conscripts, whose numbers proved to be an embarrassment once the time for action had arrived.

Athens so thoroughly dominated the rest of the fifth century B.C. that students often make the mistake of confusing all of Greece with this one polis. By its performance in the Persian War, the city of Athens won the means to political and economic domination of other Greek states—a role the Athenians accepted and interpreted with vigor for three-quarters of a century. But the Athenians had won more than money, ships, and military leadership. The circumstances of the Persian invasion cloaked the city of Athens with a moral superiority they could never forget: Athenians alone had acted courageously in time of mortal danger; Athenian fortitude had saved the rest of Greece. This moral superiority eventually lured the city into a fatally arrogant contention with other states. But without a doubt, the inspiration of victory over the barbarians also helped to arouse a generation of genius: the immortal tragedies of Aeschylus, Sophocles, and Euripides; the statesmanship of Pericles; the compelling historical logic of Thucydides; and the vision of a whole people expressed in a flurry of public building, of which the Parthenon is only the crowning example.

The fifty years after the Persian War was the zenith of Athens. But the spirit of Athena's city provoked not only admiration but fear as well. Fear of commercial rivalry led Corinth to rouse the lethargic Spartans against Athens. And Spartan fear of Athenian greatness, as Thucydides said so truly, was the principal cause of the Peloponnesian War (431–404). The result was twenty-seven years of grim and stupid struggle for which the justification was forgotten before the first battle was ended, and during which, year after year, the memory of last year's savagery was sufficient to provoke renewed hostilities for yet another season.

In 404, Athens fell from center stage, defeated and reduced to second-rate status by a triumphant Sparta. But Sparta was even less able to contribute to the cause of peace in the Greek world. Less than ten years later, Sparta's erstwhile allies rebelled and war broke out once more. This was to be the pattern in the Aegean for the next two generations as Sparta, Athens, Corinth, and Thebes in turn revealed a poverty of statesmanship as depressing as it is surprising, when we consider that this was also the century of Plato, of Aristotle, and of so many great accomplishments in science and philosophy, arts and letters, architecture, city planning, and other peaceful arts.

While petulant cities quarreled, a brilliant and ruthless monarch watched and planned in the far north. By the middle of the fourth century, King Philip of Macedon had found a pretext for entering Greek politics; clever diplomacy gained him allies and isolated his enemies. Finally, in 338, on the battlefield of Chaeronea in Boeotia, he led the

Macedonians to victory over the Athenians and the Thebans. The Spartans had lost their terrible skill in war—they crouched at home, malignant and ineffective. All other Greek states could recognize a winner when they saw one; therefore, in a triumph of expediency, they allowed Philip to appoint himself leader of a unified Greece. But Philip was not to enjoy such an exalted position, nor was he to realize his dream of leading a unified Greek nation against the hated Persians. Two years later, in 336, he was struck down by the hand of an assassin, leaving his crown, his new empire, and his plans to his son, Alexander.

This is the briefest of sketches of Greek history during the classical period. It is necessary now to take a more leisurely look at three of the more important subdivisions of the Greek people and to assess the roles they played, the contributions they made to Greek civilization, and their share of the responsibility for the *political* failure of that civilization.

Sparta: An Experiment in Elitist Communism

The valley of the Eurotas River in the southern Peloponnesus is about forty miles long. The river is one of the few in Greece to flow all year round, and the fields of the Eurotas Valley are broad and fertile. The Dorian tribesmen who settled this valley were particularly aggressive. Under vigorous kings, who were known to be descendants of Heracles, they dominated the indigenous population and reduced the surrounding mountain and coastal villages to subject status. By the seventh century, the city of Sparta on the Eurotas ruled the entire southeast Peloponnesus, an area called Laconia.

Even at that early date, the Spartans looked back to a semilegendary ruler named Lycurgus, who seems to have lived sometime in the ninth century B.C. and to have created the peculiar Spartan political and social system. This system limited citizenship to the warrior caste of Sparta— men who owned substantial lands and who could afford to devote most of their time to military training. We are unsure to what extent the "Lycurgan" system had developed by the seventh century. What is certain is that the events of that century sped up the process and created a militaristic and totalitarian state as ruthless, musclebound, and overspecialized as any dinosaur.

Two days' journey to the west of Sparta, up and across the ruggedly beautiful pine forests and rocky passes of the Taygetus mountains, one comes down into the green, well-watered hills and meadows of Messenia. Unlike the Spartans, the Dorians who had settled Messenia had succumbed to the easy life in one of the fairest districts of Greece. But three times during the seventh and sixth centuries, the Messenians were to look fearfully to the crags of Taygetus in the east. And three times

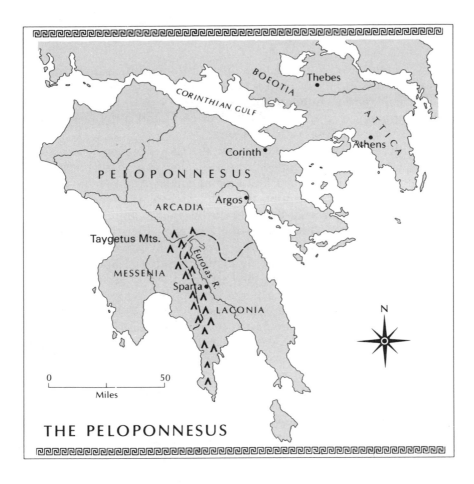

THE PELOPONNESUS

the gloomy and cruel Spartans poured through the passes and down into the plains to burn and rape and loot in an attempt to impose their rule. The last time they stayed as masters, having reduced the survivors to the same status as their serfs back home. By this time Spartan serfs—called *helots*—outnumbered Spartan warriors by more than ten to one. Some sort of rigid control was needed to avoid a continual specter of helot rebellion; the Spartan system we know is evidently a reaction to this fear.

In Laconia, a rigid hierarchy was created. At the very bottom were the helots, who were little better off than farm animals. In the middle were all Laconians other than Spartans. These people were free, except that they had to pay taxes and serve in the army when called up. At the very top was the elite body of Spartan citizens, who alone were entitled to political voice and to participation in the training prescribed by Lycurgus. Every aspect of Spartan training was devised to dehumanize the individual and subordinate him to the state. Boys were taken from their homes at the age of seven to begin a lifetime of barracks existence. From this time forward, no artistic endeavor or philosophical inquiry was allowed to distract the Spartan from military training. Virtues stressed were blind courage and obedience, indifference to pain, heat, or cold, and a contempt for the civilized niceties of other Greek states, contempt expressed in the sort of short and pithy observation that ever since has been called "laconic."

Ideally, all Spartans were social equals. They were led by two kings with equal powers, descended from Heracles. But these kings were intended to be no more than first among equals. The monarchs were advised by a board of five *ephors* (literally, "overseers") who were often the virtual ruling power of the state during the reign of weak or ineffectual kings. A council of elders—the *gerousia*—helped to give direction, and all major decisions were approved by an assembly of all Spartan male citizens. But the only distinction that meant anything in Spartan life was honor won on the battlefield. No king, no councillor could survive a moment of weakness in combat.

In order that the basic equality of all Spartans not be clouded by economic distinctions, the greatest austerity was practiced. Possessions were limited to the bare necessities, jewelry and precious metals were outlawed, and unwieldly iron spits served as currency.

These artificially created customs, perhaps because of their extreme nature, did in fact create a remarkable and enduring *esprit de corps* among Spartan citizens. This environment produced one of the most superbly trained and motivated armies the world has ever known. But the very nature of Spartan citizenship made it rigorously exclusive, so the military elite was never very large.

A famous Spartan claim was that they asked not *how many* enemies there were, only *where* they were. This was not entirely accurate, for the small size of the Spartan army led its leaders to be extremely cautious and not to commit their own citizens in large numbers unless they were almost certain to win. For this reason, the bulk of a Spartan army was usually composed of other Laconians and allies with only the position of honor on the right wing occupied by true Spartan citizens, generally led by one of the Spartan kings. Furthermore, Sparta was usually careful to have the support of as many allies as possible. By the end of the sixth century, Spartan allies were informally organized into the Peloponnesian League, formed of most, but not all, of the smaller states in the Peloponnesus. Commercial states, like Corinth, were happy to have a strong protector; others, like neighboring Argos and Arcadia, fretted at Spartan leadership.

The end of the sixth century B.C. saw Sparta drawn into more foreign adventures than the conservative elders cared for. Led by mad King Cleomenes, they were tricked into helping the Athenian aristocrats oust a tyrant (510). They were very nearly drawn into the Ionian revolt (499–494) and subsequently joined the Athenians in rejecting symbolic submission to Persia (491). They had obviously committed themselves to assisting the Athenians in any clash with the Persians. Nevertheless, when the news arrived that the Persians had landed at Marathon on the Attic coast in 490, the Spartans were careful to be celebrating an obligatory religious festival that prevented them from coming immediately to the Athenians' defense.

But ten years later the Persians came again, this time in numbers so great that they were entirely meaningless to tiny populations of small valleys and plains. The Athenians, with their usual boldness, wanted to throw the first line of defense as far forward as possible; the Spartans, with their usual lack of imagination, wished to build a wall across the isthmus of Corinth and defend only the Peloponnesus, ignoring the fact that the Peloponnesus has a coastline of more than one thousand miles and that the Persians had over 1,200 ships with them.

The Athenians finally talked the Spartans into a slightly more adventurous posture of defense, but only by promising to give them leadership of both allied armies and navies. Spartan participation in the two-year war consisted of one magnificent sacrifice—the holding action at Thermopylae—and a year later, on the battlefield of Plataea, a slaughter of the Persian cavalry that for some insane reason decided to charge the Spartan heavy infantry when it was in an unassailable position. During the rest of the war, the Spartans were kept at the front only by threats, cajolery, tricks, and outright bribery. Nevertheless, the war ended with the Spartans still in a position of leadership and with their reputation for martial skill and audacity untarnished.

But with freedom no longer threatened, the other smaller Greek states found the Spartan leaders uncongenial and asked the Athenians to assume command of the defensive alliance against possible future Persian aggression. The Athenians immediately accepted and created the more formal Delian League. As usual, the Spartans were not exactly sure of what was going on, only that in some subtle way they had been eased out of their leadership. The growing power of Athens and of Athens' league served to enhance a growing paranoia and the suspicion that no other Greek state was up to much good. They kept up a sullen opposition to Athens and the growth of Athens' empire for the next fifty years. Now and then, hostility flared into open warfare, and finally, in 431, spurred on by her allies and goaded into action by her sanguine young warriors, Sparta went to war—a moral crusade designed to force Athens to free unwilling members of her empire.

The Peloponnesian War was the making of Sparta. It turned this backward, naïve, and isolationist city into a world power, her crude generals into cunning diplomats. By the end of the war, this ignorant and distrustful state, which had once feared to send troops more than a three-day march from home and had condemned naval warfare as unmanly, now had detachments of one sort or another serving from Sicily to Ionia, supported by the largest fleet in the eastern Mediter-

The menace of a savage and pitiless fighting man
is reflected in this statuette of a Spartan warrior.
(*Courtesy Wadsworth Atheneum, Hartford*)

ranean. Her generals organized the defenses of Syracuse in the west,
and in the east conferred over banquet tables with Persian potentates.
Finally, in 405, Sparta crushed the once invincible Athenian navy. A
year later, the Athenian Empire had been liberated and delivered over
into the hands of pro-Spartan tyrants.

The war had forced Sparta to become an imperial power; now
Spartan arrogance compelled her allies to strengthen their own armies.
Athens rose again, and by 390, Aegean politics degenerated into a balance of weakness. Into this tangled situation the Persian king insinuated
himself, sending money and aid to whichever state seemed most bent
on destroying any kind of stability in the Greek world. In 387 and again
in 374, the king of Persia was able to dictate a settlement of Greek
affairs—circumstances that humiliated Greek statesmen with long
memories.

Despite momentary setbacks, one thing seemed permanent in the
Greek world: the ability of the full Spartan army to defeat any other

army in the world in infantry combat. Then came the news that shook Greece. In 371, on a battlefield near Thebes, the Spartan army was badly trounced by a superbly trained Theban army under a brilliant general named Epaminondas. More surprises were to follow: three slashing campaigns saw Theban armies penetrate the hitherto sacrosanct Peloponnesus. On one breathless day, Theban and allied troops stood on the banks of the Eurotas River and looked across at unwalled Sparta. Spartan wives, mothers, and sisters wept with shame, for no Spartan woman had ever seen an enemy soldier before. A fear of going too far kept the Thebans from attacking the city itself, but a few years later at Mantinea in the Peloponnesus, the Spartan army was humbled again and the state sank into permanent third-rate status.

Later Spartan reformers would blame the collapse on the decay of Spartan morality. In a broader sense, the truth of the matter appears to be that this monolithic, militaristic state was simply unable to adapt to changing times. But there is some accuracy in the first charge. The Spartan system was breaking down in a growing gulf between rich and poor citizens, a local symptom of a trend going on all over Greece in the fourth century. Some Spartans had become impoverished to the point where they were unable to meet their regimental dues and so had lost citizenship. Thus, at a time when population and economies were growing all over the Greek world, the Spartan military elite was getting smaller and smaller. More powerful and wealthier Spartans were demanding the rewards of wealth and power: large homes, gold, silver, goods, and luxuries never before seen in the valley of the Eurotas. They were refusing to send their sons to the barracks—and getting away with it. It would be a whole century before a reformed and purified Sparta once more struck terror into the hearts of her neighbors.

Ionia: The Greeks of Asia Minor

It often seems to us, so many centuries later, that Athens was the spiritual and intellectual capital of the Greek world, as well as its political center of gravity. But for many Greeks of the fifth century B.C., Athens was only a newcomer to fame—Ionia had a far better claim to be considered the heart and soul of Hellenic society. After all, the Homeric epics took shape in Ionia. Here lyric poetry was born. The first natural philosophers came from cities on this coast, and in the fifth century, the first historians of the Western world developed their craft here.

From the very start, the Ionian communities tended to be urban rather than agrarian in orientation; urban life in turn both encouraged and rewarded the restless intellect. In the eighth and seventh centuries, cities like Miletus, Ephesus, and Smyrna were already flourishing commercial centers, while towns on the Greek mainland, with the exception of rare emporia like Corinth, were still tied to the soil. If the Spartans were symbols of rural conservatism and simple-minded courage, the Ionians in turn had a reputation for native wit and resiliency: an ability to change with the times, to make a profit when possible, and to survive when necessary. They were, after all, originally refugees from disaster; their new settlements were established on a hostile shore. No ancestral valleys sheltered them. Instead, they became accustomed to living in the midst of barbarians—the varied peoples of Asia Minor, Phrygians, Lydians, Carians, and so forth—preserving their Hellenic identity in a strange land while adopting what was useful from their neighbors. Through the centuries, the Ionians adapted themselves to an environment of change: invaders from land and sea, visiting ships and caravans from three continents, dozens of nationalities speaking dozens of different languages and worshiping gods without number. In any situation, it could be said of the Ionians that they landed on their feet—or someone else's.

By the sixth century, most Ionian cities had come to a living arrangement with their most powerful neighbor, the growing kingdom of Lydia. The Lydians were a product of fusion of the various peoples who had crossed Asia Minor through the ages. They were horse breeders and farmers, and their last and greatest monarch, King Croesus, ruled from the magnificent capital of Sardes, a two-day journey from the coast. But Croesus grew too powerful. Hubris blinded him to the reasonable limits of his empire and he "overreached" himself, as the Greeks would put it. Challenging the new power of Persia in the East, he succumbed to the cavalry of Cyrus the Great, and in 546 B.C., Lydia was reduced to the status of a satrapy of the Persian Empire.

The Ionians enjoyed this confusion. The Greek cities of the coast chose this moment to proclaim their sovereign status and independence from any successors of their Lydian overlords. But they fell prey to the eternal Greek sickness—inability to unite for a common cause. The Persian generals were able to reduce the Greek cities one by one, and by 540, Ionia was securely under Persian rule.

In 499, Ionia revolted once more. It would be pleasant to report that they did so because of a passion for liberty. Unfortunately, the true reasons are not so inspiring. The Persian kings ruled the Ionian cities by supporting local tyrants with money and troops. One of these tyrants, Aristagoras of Miletus, offered to capture the large Aegean island of Naxos and add it to the Persian Empire—thus increasing his own power and wealth. But the attempt failed, and Aristagoras, fearing that King Darius would punish him, induced Miletus and other Ionian cities to revolt. Athens sent token aid, which served more to anger the Persians than make their revenge any less inevitable. In the face of the threat, the Ionians finally managed to unite and actually started to work on their naval tactics.

For seven days, wrote the historian Herodotus, they labored at the oars under the hot sun. Then they began to grumble:

> It would be better to suffer any fate rather than these evils and submit
> to any kind of slavery rather than what we endure now.
>   Herodotus 6. 12

Mutiny and division set in, some contingents made their own private plans, and when the Persians arrived at Miletus with an allied Phoenician fleet, the Ionians were easily defeated and once more subdued one by one.

Herodotus believed it was this Ionian revolt that brought mainland Greece to the attention of King Darius and prompted the two invasions of the Persian Wars. In 479, after the Persians had finally been driven out of Europe, the Greeks counterattacked. The allies, now led by Athens, set about liberating the Ionian cities and neighboring islands from the Persian yoke. By mid-fifth century B.C., over 150 Ionian and island city-states were members of Athens' empire, obliged to pay tribute in return for military protection, and prevented by Athenian rule from continuing their favorite pastime—quarreling with each other.

Once more the Ionian cities grew restless under foreign control. This time, the wealthier classes in the various cities, smarting under the tribute, sent secret assurances to Sparta that Athens' Ionian dependencies would revolt if only a major war between Athens and Sparta would break out. This may have been a major consideration for the Spartans on the eve of the Peloponnesian War. But the Ionians were no more dependable than usual. Only one city revolted during the first phase of the war and this challenge was swiftly put down by the Athenian navy. For the rest of the twenty-seven-year war, the Ionians clung to their individualism, cooperating now and then with the Spartans or Athenians, always separately, always expediently, and ended the war devastated, depopulated, their commerce wrecked, and their political autonomy extinguished by an even more oppressive Spartan despotism. And then, as Sparta weakened during the course of the fourth century, the cities gradually fell back into the Persian sphere of influence. One by one they began to accept the sort of role the Phoenician cities had adopted centuries before: they traded any hope of political independence for the security of lenient masters and the peaceful conditions that made trade most profitable.

It is easy to be scornful of the Ionians as a political entity. When free, they refused to unite to preserve their liberty; as subjects, they made bungling conspirators. In combat, they were capable of brilliance but never fortitude over the long run. As statesmen, the Ionians were failures—but their failure was only part of the greater Greek failure to create a lasting political stability. The conditions that the Ionians faced

The Greek schoolmaster taught reading, writing, and the rudiments of music to his charges. (*Antikenmuseum, Staatliche Museen Preussicher Kulturbesitz, Berlin*)

were more difficult and accelerated; therefore their ineptitude is more obvious.

But if the Ionians were incapable of successful group action, they certainly were able to produce superb individuals. Regardless of the ebb of their political fortunes, the cities and islands of the Anatolian coast continued to contribute far more than their share of poets, philosophers, historians, and doctors of international reputation. Perhaps one of the most famous Ionians is Herodotus of Halicarnassus. Four centuries later, Cicero was to call him "the Father of History"; there is little reason to dispute this judgment to the present day. The city of Halicarnassus is in the southwest corner of Anatolia, right on the border between the areas of Dorian and Ionian settlement. In language, Halicarnassus was Dorian, but Herodotus wrote in Ionian—the literary dialect of his day. The historian was born during the era of the Persian Wars and grew up in a generation when everyone was still talking about the wars or living their consequences—for Halicarnassus was very much on the border between East and West.

In about 460 B.C., Herodotus became a political exile, but, so far as we can tell, an exile of means. For about a dozen years, he traveled the eastern Mediterranean, probably as a merchant because he had a merchant's eye for commodities and prices. All the time of his wandering, he observed the varieties of human beings. Glorious human achievement he regarded with admiration, folly with amused toleration. At some time in mid-fifth century, perhaps residing in Athens, he began to write it all down using as his theme the Persian Wars. But the wars were only the central episode on a broad canvas that depicted the eternal division between East and West, barbarian and Greek, spanning centuries and involving all the various peoples of the eastern Mediterranean.

Herodotus saw the Ionians as the catalyst—the quickening element that brought about the inevitable clash between Greeks and Orientals. An Ionian himself, he found little to praise in his own countrymen: they made trouble perennially and then could not deal with the consequences, and they brought the wrath of the Persian Empire down on the rest of Greece. But Ionia was only part of the story. Herodotus traced the rise of Persia, ventured down the strange alleys of Babylon and into temples thronged with amateur prostitutes offering their bodies for the goddess, as every woman had to do once in her lifetime:

> And those who are fair and stately get away quickly; but ugly women
> wait a long time . . . sometimes three and four years. . . .
>
> Herodotus 1. 199

And he wrote about Egypt, where everything was the opposite of Greece. He asked the priests, why does the Nile rise every summer? And they told him about two great rocks named Crophi and Mophi way upstream, and how these rocks swung apart once a year and the water came forth. And Herodotus must have nodded his head and smiled to himself, and then like any good Greek, he must have gone out to inquire after the *real* reasons, the *scientific* reasons. Like any good Greek, he scoffed at illogical explanations, such as snow melting in the mountains of Ethiopia. . . .

And he wrote about southern Russia where the wild Scythians howled with glee in their bathhouses as they threw marijuana onto red-hot rocks and breathed the fumes. And about North Africa, where the Garamantes drove their four-horse chariots (their existence now proven by Saharan rock paintings); and about Siberia, where one-eyed Arimaspians and gold-guarding griffins lived (as yet unconfirmed by rock paintings or other means); and about the sands of Oxus in central Asia, where barbaric Queen Tomyris cut off the head of Cyrus the Great and immersed it in a bucket of blood to make her vow come true—for in Herodotus, all vows and all oracles and all dreams are fulfilled.

The *Historiê* of Herodotus is an amazing compendium of anthropology and geography, natural science and religion, history and literature. In this last respect it stands midway between the Homeric epic and the more austere and parsimonious history of Thucydides, but it is consistently true to its first word—*historiê*—which only later came to mean our sort of "history"; to the Ionian Greek it meant simply "inquiry."

This is a particularly appropriate title for the first great Ionian prose work, because inquiring was perhaps what the Ionians did best. Many pre-Socratic philosophers came from Ionia and the Ionian sphere of influence, people rather scornfully lumped together by Plato under the name of Sophists. But there were as many different varieties of Sophism as there were individual Sophists. What they all had in common was that they professed to teach something—something that could be discovered by rational inquiry. Some of the first Sophists taught science: physics, astronomy, and mathematics; others taught logic, particularly that aspect of political and legal logic called rhetoric. They became most famous for professing that they were able to make students successful at getting along in the world through the content of their courses. It is true that Plato condemned the Sophists for advocating a sort of applied materialism and equating virtue with happiness, but this was unfair. To examine any one of the Sophists in any detail is to discover a tremendous breadth of interest.

The greatest mind of his generation was Anaxagoras of Clazomenae, who flourished in Athens during the mid-fifth century B.C. He was primarily an astronomer (he said the sun was a flaming mass of red-hot metal and was as big as the whole Peloponnesus!), but he was also an elementary sort of psychologist and was reputed to have advised Pericles on political psychology. Pericles' political enemies detected sinister intent in this and tried to get at Anaxagoras by having the teaching of astronomy made illegal. Democritus, from the Ionian colony of Abdera in Thrace, discovered the real reason for the rising of the Nile, but he also wrote on virtue, reason, geometry, poetry, medical diagnosis, rhythm and harmony, tactics and infantry combat, the sacred writings in Babylon, history, and painting. In his spare time he developed the atomic theory. Clearly this was not a man to be limited by the confines of any one discipline.

One of the most famous and certainly one of the wisest of the Ionians was no Sophist at all, but a Milesian prostitute named Aspasia. We know nothing at all about her early life, but by the middle of the fifth century, she had become established in Athens as the madame of a fancy house of assignation. Socrates and other wise men used to visit her regularly simply to benefit from conversation with her. When she came to the attention of the great Pericles, he promptly divorced his wife and moved in with her. This was a union that could not be sanctioned by Attic law. Nevertheless, Pericles remained faithful to his Aspasia for the rest of his days. We are told that Aspasia was the most politically astute individual in Athens, and Plato, whether joking or not, professed in his dialogue Menexenus to have discovered a speech written by Aspasia for Pericles to deliver. (See Chapter 6, pp. 131–135 for more on Aspasia.)

Historians, educators, scientists, and courtesans are all typical of the stream of restless, energetic individuals produced by the coasts of Ionia. If this relentless individualism made it difficult for Ionians to accomplish anything by political cooperation and compromise, it at least established this part of the Greek world as an unending source of clever, accomplished, and cosmopolitan persons of both sexes who helped to make life interesting wherever they happened to travel. And in the aftermath of Alexander's conquests, it was the Ionians who first rose to the opportunity, taking advantage of new and confused times, and helped to spread their brand of Hellenism throughout Egypt and the Near East.

Athens: The Education of Hellas[1]

We are told that an Athenian king named Codrus sacrificed himself to save his city during the last Dorian siege of Athens. In the aftermath, the aristocratic families of the city felt that no future king could possibly come up to this standard of kingly behavior; they therefore decided to quit while they were ahead and to have no more monarchs.

We can only guess at what is concealed by this pleasant fiction. But we do know that with a few exceptions, the institution of monarchy seems to have died out all over Greece during the three or four centuries after the fall of Mycenaean civilization. In every known case, the aristocrats distributed the functions of the king. At Corinth, for instance, the Bacchiad clan, who had supplied a monarch for eight generations, finally decided to end the institution of one-man rule and dispense its powers over a broader area.

Aristocracy then became the standard form of government all over the Greek world. The land-owning gentry, descended from gods, made such political decisions as a simple state might require; they served as priests, generals, and judges, and if a community remained prosperous and contented, no one would question their right to rule. If the gods gave a man birth, wealth, wisdom, and warlike courage, it was altogether fitting that he should lead less fortunate folk. The Greeks were not egalitarian; they took it for granted that distinctions existed among people, and there was no natural antagonism between social and economic classes during normal times.

In their paternal role, the nobles were also a source of local credit. It has been estimated that as much as one-quarter of the grain harvest was needed to sow the crop for the next year. In times of necessity, smaller farmers would turn to their rich neighbor to borrow seed or perhaps even food during a bleak season. The normal course of events would see the debt paid off. But if an entire state became impoverished

---

[1] "In short, I say to you that our city is the education of Hellas." Pericles, in his Funeral Oration, Thucydides 2. 41. 1.

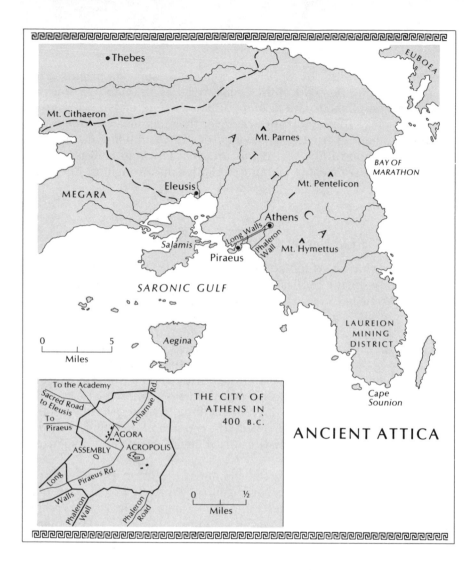

Within the map:

Thebes

Mt. Cithaeron

Mt. Parnes

EUBOEA

BAY OF MARATHON

Eleusis

Mt. Pentelicon

MEGARA

Athens

Long Walls

Salamis

Phaleron Wall

Mt. Hymettus

Piraeus

SARONIC GULF

0   5
Miles

Aegina

LAUREION MINING DISTRICT

Cape Sounion

To the Academy

Sacred Road to Eleusis

Acharnae Rd.

THE CITY OF ATHENS IN 400 B.C.

To Piraeus

AGORA

ASSEMBLY

ACROPOLIS

ANCIENT ATTICA

Long Walls

Piraeus Rd.

Phaleron Wall

Phaleron Road

0   ½
Miles

for one reason or another—a series of bad years or overpopulation—and debts could not be paid, the nobility would begin to react to long-standing debts with something less than paternal restraint, and the highly developed Greek talent for sensing injustice would become a class reaction on the part of the debt-ridden and the dispossessed. Such a crisis in the development of the agricultural economy took place in every Greek state at some time or another.

The polis of Athens was larger than most. Many of the rural districts of Attica[2] were a two-day journey from the city. During the eighth century B.C., population pressure had been relieved not by sending out

---

[2] In Greek usage, *Athens* is the name of the polis, *Attica* the name of its territory. As many as two hundred small and medium-sized villages dotted the Attic countryside.

colonies but by settling and clearing these outlying lands. But by the beginning of the sixth century, we are told that the aristocrats had gained control of most of the land and were forcing the dispossessed to work as sharecroppers. Worse still, many Athenians had pledged their own persons as surety for their debts and when unable to pay had been sold abroad into slavery.

When it seemed that the rage of the oppressed might erupt into violence, both rich and poor agreed to put matters into the hands of a man named Solon, who, although young, had already acquired a reputation for both wisdom and honesty. A child of the Archaic Age, Solon took the unusual step of explaining and promoting his political and economic reforms in a series of poems, some of which have survived. Unfortunately it is not always easy to define exactly what he did, since the language of the verses is obscure and because we know about the Athens of Solon only from accounts of writers two hundred years later, who were often as puzzled by his poems as we are.

The worst injustice was the sale of fellow citizens into slavery for debt and there seems to be no doubt that Solon both raised funds to purchase their freedom and made a law forbidding anyone to offer his own person as security. Second, in some way he relieved the burden of those who were oppressed by the debts on their land. In one poem he claimed to have liberated black Earth (whom he refers to as a woman) by pulling up the mortgage markers, but how he accomplished this he did not say. Many other economic reforms are attributed to him, but because a commercial economy of any sort was still virtually unknown at Athens, it would seem that our sources are projecting market conditions of their own day backward into a far more primitive era.[3]

Most lasting were Solon's political reforms, or—as it would be more accurate to say—his political creations. For it was Solon who really created the concept of the impersonal state at Athens, in contrast to the personal and arbitrary leadership of a handful of nobles. First of all, he regularized existing institutions and offices, defining their responsibilities and setting limits to their powers. Then he created a tribal council and generally broadened the political base, guaranteeing that if hard times should come again, all classes would at least have some opportunity to alleviate their distress through constitutional means. His settlement was entirely pragmatic, rather than ideological. When asked if he had given the Athenians the best possible laws, Solon replied, "No, the best they would accept." Significantly, the laws of Solon were inscribed permanently for all to see. This is the beginning of what

---

[3] During the past thirty years numismatists have been able to show that the Athenians did not even produce a coinage until after about 550 B.C. What commerce existed was a matter of barter.

The ferociously competitive nature of the young Greek aristocrat is illustrated by the footrace depicted on this sixth-century black figure vase. (*Lee Boltin Picture Library*)

became an enduring conviction among Athenians that all government business ought to take place in public.

When strife broke out again in Athens, it was between rival noble families rather than between economic classes. Finally, in 561 B.C., an aggressive and ambitious aristocrat named Peisistratus recognized the power inherent in popular support, particularly the support of the countryside against the entrenched great houses in the city of Athens. Courting the aid of the rural districts, he seized control of the state from the annually elected magistrates, and except for two brief periods, he and his sons ruled Athens as tyrants until 510.

Peisistratus illustrates many of the aspects of "tyranny" as it was later to be defined by Aristotle. He came to power and remained in

The sons of the Athenian rich, who could afford to raise horses, served as the cavalry and are perhaps shown here in a processional scene from the great frieze of the Parthenon, looted in the last century by Lord Elgin and now in the British Museum. (*Lee Boltin Picture Library*)

power unconstitutionally, but otherwise preserved constitutional forms. Like so many other tyrants, his ultimate power base was popular support, and he nourished this support by distributing the estates of his exiled enemies among the poorer citizens of Attica—a redistribution, incidentally, that contributed to greater economic stability in the countryside for the future. Peisistratus and his sons were also patrons of the arts, inviting poets and artists from all over the Greek world to come to Athens. The later sixth century thus saw the beginnings of an Athenian cultural primacy that would rarely thereafter be challenged by other Greek cities.

But as was the case with so many tryants, Peisistratus was unable to bequeath his popularity to his sons. Rival aristocratic families grew restless once more and in 510, with Spartan help, successfully expelled the tyranny for good. Two years later, a man named Cleisthenes, leader of one of the grandest aristocratic houses of Attica, put together the democratic constitution by which Athens was ruled for the next two centuries—a record of stability unmatched anywhere else in the Greek world.

The city of Athens entered the fifth century B.C.—the century of her greatness—in form a democracy, but an aristocracy in function. It was true that all officials were elected or chosen by the people, that all public business was administered by a representative council of 500, and that all final decisions were made by an assembly in which all male citizens could speak and vote. But the leaders of the noble houses continued to dominate political life at Athens for three-quarters of a century. The common people listened to the arguments of rival aristocrats in the assembly, they chose among aristocrats when electing people to office, and they followed aristocratic officers into battle and sent them as diplomats to other states.

The continuing primacy of the noble houses of Athens is easy to explain. The heads of the great land-owning families accepted leadership as a natural responsibility handed down from father to son. They were the only members of the state trained to lead. They were the only citizens who received a formal education, rudimentary as it may seem to us. And of course, they were descended from gods and presided at all the religious rites that occupied such an important place in the life of any Greek community. Although we are told—most notably by Aristotle and Karl Marx—that a natural hostility exists, or ought to exist, between nobles and commons, the aristocratic monopoly of the direction of the state was not challenged for several generations. Athenian nobles covered themselves with glory during the Persian Wars. It was Miltiades who commanded on the fateful day at Marathon when Greeks first defeated Persians in set battle. Themistocles, Aristeides, and Xanthippus, leaders of rival clans, competed with each other during the invasion of Xerxes in supplying courageous leadership and good counsel to the state. After the war, the Athenian aristocracy accepted leadership in the new league against Persia without hesitation. It was their incentive, ambition, and foresight during the next thirty years that eventually put Athens at the head of an empire containing over 200 states, large and small.

In the long run, it was this empire that was most responsible for the decline of the aristocracy at Athens. Before the Persian Wars, the city of Athens had been little more than a minor port and a marketing center for the surrounding farmlands. "Government," in our sense of the word, scarcely existed and must have been much like a New England town meeting. And now, suddenly, the volume of public business began to increase at a geometric rate. Records had to be kept of the financial obligations of the cities in the league. Boards of treasurers had to administer the tribute. The courts were vastly expanded to deal with disputes between cities of the empire. And a permanent military establishment kept fleets voyaging from one end of the Aegean to the other to remind members of the empire of the ultimate justification for Athenian rule. According to Aristotle, there were 1,500 minor officials of various types at home and abroad by the middle of the century, and we would assume that by the very nature of bureaucracy, these numbers would have continued to increase.

No less extraordinary was the expansion of the economy. Athens had always had a great potential source of wealth in the state-owned silver mines at Laureion, but they had never truly been exploited; the surplus was simply coined and handed out in a public distribution. But when a rich vein was discovered in 483, the Athenians accepted the advice of Themistocles and used the money to build a fleet of warships. Thus was born the public sector of the economy at Athens.

Because a growing coolness to Sparta developed after the war, the land fortifications of Athens were greatly improved; this had the effect of putting scores of stone masons, muleteers, and day laborers on the public payroll. Finally, in 449, the Athenians decided to use part of their imperial revenues to rebuild the temples burned by the Persians. Because all state business was let out to private contractors, scores of opportunities were created for budding entrepreneurs willing and alert enough to take advantage of them. Shipbuilders kept the Athenian navy at full strength while building contractors bid for their share of public works. All this construction put a premium on materials that either had to be imported, such as wood and hemp for the boatyards and gold and ivory for the adornment of temples, or produced locally, such as cut stone, leather goods, armor, woolens, and fleeces for troops on bivouac. It is no coincidence that, in 424 when the comic poet Aristophanes parodied the new breed of tradesmen risen to political prominence, he named a dealer in sheep, a rope maker, and a tanner—all professions that profited from the demands of public works and the military establishment.[4]

This twin growth of governmental apparatus and economy cannot be overemphasized. It had the most profound effects on social classes at Athens. The first to feel the effects were the aristocrats, who had run the public life of Athens for years. The empire, by creating hundreds of new public officials, diluted aristocratic control of public business. And by creating a new class of wealthy people outside the nobility, it diluted aristocratic control of the economy.

For a long time, the people of Athens continued to elect and appoint nobles to the top posts in government. For fifteen consecutive years, from 443 to 429, they put their trust in Pericles, an aristocrat of austere demeanor, irreproachable standards of financial honesty, and proven ability in foreign affairs and military leadership. During this period, Pericles himself boasted that Athens had become the "education of Hellas." But toward the end of Pericles' primacy, there were probing attacks by the new bourgeois leaders. In one generation, common people of ability had acquired wealth and influence; now they intended to have power as well, not only minor magistracies and junior military posts, but the political prominence once reserved for nobles only.

The Indian summer of the aristocracy came to an end with the death of Pericles in 429 during the second year of the Peloponnesian War. It has often been observed that war has the tendency to accelerate social trends. For the first time, the electorate turned to one of its own— Cleon the tanner—a man who was a contrast to Pericles in every way,

---

[4] *Knights* 128ff.

except in political aptitude. He was the first to use the language of the streets and the marketplace while addressing the assembly. He tucked up his tunic and he made coarse gestures. And he attempted to stir up in the people a resentment against the class that had led them so long, against the wealth, privilege, and above all, the *style* of the aristocracy. The Athenian voters admired the novelty of Cleon, and they were impressed by his energy, but with their characteristic moderation they refused to follow him into any class vendettas. The election of Cleon to high office was only a symptom of evolutionary social change; it was not to herald a sudden toppling of one class and the revolutionary ascendancy of another. (See Chapter 6, pp. 123–127 for more on Cleon.)

Throughout the long years of the Peloponnesian War, the exigencies of conflict helped elevate the commoners in Athens to a commanding position. Both ancient and modern critics have railed at the tyranny of the mob; in fact, one must admit that at times demagogues did in fact goad the popular assembly into foolish decisions. And from time to time, the popular courts were used as political weapons— usually against people of wealth and prestige. But from our perspective, we can only marvel that the first popular sovereign assembly in the history of the Western world did as well as it did.

Toward the end of the war, the most bitter and violent opponents of democracy in Athens formed a conspiracy that became not only oligarchic in theory but pro-Spartan in reality. As a result, when the Athenians were forced to surrender to Sparta in 404, the government of the state was handed over by the Spartans to a committee of thirty Athenian oligarchs—the "Thirty Tyrants," as they came to be called— headed by an unscrupulous political adventurer named Critias.[5]

The exciting story of the next year is told in some detail by the historian Xenophon, who also participated in some of the action (*Hellenica* 2). A handful of the democratic leaders fled Athens as the gates were opened to the Spartans. They were given refuge in neighboring Thebes and were soon joined by other exiles fleeing from the reign of terror instituted in Athens by the Thirty Tyrants. Then one night, they recrossed the border and seized a fort in the mountains north of Athens. This became a rallying point for Athenians of all classes who hated the Spartan-supported tyranny. Once again, the democrats moved at night, this time to seize the harbor district of Piraeus. The next day, a battle broke out between the democrats and the supporters of the Thirty Ty-

---

[5] Critias was a fascinating, if rather unsavory, person. He was Plato's kinsman, an aristocrat of impeccable background, a descendant of Solon. Just prior to his career as an oligarchic leader, he had been in the north attempting to organize the serfs and other dispossessed factions against the rulers of Thessaly.

rants. Critias himself was slain, the oligarchs lost their direction, and soon the Spartans agreed to let the Athenians have their old government back. Once more, the Athenians displayed their usual good sense and moderation. Instead of avenging themselves on the oligarchs and their supporters with a bloodbath—so ordinary in the political turmoil of other Greek cities—one of their first acts was to pass a bill of amnesty making it illegal for anyone publicly to mention any crime committed during the time the Thirty had been in power.

But the Peloponnesian War was over in name only. Sparta's erstwhile allies, Corinth and Thebes, soon turned against her, and the Athenians, seeing Sparta occupied on every hand, soon regained their old confidence and began to rearm. In 396, hostilities broke out once more and continued in desultory fashion for nearly forty more years, involving Sparta against a shifting coalition of Athens, Thebes, Corinth, and their allies. The clashing of arms year after year after year finally had one very understandable effect: it tended to drive the war-weary common people, wherever they lived, out of the business of making war. As a result, most Greek states with any pretensions to a commercial economy had difficulty interesting their citizens in direct participation in military adventures; therefore, they turned instead to mercenary troops and professional commanders. Athenians in particular more than once betrayed their lack of enthusiasm for foreign war by authorizing a general to hire troops and to go off campaigning, and then forgetting to appropriate any financial support for the venture. There is the ludicrous example of one body of troops forced to take jobs as farm laborers on a distant island simply to earn enough to stay alive.

By 357, Athens was ready for a long respite from war. A brilliant statesman attempted to perpetuate this antiwar attitude by committing all unexpended funds in the state budget, present and future, to public services and public welfare. After a century and a half of living under a democratic constitution, the Athenians had become accustomed to the concept of the state as public servant; a glance at Aristotle's *Constitution of Athens* reveals the extent of the services and safeguards private citizens expected from their government.

By mid-fourth century, Athenian citizens could actually feel confident that they *were* the state. All decisions were made by the assembly of Athenian male citizens—and those who attended the assembly were paid for their time. Moreover, any Athenian citizen might aspire to political leadership in some state office, for there was no longer an unwritten understanding that the top posts should go to men from noble houses. All disputes and judgments were the responsibility of juries of citizens, chosen by lot and paid for their services.

Athenians might expect to be guarded at night by state watchmen. During the day, they went to market on streets kept in repair by the state and kept free of refuse by garbagemen on the public payroll. And when they got to the marketplace, they could expect the weights and measures used by shops to be honest, subject to state inspection; their food, too, was inspected for purity by employees of the state. Public baths and gymnasia contributed to the enjoyment of life, and during the great religious festivals, the state paid for admission to the theater. Aristotle could truthfully say that Athenians were in control of their state and had consequently made life pleasant for themselves.

Naturally, for such a variety of public services, payment was required. In the prosperous days of the fifth century, Athenian revenue came from the tributary states of a huge empire; in the fourth century, resources were more constricted. The state owned silver mines and some land from which rents were collected. Flourishing overseas trade put money in the treasury in the form of duties and tariffs (although we are imperfectly informed about the details), and direct taxes were levied in a variety of ways on the richest citizens of Athens. But sources of revenue were generally strained throughout the fourth century, which may help explain Athenian forgetfulness when it came time to appropriate money for military purposes.

In the middle of the fourth century, the rise of King Philip of Macedon led to a bitter political struggle in Athens. A brilliant young orator named Demosthenes insisted that Athens should take military steps to defend her sphere of influence overseas against the ambition of this monarch. But a peace party in Athens believed that Macedon could be accommodated without war. It was inevitable that the spirited foreign policy recommended by Demosthenes would bring about a budget crisis. Athenians could afford either a full round of public services and comforts at home or military adventures abroad—but not both. Realizing this, the wily king of Macedon timed his expansionist policies at just a slow enough rate to keep calmer heads prevailing in Athens until it was too late. In 338, unaccustomed to the rigors of total war, the citizens of Athens fought their last great battle on the field of Chaeronea in central Greece. Although they fought valiantly, hastily converted civilians were no match for the tough, confident veterans of Macedon—and there were too few mercenaries and better trained Theban allies. Even Demosthenes threw away his shield and ran for his life.

A magnanimous King Philip freed all Athenian prisoners without conditions and allowed Athens to keep a tenuous sovereignty. But the day of the influential and independent city-state was past. In coming centuries, Athens would be satisfied with being recognized as the ancient and august center of learning and culture in the Greek world—the true education of Hellas. Political strife would be left to others.

SUGGESTIONS FOR FURTHER READING

The histories of Herodotus, Thucydides, and Xenophon provide a connected narrative from about the mid-sixth century to 362 B.C., supplemented most significantly by Plutarch's *Lives* of the period and the history of Diodorus Siculus. Those authors both lived much later and were uncritical. Our evidence for the period of the Peloponnesian War is enlivened by the comedies of Aristophanes. From 362 to 310, historians must rely on Diodorus for a narrative, supplemented primarily by the speeches of the Athenian orators, by Plutarch's *Lives* once more, and by Arrian, the most important surviving biographer of Alexander the Great. Three fine collections of original sources are volumes in the series, *Translated Documents of Greece and Rome: Archaic Times to the End of the Peloponnesian War*, edited by Charles W. Fornara (New York: Cambridge University Press, 1983); *From the End of the Peloponnesian War to the Battle of Ipsus*, edited by Phillip Harding (New York: Cambridge University Press, 1985); and *The Greek City States: A Source Book* (Norman: University of Oklahoma Press, 1986) edited by P. J. Rhodes. N. G. L. Hammond's *History of Greece to 322 B.C.* (Oxford: Clarendon Press, 1967) is a well-annotated general history. A novel perspective is furnished by 140 aerial photographs of ancient Greek sites in *Wings over Hellas: Ancient Greece from the Air*, edited with commentary by Raymond V. Schoder, S.J. (New York: Oxford University Press, 1974).

4 The Economies of the Greek World

The Means of Exchange

THE FIRST CURRENCIES all over the ancient world were pieces of precious metal with no fixed value: copper, bronze, silver, and infrequently gold. The only way one could evaluate such a piece of metal was to weigh it using a standard set of weights; in time, merchants began to guarantee the purity of the bullion they used by stamping a recognizable device on each unit. The earliest examples of such private coinage come from Ionia. We are told that in mainland Greece, in the archaic period, minor exchanges were negotiated by means of *obols* or spits of metal, iron, or bronze, and that six obols equaled a *drachma*—literally, a "handful," derived from the Greek verb meaning to grasp. But until the first half of the sixth century B.C., the Greeks lived in a largely premonetary society, relying on barter to obtain items they could not grow or make themselves. Only a growing class of merchants in-

The famous Aeginetan "turtles" circulated all over the Mediterranean as the currency of one of the first great mercantile powers. (*Hirmer Fotoarchiv*)

volved in overseas trade was accustomed to deal on a daily basis with precious metals. Coinage was eventually adopted not because it aided commerce but because it was part of a general trend all over the rapidly developing Greek world to replace traditional and arbitrary values with rational and consistent ones.

The kingdom of Lydia was the first state to guarantee both the weight and purity of pieces of metal by turning out standardized currency marked with the symbol of the realm. By the late seventh century, Ionian Greek neighbors had adopted this custom, and it quickly spread to the islands and to mainland Greece, particularly to the highly commercialized island of Aegina, just south of Athens.

The discovery of coin hoards all over the ancient world helps to inform us of the relative prosperity and commercial activity of the Greek states that competed in trying to make their currencies universally acceptable. The criteria were first, the extent of foreign trade in which the city was engaged, and second, the purity of the city's precious metal resources. Many Near Eastern states used gold, and the Lydians coined electrum (a natural alloy of gold and silver); but pure silver was by far the most common precious metal in the Greek world, thus all early coinage is of this metal. From the evidence of the first large coin hoards, it would seem that Aegina, Corinth, and Chalcis (on the island of Euboea) dominated Aegean trade until the first part of the fifth century.

Sometime in the middle of the sixth century B.C., the Athenians adopted the coinage standard of Chalcis, which was gaining wide acceptance in Aegean trading. Athenian commerce then began to catch fire, and fifty years later the Athenian tetradrachm (four-drachma coin) had become one of the "universal" currencies of the eastern Mediterranean. Statistical counts of coin hoards show Athenian currency dominating the Greek world and the Near East during the fifth century, rivaled only by the gold Darics of the Persian Empire. Even after the disastrous Peloponnesian War, the drachmas of Athens retained their popularity, with only the currency of Corinth once more a serious rival. Attic coins have been found from Spain to India, and inscriptions giving

66

This Athenian vase of the late sixth century was found in Sicily. It shows a merchant making up containers of equal weight. (*The Metropolitan Museum of Art, Purchase, 1947, Joseph Pulitzer Bequest*)

the official rate of exchange in Panhellenic centers like Delphi show that sheer demand made them acceptable at as much as a ten percent premium over their actual content of silver.

Athenian coinage can serve as a model for the currencies of other Greek cities issued in more or less the same denominations. The smallest coin was a tiny bit of silver (or a larger slug of copper or bronze) worth one eighth of an obol. Larger divisions of the obol were one-quarter, three-eights, one-half, and three-quarters. Six obols equaled one drachma, one hundred drachmas made a mina, and sixty minas a talent. The major denomination for larger transactions was the tetradrachm, or *stater*.

It is almost impossible to equate Attic or other Greek money with modern currency. The Athenian tetradrachm weighed 17.5 grams; the old American silver dollar weighed 27 grams. But such a comparison is meaningless when one considers that in mid-fifth-century Athens, a day laborer earned an average of two obols a day. In terms of weight of silver, this would be equivalent to about five and one-half cents. The only way to approximate the Athenian standard of wages and prices is to compare the average daily wage of the working person against prices of food, clothing, and other commodities.

By the last decade of the fifth century, no doubt due to war-caused inflation, the daily wage of a laborer had gone up to one drachma, and it is against this standard that we must measure prices. In 414, a number of Athenians (mostly wealthy young men) were convicted of impiety. They were executed and their property was confiscated and sold by the state. The proceeds from this sale were inscribed on marble stelae like any other piece of public business at Athens, and having fortunately survived the centuries, now provide an invaluable record of prices in Athens near the end of the fifth century. In addition, contemporary literature from time to time lets slip a remark about prices, as do other inscriptions. These various types of evidence, where they confirm each other, help us make fairly confident statements about the prices of a wide range of items.

We might begin with a citation from Plutarch's *Tranquillity of Mind* (470F), which is often accepted as authentic tradition:

> When Socrates heard one of his friends say that the city was expensive: "One hundred drachmas for Chian wine, three hundred for a purple robe, a half pint of honey for five drachmas!"[1] he took him and led him to the barley market—"eight quarts of barley meal for an obol, the city is cheap"—then to the olive market—"a quart for one-eighth obol"—then to the tunic stall—"ten drachmas, the city is cheap!"

If we assume the Athenian laborer's daily wage during Socrates' day to have been one drachma and his modern American counterpart's to be about $100.00 (average, after taxes and other deductions), we see immediately that by our standards, the city was by no means cheap. A quart of olives by this equation would cost about $2.08 and eight quarts of barley meal $16.67—reasonable enough—but the tunic, a simple woolen sleeveless garment worn by the poor, would cost $1,000.00!

We can compare the range of prices at this time by looking at the accompanying table. As can be seen, Athenian prices bear little relationship to present-day U.S. prices. The cost of a few things like furniture and livestock may be more or less equivalent, but any American would find food prices (with the exception of figs, olives, and other staples), as well as the cost of the simplest kinds of garments and shoes, wildly exorbitant.

But one must always bear in mind that the Athenian style of life was entirely different from that of twentieth-century America. Very few Athenians had large, fixed, monthly expenses like rent, and of course none of them had utility bills, insurance, car payments and so forth. A large part of the diet of every working class Greek was barley boiled up into porridge or made into barley cake, and one could buy a quart

---

[1] Actually, according to the inscription mentioned previously, a half pint of honey would cost only three obols. Perhaps we are to think of vastly differing qualities of honey.

PRODUCT	ATHENIAN PRICE	MODERN U.S. EQUIVALENT
	(To Be Measured Against a Daily Wage of 1 Drachma)	(To Be Measured Against $100.00 a Day)

food

one quart figs or olives	1/8 obol	$ 2.08
five lbs wheat	2 obols	33.33
a gallon of domestic wine	3 obols	50.00
a gallon of olive oil	3 drachmas	300.00
a loaf of bread	1 obol	16.67
one salted fish	1 obol	16.67
a small pig	3 drachmas	300.00

clothing

a woolen cloak	5–20 drachmas	500.00–2,000.00
a pair of shoes	6–8 drachmas	600.00–800.00

furniture

a stool	1 drachma, 1 obol	116.67
a table	4–6 drachmas	400.00–600.00
an imported bed	8 drachmas	800.00

livestock

a cow or ox	about 50 drachmas	5,000.00
a sheep or goat	10–15 drachmas	1,000.00–1,500.00

slaves

a Carian goldsmith	360 drachmas	36,000.00
a Macedonian woman	310 drachmas	31,000.00
Syrians	240–300 drachmas	24,000.00–30,000.00
Thracians and Illyrians	about 150 drachmas	15,000.00
a donkey driver	140 drachmas	14,000.00

miscellaneous

a ring, proof against snakebite	1 drachma	100.00
a woman's cosmetics	2 obols	33.33
a small jug for oil	1 obol	16.67
to have a dream interpreted	2 obols	33.33
to sleep with a prostitute	about 4 drachmas	400.00

(enough to glut a family of five for a whole day) for one copper, that is, one-eighth obol or about $2.08 by our scale. A loaf of bread also lasted a day for the same family, and although the price to us seems absurdly high, we must remember that the Athenian family was accustomed to eating very little else: some garlic or onions and cheese to flavor the bread or porridge, beans and other legumes, figs and olives, on occasion a little fish, octopus, or meat. Furthermore, one must remember that not all food had to be bought. Almost everyone tried to maintain a kitchen garden and a few sheep or goats for milk and cheese. Gray mullet, anchovies, and octopus were free to anyone who could lay his hands on a net or a barbed spear.

Cloaks, tunics, and shoes seem very expensive when measured against daily income. But the average Athenian generally possessed only one set of garments and one pair of shoes; this wardrobe was made to last a lifetime, with repairs. Once again, most Athenian families would not have had to pay the full retail price given in the accompanying table, because there were usually females present who could card, spin, and weave wool.

Our sources show that Athenian life was quite frugal. There was an upper stratum of great wealth: we read of families being able to pay 50-talent fines, estates valued at 80 and 100 talents, women buying 1,000-drachma dresses, and young men spending fortunes on horses. But for the most part, even the rich lived modestly, wore simple clothes, and built houses not much more elegant than those of the poorest citizens.

Far more is known about the Athenian currency and price structure than about the exchange of any other city. But we assume that other commercial city-states of the same period had more or less the same values, and the same proportion of cash was in circulation. The more doggedly agricultural communities of the Peloponnesus and Boeotia continued to rely heavily on simple barter and payments in kind.

Real Property

Land was the essence of property in the Greek world as in every other country of the ancient Mediterranean. The broad fields of the gentry testified not only to their present wealth but to their ancestral identity as well. Peasants gained a sense of dignity from their small plots of land that set them apart from the landless rabble of the cities. One of the first responsibilities of embryonic governments throughout the Greek world was recognizing and protecting landownership. The first vestiges of civil law, for instance, were simply an extension of the state's tacit admission that it was responsible for safeguarding property rights. The single greatest cause of civil disorder in early societies was property

A merchant supervises the loading of goods for export. (*Hirmer Fotoarchiv*)

dispute; custom, tradition, and law combined to surround the institution of property with rules and regulations, oaths, affidavits, and public registration of deeds, hoping thereby to make such disputes impossible or at least easily adjudicated.

In many states, real property was not originally a commodity to be bought and sold like any other object, but was only passed on by inheritance or sometimes as dowry. In Athens, for instance, unwed heiresses were required to marry a male relative to prevent adventurers from marrying them and then claiming part of their family land. As the agricultural economy in the Greek world began to yield its monopoly to urbanization and a cash economy, old strictures against alienation of land began to relax. The natural result was that land then became a profitable sort of investment. Differing social organizations led to different types of land distribution. In northern Greece, in the western Peloponnesus, and in Sicily, huge estates became the rule, whereas in Attica they were the exception. Our data are not really sufficient to provide satisfying explanations of agricultural trends; we can merely report the patterns as our sources show them.

The once rigorously antimaterialist Spartan Empire in the southern and southwestern Peloponnesus was thoroughly corrupted by the enticements of a monetary economy by the mid-fourth century B.C. The state that had once outlawed anything but iron money had unfortunately won a war that brought vast amounts of gold and silver into the valley of the Eurotas. No one can say for certain what the processes were in Sparta that made one person rich and the other poor, but as early as the 390s, the number of disenfranchised and embittered former Spartans was great enough to make the idea of violent revolution attractive. An uprising that was caught before it could gather momentum was put down with memorable Spartan severity, so the individual estates of Spartan entrepreneurs continued to grow in size and dwindle in number.

The large estates of Sparta continued to be worked by helots; elsewhere in the Peloponnesus, in Thessaly, and on the broad fields of Sicily, many of the great estates were cultivated by tenants, serfs, or outright slaves. No doubt such great size made agriculture more efficient and productive, but the great landowners were not secure in their prosperity. Each generation was faced with the threat and sometimes the realization of social upheaval.

In Attica, the opposite pattern prevailed. When speculation in land became popular in the fourth century, the new owners tended to hold it for capital gains or for rents rather than for crop income. We are told of some investors who bought unimproved land and developed it for profitable resale. Others thought of the land as income-producing property from rents and had little interest in farming. The large estate, therefore, was a rarity in Attica. We know of people who had large land holdings, but these consisted of many different parcels in different parts of Attica.

Despite urbanization, Athenians still clung to an agricultural economy. It has been estimated that as many as three-quarters of Athenian families continued to own at least some land, right down to the end of the fourth century. A revealing aspect of landownership in Attica was the relative smallness of plots of land: some were valued at as little as 45 drachmas, whereas the average of a whole list of parcels, drawn from epigraphical and literary testimony, was about 2,000 drachmas. Athens was thus spared both a class of land barons and the specter of agrarian revolt.

Although little of the Greek world was blessed with fertile plains or adequate rainfall, with intelligent planning even small plots of poor land were made to turn a profit of some kind. Stony, sun-baked hillsides produced the sweetest grapes; lentils, beans, and barley grew almost anywhere; fig trees sprang from the very rocks. As usual, the greatest problem of the farmer was not making things grow, but distributing them. In bumper years, the crop might be worthless as soon as supply exceeded demand. Export could solve some of the problems, but the

One of the big events in the farming year was the fall olive harvest. (*Reproduced by Courtesy of the Trustees of the British Museum*)

cost of transportation could eat up the profits of a bulk crop within a dozen miles. To anyone driving across the wide fields of Boeotia today, it is obvious that Boeotia must have produced a grain surplus. But thirty miles south, across the mountains in grain-hungry Attica, wheat imported from Egypt or southern Russia was cheaper than the Boeotian crop. To meet such problems of supply and demand, some states even legislated which crops might be exported or imported.

Wine was the universal beverage of the Greeks, who customarily drank it diluted with water for reasons of temperance and economy. Every district in the Greek world produced a local *vin ordinaire*, even if it were a vile and corrosive fluid that had to be soaked up with bread crumbs or mixed with flour and honey to make it potable. But in general, southern Greece and the islands annually produced a tremendous surplus of good cheap wine for export—just as the same areas do today. From famous wine-producing districts came some spectacular vintages that only the very rich could afford.

It would be a mistake, however, to view Greek farmers as entrepreneurs, treating land as a capital investment to provide an annual income. To these hardy and independent souls, whose values had changed little since the Dark Age (see p. 23), land was of inestimable value because (1) it allowed them to work for themselves rather than for others while permitting them enough leisure time to participate in the social life of their communities; (2) it enabled them to provide their daughters with dowries and to leave their sons a source of livelihood;

and (3) some of their income from the land enabled them to meet traditional obligations by making noteworthy dedications and sacrifices at community religious celebrations. These were the advantages of land-owning that permitted people to hold their heads high and enjoy the respect of their neighbors. Only after these requirements were satisfied would farmers consider the various methods of converting a surplus into commodities they could not provide for themselves: steel tools, fine pottery, or perhaps an additional household slave.

Farming of this kind is admittedly inefficient, but efficiency is not a concept Greek farmers would have understood or thought important as long as they could claim to be beholden to no one for their grain, meat, cheese, fruit, oil, wool, leather, and wine.

The Rise of Commercial Economies: Trade

As a previously agricultural community develops an urban, commercial economy, a correspondingly large share of the community's wealth begins to be converted to "venture capital"; that is, it is invested in enterprises promising a brisk return and bearing a risk whose degree can be measured by the amount of interest charged. Some modern economists have estimated that when the amount of venture capital invested by a given community is equivalent to ten percent of the gross national product, that community has reached the economic "take-off" point—a theoretical stage after which a mild inflationary spiral makes economic growth self-perpetuating. Nowhere in the Greek world during the classical period did the economy even remotely approach such a stage of development. Nevertheless, in every polis undergoing increasing urbanization there was a small but active entrepreneurial class whose activities can be compared to business practices through the ages.

Everywhere in the Greek world, the first form of what we would call venture capital was the maritime loan, which grew directly out of the needs of traders for financial backing after piracy had begun to decline as the most popular method of capitalization.

During the archaic period, the first great trading fortunes were made as merchants sought out markets and established trade routes all over the Mediterranean. To find a "virgin" port was the dream of these earliest shipowners. The riches of Tartessus outside the straits of Gibraltar, for instance, were well known to the traders of the Near East, as Ezekiel knew already in the early sixth century: "Tarshish was thy merchant by reason of the multitude of all kinds of riches: with silver, iron, tin, and lead, they traded in thy fairs." And Jonah was headed for this same destination before his unhappy transfer to another kind of transport.

So when Colaeus of Samos, blown off course by a storm, became the first Greek to discover Tartessus, he returned with one of the most profitable cargoes in history—a *net* profit of sixty talents. We have no idea what trade goods Colaeus carried, but he probably bartered them for Spanish silver, which was so common locally that the natives used it for furniture and visiting Phoenician ships used ingots of the precious metal for ballast.

By the fifth century B.C., most of the glamor had vanished from the shipping business and numerous middlemen had begun to share both profits and risks. The Athenians imported more than two-thirds of the grain they consumed, so naturally enough their most common form of maritime loan was made on grain futures. The three most important

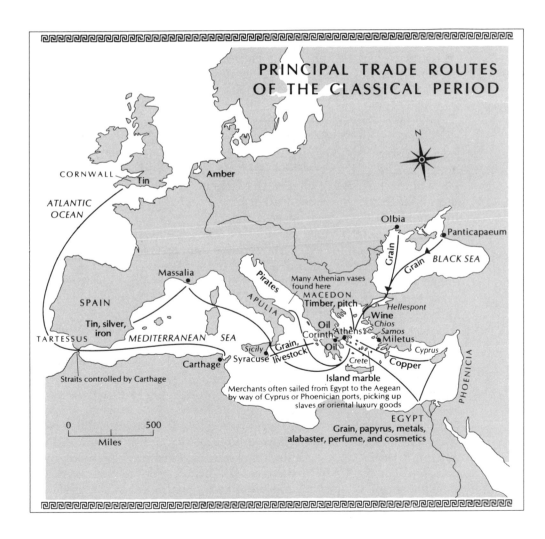

granaries in the ancient world were Egypt, Sicily, and southern Russia; Athens dealt primarily with the cities of the latter area.

Normally a transaction would proceed as follows: a merchant would borrow money from a banker in order to purchase a load of grain in the Crimea. Generally, the only security was the cargo itself and the reputation of the merchant both for trustworthiness and past success. The merchant would then make a contract with a shipowner to hold space on his ship for the voyage back from the Black Sea to Athens (the shipowner might have contracted with another merchant to carry wine from the Aegean to the Black Sea on the outward leg of the journey). Usually, the merchant went right along on the venture to make sure all went well. When the ship returned to Piraeus, the harbor of Athens, all grain had to be delivered to the Long Colonnade, where the grain wholesalers would bid for the cargo.

Now and only now could a profit be realized on the grain, and such profits were measured by the astuteness of the merchant. If he had correctly gauged the demand for grain at Athens and the relative cheapness of Black Sea grain, he could triple his money. But if he had gone off to the Crimea and came back only to find that Sicilian wheat or Egyptian wheat was far cheaper, he might have to sell at a loss, after paying the shipowner his contract. The banker, of course, took the loss right along with the merchant; this is one reason interest rates were high. Rates varied between 225 and 600 drachmas per 1,000, depending on the nature of the cargo and the time of year, and were not charged per annum, but for the term of the voyage. Therefore, during a seven-month sailing season, a fortunate investor could hope to double or triple his investment.

Such a lucrative business invited sharp practice, and much of our information about the grain trade comes from lawsuits for which Athenian orators wrote speeches. Although we have no such literary evidence for other great commercial centers, archaeology has provided clues to the sort of traffic they enjoyed. In the sixth century, Corinth and Aegina dominated the Aegean west to Sicily and southern Italy, whereas Ionian emporia like Samos, Miletus, or Chios exploited the markets of the Near East and Egypt. At Corinth, it was even possible for ships to be hauled across the narrow isthmus between the Corinthian and Saronic gulfs, thus avoiding the long sail around the Peloponnesus where adverse winds might hold up a ship as long as three weeks.

As late as 487, the Athenians had to borrow twenty warships from Corinth in order to continue a war against Aegina. Not until the Persian Wars and after did the city have a large navy. And only then did the Athenians learn what countless mercantile states have learned since: that the overseas trade of their merchants prospers to the extent the state is prepared to protect and promote it—with force if necessary. By mid-fifth century, all the states of the eastern Mediterranean knew that

Athens had such force and was prepared to use it to further the interests of her maritime empire.

Crucial to any such empire was a ready supply of shipbuilding timber, but the bony spine of Attica was devoid of such resources. Therefore, the great forests of Macedonia and Thrace, which supplied both lumber and pitch, were controlled by exclusive treaties with the rulers of those areas; when these petty princelings became obstreperous, the Athenians backed pretenders to the throne. An inscription shows that three cities on the island of Keos pledged their entire production of vermilion (mercuric sulphide) to Athens; this was an essential component of the paint used on ships.

All along the route to the Black Sea, the Athenians kept a close eye on cities that might, by their strategic location, interrupt maritime commerce. Athens interfered as a matter of course with the internal politics of such states as the islands of Lemnos and Imbros, in front of the Hellespont, and the city of Lampsacus, right on the straits. Athenian diplomats skillfully cultivated the despots of the various kingdoms of southern Russia in order to extract and maintain the most favorable commercial treaties. At the first sign of trouble anywhere along this grain lifeline—extortionate prices, a confiscated vessel, a sudden challenge to rights of passage—a mission of inquiry would be on the scene, and if the envoys were not successful, a squadron of triremes (galleys with three banks of oars) might swiftly arrive to lend poignancy to their arguments.

In the same way, Corinth jealously guarded what she considered her sphere of economic influence: the Ionian Sea west of Greece, Sicily, and southern Italy. Successful Athenian attempts to penetrate the Corinthian markets during the fifth century B.C. led to an outright break between the states, which was one of the causes of the Peloponnesian War. Massalia, in turn, was coming to dominate the shipping of the western Mediterranean to such an extent that the Carthaginians in Spain closed the Straits of Gibraltar, probably to keep Greeks out of the tin and silver trade they found so profitable.

Such restrictions on trade as existed, however, were generally minor and were designed to protect that portion of a state's trade considered vital. For the most part, the Greek instinct for free enterprise and the law of the marketplace reigned supreme until the more rigorous control of the Hellenistic monarchies. During the classical era, when the exclusiveness of the polis often fostered a stifling parochialism and xenophobia, the real cosmopolitans were the merchants. In the great ports of the Greek world—Massalia, Syracuse, Corinth, Athens, Samos, and so on—perhaps a majority of those engaged in the import-export business were *metics*, or resident foreigners, who enjoyed the protection of local law as well as the "right" to pay taxes and serve in the military, but who were denied citizenship and the right to own land. Two of the scoundrels prosecuted by Demosthenes were from Massalia, two others were from Phaselis in Lycia. A worthier man was Heracleides, from the Cypriot town of Salamis. The city gave him the status of a *proxenus*, which in Athens included the valuable right of landownership as well as the other advantages of citizenship, for various donations and subsidies during a grain shortage.

Both literary and archaeological evidence testify to the principal imports and exports of the Aegean area. From the Black Sea coasts, in addition to grain, came highly prized tuna, smoked and pickled. Scythians and Thracians who had fallen into slavery were a relatively cheap, if primitive, labor supply. Illiterate, but strong and hardy, they served as miners and farm workers. The wide steppes of Thrace also produced superior horses—mounts that were faster and stronger than the ponies to which the Greeks were more accustomed.

From the eastern Mediterranean came copper, glass, and in general, products of a higher technology such as medicines and dyes. The ships that brought grain from Egypt also carried papyrus, a fundamental necessity for a world without paper. But also from the valley of the Nile came a whole range of exotic goods, from ivory to magic amulets; cheetah cubs for pets and black slaves; alabaster, cosmetics, and fine linen.

The Greeks of the western Mediterranean were the middlemen carrying Baltic amber and Cornish tin to the eastern Greeks. One of the strongest commercial bonds was that between the Etruscans in Italy and Athens, demonstrated by hundreds of choice Athenian vases found in Etruscan tombs. No one is exactly sure what the Etruscans sent to Athens in return, perhaps iron from the mines of Elba.

As one might expect, exports from the Greek cities were less raw materials than finished products—the results of labor and ingenuity. One of the Greek products most in demand was olive oil, and there were many areas of the Mediterranean that regularly imported oil from Attica, Laconia, Samos, and the western city of Thurii on the Gulf of Taranto. Every Greek community made wine of a sort, but a few states shipped their great wines all over the ancient world. The islands of Thasos, Chios, Icaria, and Samos were among the most famous for their vintner's art. Their vintages were carried in characteristically shaped amphorae, and these containers, found from one end of the Mediterranean to the other, have helped to indicate the routes and the volume of the wine trade.

The painted clay pottery of Greece had an intrinsic value beyond the simple value placed on it as a container, and its frequency in the non-Greek world is used as an index of the esteem in which various national pottery industries was held. By the end of the sixth century, Athenian pots had begun to replace Corinthian ones as highly prized works of art. That their value was aesthetic rather than practical is proven by the fact that wherever Attic red or black figure wares appear, one also finds local attempts to copy them, particularly in the Etruscan settlements of eastern Italy and in the Black Sea area.

The coasts of the Aegean are built on a skeleton of solid limestone, which in certain areas achieves a degree of beauty or uniqueness that makes it exportable as a building material highly in demand. Sparkling white marble came from the island of Paros and from the quarries of Pentelicon in Attica. The red and green porphyries of Laconia were also especially popular. Some states, such as the island of Seriphos, which is practically a lump of iron ore, were famous for just one product. The vermilion of Keos has been mentioned and to this should be added the various rare earths used by the fuller's trade that come from Kimolos and Mykonos.[2]

Some of the Greek states became prosperous not through any products of their own, but by carrying the goods of other states. Massaliote and Rhodian merchants, for instance, roamed the Mediterranean seeking new markets, buying cheap in one port and selling dear in another. The city of Rhodes was a new settlement at the beginning of the fourth century, but 100 years later it had the largest merchant fleet in the Mediterranean; her prosperity had come almost entirely from the carrying trade.

Banking and Other Forms of Investment

The growth and maturity of maritime trade was made possible by the simultaneous development of investment banking, which gradually emerged from two very disparate institutions: the temple on the hill and the currency table in the marketplace. As far as exchange banking is concerned, the first "bankers" were simply money changers who sat at tables in the market or down at the harbor. These men would weigh and appraise foreign currency and change it into a local means of exchange. The Greek word for table was *trapeza* and a money changer was called a *trapezites*.[3] As one of the few individuals around with a ready store of capital, the *trapezites* began to make small loans and to act as a go-between for large loans, locating men with available capital to invest and collecting a finder's fee. Because larger ventures were often beyond the capitalization one individual would want to risk, partnerships gradually were formed to provide a fund of capital, not

---

[2] The rare earth of Mykonos has been found to be a perfect component of drilling mud for the oil industry and has become one of the major modern exports of Greece.

[3] *Trapeza* and *trapezites* are still the modern Greek words, respectively, for bank and banker.

only for merchant ventures, but for contractors of public works, tax farming corporations, mining companies, and every sort of commercial enterprise.

The other primary function of banks is deposit, and this service was first rendered by temples. Since time immemorial, temples had doubled as treasure houses, and at some early date, individuals began to take advantage of the great security offered by the implied protection of a god or goddess. Money or precious metal was stored in various types of sealed containers, which were then stacked up in the interior of the temple. Depositors had to pay a certain fee for safeguarding their money. This practice might be compared to the modern rental of a safe deposit box.

But temples also engaged in the money-lending business. "Open" deposits could be made that simply became part of the temple's lending capital and therefore returned a certain interest to temple and depositor alike. The great temple of Artemis at Ephesus, for instance, engaged in both forms of banking. The goddess loaned a large sum to King Croesus of Lydia as early as mid-sixth century B.C., and later inscriptions bear witness to the activity of the temple as a lending institution throughout its history. An example of the "closed" deposit is the not inconsiderable fortune the great Athenian soldier-adventurer Xenophon left with the treasurer of the temple, not at interest, but simply for safekeeping. Later in life, when he had been exiled from Athens and was living in Elis, Xenophon was visited by the treasurer who had come to see the Olympic games and had thought to bring Xenophon's money with him—an inspiring example of trust in an age of opportunism.

The money changers of the marketplace began to take over various functions from the temples in the fifth and especially the fourth centuries. Negotiations with a *trapezites* were no doubt quicker and simpler than the same arrangements with a temple. In an era of growing insecurity and waning piety, temples were no longer the sacrosanct treasure houses they had been in the days when people believed in plagues, blights, and thunderbolts as evidence of divine displeasure. Instead, the temples had become the first and most logical target for an army intent on looting; during the fourth century, not even Apollo's sanctuary at Delphi was preserved from unauthorized withdrawals.

By the end of the fourth century B.C., there were banking corporations in every commercial city of the Greek world from Emporion in Spain to the new Hellenistic settlements of Alexandria in Egypt and Seleuceia in Mesopotamia. These establishments performed almost every service found in modern banking houses: they kept deposits for both security and for profits, and they loaned money to individuals and to other corporations, sometimes even to sovereign states. They sold shares and invested the bank's capital in every enterprise from real estate to bottomry. Although the day of the checkbook had not arrived, it was already possible to transfer funds by means of a letter of credit from Marseilles to Rhodes, for instance, making it unnecessary for a vulnerable individual to carry large sums of precious metal on a long sea voyage.

The most common form of investment for the middle classes was slave owning. We are told that the elderly or widowed often provided for a leisurely old age by investing their savings or an inheritance in a sturdy and dependable workman, who would be sent out to find work for himself. When he returned in the evening with his wages, he would keep a certain amount for himself, greater or smaller depending on whether or not he was expected to feed himself. One might call this subsistence slave owning; more normally, a man might own two or three slaves to help him with his business. When business was at its peak, they would be kept busy. When the slack season arrived, they too would be sent out to look for casual work elsewhere. No doubt many of the slaves whose daily wage is recorded in Athenian public building accounts were the property of small-time slave owners of this type.

"Industry," as such, never really existed in the Greek world. The Greek workshop was merely an extension of slave owning on the one hand and cottage industry on the other. Slave labor in the workshop was usually organized vertically, rather than horizontally. The slave did not stay in one spot, performing the same task over and over. In a typical establishment, let us say, a shoe factory, the slave came to work in the morning and drew so much in raw materials and tools from the owner. He then spent part of the day making shoes and the remainder selling them. The slave was therefore himself an entrepreneur—he would try to get the best possible price for the wares he made in order to keep a proportionally larger share of the price for himself.

A skilled workman at Athens in 415 B.C. could cost as much as 300 drachmas, but an investment in skilled slave labor was potentially far more profitable than lending out money at interest, as the following example will show.

Let us say that ten slaves cost 3,000 drachmas. Each slave turns an average of three obols a day over to his master. Thus the owner *nets* five drachmas a day from his ten workmen, for they must feed and clothe themselves. On the other hand, 3,000 drachmas lent out at the usual rate of one percent simple interest per month would earn only one drachma a day. Even if the slaves worked less than three hundred days out of the year (which would be normal), the return on their labor would have been far greater.

Foreign entrepreneurs in search of profits began to open workshops in Athens in large numbers in the fifth century. The orator Lysias, prominent at the end of the fifth century, was the son of just such a man. Lysias and his brothers continued to run the business established

The same vase depicts these two scenes: a shoemaker's shop with a customer being measured for shoes (top) and a blacksmith's shop with the various articles available displayed on the wall (bottom). (Courtesy, Museum of Fine Arts, Boston)

by their father—a shield factory down in the Piraeus. This was one of the largest industries known to us from the classical period. At one time, under the accelerated demands of wartime, there was an inventory of over 700 shields, and perhaps as many as sixty slaves were working there. But an operation like this remained an exception during the classical period; in most of the Greek world, a shop employing twenty slaves was considered a major industry.

On the fateful day when Alexander crossed over to Asia, the economies of the Greek cities were, with a few exceptions, enjoying rapid growth and increasing sophistication. Manufacturing was no longer left to the haphazard production of cottage industry but was in the hands of entrepreneurs whose wares might have had an international reputation. The public works at Argos, Epidaurus, and Delphi attracted contractors from as many as five or six foreign cities. "Attic" vases were being mass-produced in Sicily and southern Italy. International cartels were beginning to sell shares in agricultural or mining ventures, and banks in Corinth had depositors from Egypt to Syria.

Cosmopolitan commerce was one of the major factors eroding the old particularism and xenophobia of the polis. Both Plato and Aristotle realized this, although with their idealized view of the polis, they were highly critical of the trend. Both favored a city built a moderate distance away from the sea and harbors, where wily and unreliable foreigners could congregate from all over the globe and infect the local population with dangerous ideas. But the majority of Greeks delighted in just those enterprises viewed most morbidly by Plato and Aristotle: commerce, foreign trade and association with foreign traders with news from all over the world, making things for profitable sale, and the sales transaction itself—one of the most enjoyable ways of spending time and a pursuit that brought to the surface all the effervescent competitive spirit of the Greek.

And the spirit in which the thing was sold was an extension of the spirit in which it was produced. It is described best by the great economic historian Gustave Glotz, writing in the years between the World Wars and contrasting Greek manufacturing particularly with the sordid and depressing factory system in the industrial Europe of his day:

> One would have a very incomplete impression of Greek industry were one to ignore its moral aspect. Among a people of lively imagination and spontaneity, the artisan class easily acquired an aesthetic character. Here was no machine which mastered its operator and made him repeat the same action over and over as if he were himself a servo-mechanism. The job was not of necessity monotonous; it might even encourage natural aptitudes. Here was no mass production, rushed and feverish, piled up in darkness by faceless workmen. The skilled craftsman did his work in a little shop, in full view of passersby. He did not labor furiously from dawn to dusk, but took the time to finish everything that passed through his hands. Articles of value were de-

manded even for export. Eye and hand worked in leisurely fashion; self-esteem was aroused; technology advanced at a happy pace. This joy of workmanship, this partnership of creative thought and obedient tool, this taste for free play which ennobled daily labor—all this seemed to illuminate the commonest object and made an artist of the laborer.[4]

SUGGESTIONS FOR FURTHER READING

Ancient authors rarely concerned themselves with economics, although Xenophon's *Ways and Means* may be considered an exception. Most of the evidence is numismatic or epigraphical with literary sources supplying only occasional insights. The section on prices is derived from the research of W. K. Pritchett et al. in "The Attic Stelae," *Hesperia* 22 (1953) 225–229; 25 (1956) 178–328; 27 (1958) 163–310. F. M. Heichelheim, *An Ancient Economic History*, vol. 2 (Leiden: Sijthoff, 1964), is a thorough survey with extensive bibliographies. Still fundamental is Gustave Glotz, *Ancient Greece at Work* (New York: W. W. Norton & Co., 1967). A number of scholars have contributed to *The Muses at Work* (Cambridge, Mass.: M.I.T. Press, 1969), edited by Carl Roebuck, which surveys ancient trade and industry. Lionel Casson's *Ancient Mariners* (New York: Macmillan Co., 1959) is a history of ships and maritime commerce from the beginnings to the end of the ancient world. M. I. Finley puts many ancient terms and practices in perspective in *The Ancient Economy* (Berkeley and Los Angeles: University of California Press, 1973); many of his essays on the Greek economy are collected in B. D. Shaw and R. P. Saller, eds., *Economy and Society in Ancient Greece* (New York: Penguin, 1983). The fundamental study of ancient Greek agriculture and its essential role in every aspect of Greek life is T. W. Gallant, *Risk and Survival in Ancient Greece* (Palo Alto, Calif.: Stanford University Press, 1991).

---

[4] From Gustave Glotz, *Le travail dans la Grèce ancienne* (Paris: Librairie Félix Alcan, 1920), p. 328.

5 Greek Society in the Age of the Polis

THE WORLD OF Archilochus was one of change and opportunity. But the great population explosion that took place on the coasts of the Aegean between about 750 and 500 B.C. tended to lessen the land available to settlers, even on far frontiers. At the same time, an increasingly complex economy began to change the nature of economic opportunity, while a rising tide of bourgeois politics and bourgeois values stifled the spirit of adventure. If Odysseus had landed in fifth-century Athens, he would have been viewed with the darkest suspicion, forced to register his presence with the Polemarch, and in fact would have been lucky to escape being hanged as a common pirate, a fate he more than once richly deserved.

Two centuries later, on the eve of Alexander's conquests, an astute observer would have been able to detect the dawn of a new era of individualism and opportunism, which would reach maturity during the Hellenistic age. Once again, great movements of population took place: simple soldiers became kings, potters ruled whole islands,

Phoenician immigrants founded schools of philosophy in Athens, and people born slaves counted their millions in teeming cities sprung from the sands during their own lifetimes.

The polis was a decided contrast both to what went before and what came after. The efforts of the poleis to establish themselves and to maintain their independence had fostered civic spirit and the notion that the needs of the whole city were superior to those of any one individual. This in turn had the effect of making the polis a tight little enclave, jealous of its autonomy, distrustful of its neighbors, and critical of individualism and unorthodoxy at home. The polis was idealized by the most influential writers of antiquity and has been romanticized ever since by uncritical philhellenes. It is true that there was a certain pride and nobility of purpose about the polis—this was true of every Greek endeavor (including their wars)—but there was also quite a bit of hypocrisy and narrow-mindedness, not least of which was the fact that a good two-thirds of the population of every polis was regularly excluded from public life. Therefore, any survey of Greek society ought to include a good look at those lower orders that contributed so much to Greek life and received so little recognition.

Slaves

A slave was legally a piece of property, just like a house, a farm animal, or a wife. A slave might have been born a Thracian prince or a third-generation slave from some Syrian metropolis. Or the slave might have been an unfortunate fellow Greek, a prisoner of war whose family back home was unable to raise the ransom. Greek and Phoenician traders carried all varieties and nationalities of slaves from one end of the Mediterranean to the other, and every large city had a slave market, usually located somewhere near the waterfront. At a large market one could find slaves of every age, sex, and national origin. The price would depend on all these factors. Our evidence from Athens at the end of the fifth century shows that an expensive slave cost 360 drachmas, a cheap one 140; in U.S. dollar equivalents this is a range of $14,000–$36,000.

Slaves from the Near East were generally skilled at some craft and were eagerly sought by the owners of workshops. Moreover, they came from societies whose economies had been based on slave labor for thousands of years. Slaves from such origins were therefore docile and easily managed. The unskilled who were either intelligent or good natured or who merely looked promising would find employment in the middle ranks as domestics: grooms, maids, cooks, errand boys, and pedagogues (a term now associated with education, but originally meaning literally the highly reliable servant who accompanied a boy to and from school).

Blacks were rarely encountered in the Greek world. They tended to be slaves imported through Egypt. (*Courtesy, Antikenmuseum, Berlin*)

The lowest variety of slave came from the northern lands: Thracians or Scythians from the frigid plains of southern Russia, Illyrian mountaineers from the Adriatic. These were frightening savages of great size and strength. A picked corps of Scythian archers was employed by the Athenian government to keep order within the city—the only equivalent of a modern police force—but for the most part, these barbarians were thought fit only to work in field or quarry under close supervision. A recalcitrant slave of this type would be sent in chains to work in the mines—a living death that took the lives of the sturdiest within a few years.

The *function* of slaves in antiquity has been widely misinterpreted. It was once popular to picture the citizen body of any Greek city as a leisure class, freed from care and tiresome work by the labor of slaves. This way, it was argued, the average Greek citizen was able to sit around discussing politics all day or debating truth and virtue with Socrates.[1] The fact is that a class did exist that could have avoided work, had it so wished. But Greeks have always been both energetic and ambitious. To own a slave meant only that one was freed from one sort of task— generally an onerous and routine job—in order to engage in more creative and lucrative forms of activity.

The housewife had a maid to keep the house clean, permitting her to care for children, to cook and preserve food, and to weave the family textiles. A middle-class family in the present-day United States will purchase a dishwasher, a washing machine and dryer, and a vacuum cleaner in order to make daily housework a matter of minutes rather

---

[1] Naturally enough, this was a popular conceit in the antebellum American South.

than hours. The Greek housewife had a slave girl for the very same purpose. But possessing a slave, although freeing the woman of the house from drudgery, saddled her with responsibility—and the wealthier the household and the larger the servant establishment, the greater the responsibility.

In the same way, a Greek farmer owned field hands to do the sort of work that would be performed today by machines. But the time he gained because of slave labor was not leisure time. It amounted to hours that he could spend developing new acreage or tending to business in town or in supervising the management of his property. A slave was, after all, a piece of labor-saving machinery, and every modern businessman knows that labor-saving machinery, while saving hours of tedious and witless work, creates new responsibilities and quickens the overall pace of whatever operation is taking place.

In a thriving community like Athens, Corinth, or Miletus, the slave-owning class would have been equivalent to the modern American automobile-owning class. All poorer families would have looked forward to the day when they could afford a boy or girl to lighten the load: to watch the goats, run errands, fix the roof, clean the floor, and in general free the adult members of the household for more productive and remunerative occupations. Some slaves even owned slaves.

Greek authors did not write biographies of slaves, but it is not difficult to describe the career of the typical upwardly mobile slave, building a composite picture from the available evidence. A Carian farmer, pushed to the wall by a succession of bad years and needing a bit of capital to get his oldest son started, would take the younger children to the nearest city and sell them. Callous and brutal as this may seem to us, it was evidently a traditional method of raising money for many Anatolian peoples. Greeks found the idea repugnant, especially the common practice of castrating boys in order to fetch the high price brought by eunuchs, but they had nothing against buying such children.

A bright Carian lad would bring a good price because he could be trained in any number of skills and sold as an apprentice to an artisan. His sister, if she were fair, would probably be snapped up by a procurer for schooling in the arts of prostitution, which included flute playing and dancing. The boy, if lucky, would be purchased by a businessman, perhaps a merchant looking for a youth to keep his office in order, mix ink, sharpen pens, fetch refreshments for visitors, run errands, and perform the countless odd jobs required in a mercantile establishment. An ambitious office boy of this type would teach himself to read and write—and would be encouraged to do so by his master. Once he became even partly literate, he could be put to work filing contracts, marking consignments, and checking accounts. With ten years or so of experience, an ambitious young man would be on the move. He would

A domestic servant kneads the daily bread. (*Courtesy, Museum of Fine Arts, Boston*)

now be trusted to go down to the harbor and give orders to ship captains or perhaps even accompany cargoes on short trips. He would know how to run the office when the master was out. As far as finances were concerned, he would have both a small stipend from his owner and a number of other opportunities for filling his pocket. Did a customer wish an immediate appointment with the merchant? A few drachmas would put him at the head of the waiting list. Would it be possible to rent space in one of the merchant's sheds? It could certainly be arranged, for a small fee. What kind of prices were other merchants having to pay for Black Sea grain? These were tightly guarded secrets, but a casual walk through the marketplace and a few words with fellow slaves might at least provide a clue; information was valuable and an astute master would pay well for it.

An enterprising slave would soon be able to rent quarters for himself, to buy a woman, and to start his own family; in fact, he would be encouraged to do so by his master because these would ensure stability and responsibility. With proper management, such a slave would eventually be able to buy his freedom and perhaps with his freedom a share of his master's business.

Such a slave was Pasion of Athens. Bought off the slave block as a young man by the bankers Antisthenes and Archestratus, he soon gained a reputation for industry, honesty, and business acumen. After he had become indispensable to the partners, he was given his freedom; when they retired from the banking business, they turned it over to him. The acquisition of great wealth, freedman status, and far-reaching political influence would be enough to satisfy the usual ambitions of a man who was born a slave. But Pasion aimed at the unobtainable: full Athenian citizenship.

This was one of the most exclusive, most jealously guarded possessions in the Greek world. The orator Lysias, a wealthy manufacturer of Sicilian origin who became a hero of the democracy in the aftermath of the Peloponnesian War, was never quite able to persuade the assembly to make him an Athenian, despite a multitude of sacrifices and services. Athenian citizenship was generally granted only as a cynical political maneuver, bestowed with a maximum of pomp on Thracian and Black Sea potentates as a reward for commercial treaties. It therefore seemed that citizenship would be granted only to those who could be counted on not to exercise it. But Pasion persevered. He made the city a gift of a thousand shields and equipped five naval vessels, although wealthy men were never expected to supply more than one. Finally, the impressed Athenian assembly voted citizenship to him and to his descendants. Eligible now to own and speculate in real property, Pasion ended life the richest man in Athens by contemporary estimate.

Such a career was unusual but not unique. During his presidency of the bank, Pasion had himself acquired a slave named Phormion who became the protégé of his owner, and who in turn gained his freedom and the management of Pasion's many enterprises. When Pasion died, he provided in his will that Phormion should marry his widow—a not infrequent device used at Athens and elsewhere to reward a faithful associate and to protect the interest of the family.

Stories of freedom and other honors given to slaves were common in the Greek world. The Faithful Slave, a stock figure in literature, was often shown to be more loyal than members of his owner's family. Slaves walked the streets in better clothing than many of the citizens. And after their working days were ended by old age or infirmity, custom required that they be supported for the rest of their days by the family that they had once served. One sees the usual humanitarian attitude in Plutarch's indignant reaction to the parsimonious Roman notion, expressed by Cato, that old and sick slaves ought to be resold, even for pennies, to avoid having to feed them further.

But the relative security and possible advantages of servile status should not blind us to the fact that slaves were, in fact, only property, unprotected by law and subject to the whims of their masters.[2] Slave

---

[2] It was illegal in most states to *kill* a slave, but only because any kind of murder was considered a religious pollution.

girls—and boys as well—were sexually abused as a matter of course and were often sold for this purpose. A slave unlucky enough to be bought by a sadist or degenerate could find solace only in death. Escape was possible only for sturdy males who intended an outlaw existence, for no city would admit a stranger who could not prove his free status, and all cities cooperated in returning escaped slaves. Greeks were normally a humanitarian people, but they could turn a blind eye to occasional barbarity—such as that evidenced by the skeletons of children unearthed by archaeologists from the cramped and airless burrows of the silver mines where their lives had ended. And in even the most trivial cases at law, the testimony of slaves was accepted only if given under torture.

Women

Defining the position of women in Greek history is a complex problem. First of all, the very notion of "status" is a modern one and we tend to compare the status of Greek women not only to that of women in modern urban society but also to what we think that status ought to be. There is, therefore, a continual temptation to make judgments about the roles and lifestyles of Greek women. But for a balanced understanding of the roles women played in the Greek world, it is best to adhere strictly to what can be interpreted from the available evidence. Only after the nature of the evidence is defined and analyzed can we begin to speculate about the goals, the gratifications, and the frustrations of what often seems to be the invisible half of the Greek people.

The first category of evidence is Greek literature. Anyone who even casually begins to look through Greek writers for their views on women will immediately note the tremendous range of opinion. Of course, with a rare exception like the poems of Sappho, this body of literature was written by men and so what we have, essentially, are the views of men who had very different notions about the roles of women. On the one hand, we have the classically antifeminist opinions of early poets like Hesiod or Semonides (see Chapter 6). Again, even male writers who professed to recognize the true value of women could be insufferably patronizing, at least from a modern point of view. On the other hand, we have literary portrayals of women in both tragedy and comedy. Some of the female characters so presented demonstrate such aggressive character and moral strength that some critics are inclined to doubt the mass of evidence showing women as subservient and inferior.

The second class of evidence is more objective. Painters and sculptors pictured women of all classes engaged in various activities and although these artists were also exclusively male, they were depicting what they saw rather than expressing an opinion. Through their works

we can get impressions of women at work and at play with less pos-
sibility of male prejudice entering the picture. Finally, we cannot ignore
the most poignant sort of documentary evidence: those epitaphs, often
accompanied by a portrait in relief, dedicated by grief-stricken Greek
men to their lost wives, mothers, and daughters.

Using all these categories of testimony with great care, it is possible
to make a few observations about the roles of Greek women, including
the change in these roles through the centuries.

Earliest Greek society was dominated by the deeds and values of
the warriors and heroes who ruled the land during the Bronze Age and
well into the era described by Homer in the *Odyssey* (ca. 750 B.C.). A
warrior society naturally places the greatest importance on masculine
virtues: great strength, skill in battle, and physical courage. It was a
thoroughly patriarchal society that was described by Homer and by
later Greek authors who turned old traditions and legends into literature. Nevertheless, from this period we get an impression of women
who had many heroic virtues themselves and who often seemed to deal

Proper marital affection is contrasted with sexual outrage in two scenes from the same
vase. (*Reproduced by Courtesy of the British Museum*)

with men as equals. First of all, goddesses like Athena, Artemis, Hera, and Aphrodite seemed in no way inferior to their peers among the male Olympian deities. Epic poets did not simply invent patterns of human behavior that did not exist in their society; therefore, one must assume that Homer's audience could imagine outspoken and strong-willed women acting in an aggressive fashion. Of course, the women of this society were in fact the mothers, wives, and daughters of warriors and were therefore entitled to at least vicarious respect. But these were the people of highest station, the rulers and leaders of their society.

To the farmer Hesiod, who lived not long after Homer, all the great women had lived in the mythological past. His advice to his brother was simply to get a young wife who could be trained, not one who wiggles her behind: "She is after your barn." We also owe to Hesiod the earliest account of the tradition that saw women as an affliction imposed on a previously happy and exclusively male human race. Zeus grew jealous of mortals, especially after Prometheus had given them the forbidden gift of fire. So he created the female and gave her to unsuspecting mankind, accompanied by a great jar containing all the evils that have come to afflict the human race. This first woman, named Pandora, took the lid off the jar and loosed these evils to torment man from that time on.

In the period between Hesiod (ca. 700 B.C.) and the Persian Wars (490–479 B.C.), there were some examples of exceptional women who were models of feminine accomplishment not only to contemporaries but to succeeding generations as well. First and foremost, of course, was Sappho, but there were other famous women poets. Telesilla of Argos was not only admired for her art, for when the Spartans killed almost the entire male population of Argos in battle, Telesilla assumed leadership of the Argive women, distributed weapons, and made such a vigorous stand against the Spartans that their king decided to call it a day and go home (ca. 494 B.C.). Corinna of Tanagra, who lived in Boeotia about the same time, supposedly defeated the great Pindar in verse competitions five times. Another martial woman was Artemisia of Halicarnassus. Her husband was the tyrant of the city with Persian support, and when he died, the Persians not only allowed her to assume her husband's role but even to command the Halicarnassian contingent that joined the expedition of Xerxes against Greece. Herodotus says that the Athenians put a price on her head because they were angry that a woman should come against them in war. Evidently all Greeks did not appreciate the martial spirit in women.

But in general, Greeks of this era seemed to agree that a woman was a necessity. If she were a good wife you were lucky, if not you were stuck. This point of view was explained by the poet Semonides in a catalogue of female types and the various ways they distress their mates. There is the gross Sow-woman whose house is always filthy;

the unreliable Sea-woman; the Donkey-woman who never finishes a job and will lie with any man; the Mare-woman, all vanity and a stranger to housework. Only the Bee-woman is a joy to men; it is revealing that the only specific attribute Semonides gave her was negative: she never sits around with other women talking about sex.

For the fifth and fourth centuries, most of our evidence for the status of women comes from Athens. Legally and economically, they had virtually no status at all. They were under the control of a man their entire lives. In her father's home, a maiden was a burden because he had to raise a dowry—a significant expense—to get her married. Because of the value placed on a landed estate, Athenians were greatly concerned with the status of heiresses: women whose fathers had died with no male heirs in the direct line of succession. In this case, the father's nearest male relative could claim the heiress in marriage to ensure that the estate remained in the family. A woman had no control over choice of a husband, all the more so because it was customary to marry a maiden off a few years after puberty. In a few Greek city-states, it would appear that women had the right to own and dispose of landed property; but in Athens the lawmakers seem to have been preoccupied with exclusive male ownership and disposition of property. On the other hand, the testimony of inscriptions shows that some women of the tradesman class could own and operate small businesses in Athens such as food stalls and laundries.

Social status depended on class and station. In two realms, women could rise to equal or surpass men in influence and competence: as priestesses and prostitutes. Probably the most emancipated women from our point of view were the *hetairai,* or courtesans (the word means literally "female companion"). These were far more than simple prostitutes, who were usually slaves. A *hetaira* might have started life as a slave, but through unusual intelligence or simply good luck may have attracted a benefactor whom she could talk into purchasing her freedom. The most famous *hetairai* in Athens mixed freely in male company and are said to have discussed politics, drama, and philosophy with their clients in addition to providing the usual professional services. On the other hand, although they had freedom, wealth, and an exciting life, their success did depend on the fact that they provided sex for sale and their profession was regarded as shameful by most citizens.

The most respected women were priestesses of the various female cults. These were of two types: cults devoted to one of the Olympian goddesses such as Athena, Hera, or Artemis, and the older mystery religions, which had roots in what may have been pre-Greek cults of the Mother Goddess. The priestesses of Hera at Argos were such a universally recognized institution that their terms of office were used to date events. Thucydides precisely dated the beginning of the Peloponnesian War "when Chrysis had been priestess at Argos for forty-

The women of the Greek household were entirely responsible for all steps in the manufacture of the family's clothing and other textiles, from spinning the wool to weaving and sewing. These scenes appear on two sides of a black figure Athenian *lekythos*. (*The Metropolitan Museum of Art, Fletcher Fund, 1931*)

eight years." The rites of Eleusinian Demeter were an example of the latter type (the name Demeter means "Earth Mother"). These rites were the established state cult of Athens. Every year at the Great Mysteries, Athenians celebrated the return of Demeter's daughter Persephone, a rite that probably originally symbolized the annual rebirth of life-giving crops. Some of the chief priestly officials of the Eleusinian mysteries were men, but women still presided over the even older rites celebrating the Great Goddess at Phlya, outside the city of Athens. Even under the Roman Empire in the third century A.D., the office of priestess of the Great Goddess was being handed down from mother to daughter—a practice that may, by that time, have been 1,000 years old.

The high status of priestesses reflected a deep-rooted Greek conviction that women, if not as intellectual as men, possessed a spirituality that brought them in closer communication with the divine element. Only women were thought capable of entering into the inspired frenzy bestowed by Dionysus on his most favored worshipers. And perhaps the single most influential Greek at any given time was the priestess at Delphi. When the Olympian god Apollo came to the ancient pre-Greek shrine at Delphi, which at the time was ruled by a sacred female snake, he was unable to prevail completely. From that time onward, Apollo's servants shared the site with its previous occupants who preserved their aspect in the person of the Pythoness. She

was always selected from among the local peasant girls who had revealed a tendency to hysteria and irrational behavior, thus indicating
that her mind had been touched by the god. Seated on a tripod over a
rift in the ground from which noxious gases were supposed to have
emerged (although no trace of such a rift has ever been found) and
chewing poisonous laurel leaves, the Pythoness entered a state of divine
intoxication. While in a trance she became the vehicle for the voice of
Apollo, uttering prophecies capable of changing the history of the Greek
people.

But when scholars debate the status of women in classical Greece,
they are talking not about priestesses and prostitutes but about the
mothers, wives, and daughters of the average city dweller. The fifth
century B.C. saw the growth of a large middle class in Athens and as
usual, middle-class values tended to be conservative and intolerant of
unorthodox behavior. It is often suggested that the lowest ebb in the
social status of Greek women came about the middle of the fifth century—which in other respects used to be regarded as some kind of
golden age.

In the Homeric era, women were after all the companions of warriors. In succeeding centuries, women poets could still win a reputation.
Even women on the typical Greek farm could feel that they contributed
something to the common effort—that they were partners of their men
in the unrelenting struggle to make the land produce a living. But the
urban, middle-class Athenian woman had lost her feeling of usefulness
and our sources speak of a virtual seclusion in the women's quarters
of the house. "The effect of urbanization upon women was to have their
activities moved indoors, and to make their labor less visible and hence
less valued."[3]

The home was the woman's domain and in an average household
three generations might be represented: mother-in-law, wife, and
daughter. The housewife was expected to master the arts of cooking,
spinning, weaving, and child-rearing, and to be able to direct and supervise the household servants. It was not thought proper for a woman
of the "better" classes to leave her house unaccompanied by a male
guardian or chaperone. Even women of the poorer classes were better
off because by necessity they had to go to a well or fountain to draw
household water or go shopping in the markets. Any woman whose
husband could afford a domestic slave was expected to send the slave
on such tasks. While men entertained each other at meals and drinking
parties, wives ate their meals with the children and female servants. It
was considered socially acceptable for men to pursue affairs with pros-

---

[3] Sarah Pomeroy, *Goddesses, Whores, Wives and Slaves* (New York: Schocken, 1975),
p. 71.

titutes or relationships with younger men, but every possible obstacle was erected to keep the Athenian wife from adulterous temptations. It is little wonder that our sources so often mention adultery. We can only guess at the desperate boredom and frustration of women whose intellectual capacity and curiosity might be, despite their inadequate education, in no way inferior to those of their male counterparts. In a life of such tedium, an illicit sexual relationship might have offered the only excitement. It is revealing that Athenian men thought so little of feminine character that a wife caught in adultery was held practically blameless.

Some of the rationale for the attitude toward women can be seen in the story of Teiresias. This ancient prophet had once been changed into a woman for seven years and thus was the only person who had experienced sex both as a man and a woman. Zeus and Hera were once having an argument over who enjoyed sex more and decided to let Teiresias settle the question. He replied that if there were ten parts of

The poet Semonides wrote of the proud and fastidious wife who "would never sit over the oven dodging soot." The housewife depicted in this figurine sets a more diligent example. (Marburg/Art Resource, NY, 1.199.878, Hellenistic Baking Figurine, Berlin)

pleasure in the act of love, woman had nine of them. Hera was furious at this disclosure, but forever after, all Greek men believed that women were uncontrollably passionate and needed to be guarded continually against temptation.

Our impressions of middle-class women tend to derive from what might well have been the wishful thinking of male spokesmen. Pericles said that the best woman was the one about whom there was the least talk, either of praise or blame, but this is a rather strange sentiment to attribute to Pericles, considering that the statesman's consort Aspasia was probably the most talked-about woman in Athens (see Chapter 6). Xenophon shows us Socrates talking to a man named Ischomachus, who praised his young wife because of her docile acceptance of household management as her only role in life and her swift obedience to his will when he criticized her for wearing too much makeup.

But if the modest, secluded, diligent housewife was the ideal to civic leaders like Pericles and Xenophon, there must have been many exceptions in reality. Our literary sources portray women in roles far different from those of the cloistered majority. Sophocles did not create Antigone entirely from imagination, and the audience who saw her stubborn and self-righteous opposition to an unbending despot must have had women just as outspoken in their families. Of all the playwrights, Euripides might have come closest to recognizing a woman's frustration at her limited existence as we hear Medea complain:

> A man, when he's bored with being at home
> Can go out and escape depression
> By turning to some friend, or whatever.
> But we have our one soul to look to.
> They say we lead a safe life at home
> While they do battle with the spear.
> What imbeciles! I'd rather stand to arms
> Three times than bear one child.

Medea 244–251

Then there are the women pictured in the comedies of Aristophanes. They gossip, intrigue, and cheat on their husbands. But they can also be loyal, loving, generous, and forgiving. In a number of plays, they seem to be smarter than their husbands. While this is comedy and fantastic comedy at that, we must suppose such women to have been at least recognizable; otherwise many of the jokes would have lost their point.

A recent book blames Athenian men for a purposeful and concerted effort to keep women in a permanent state of social and sexual repression.[4] But anthropologists have shown that in many traditional soci-

---

[4] Eva C. Keuls, *The Reign of the Phallus: Sexual Politics in Ancient Athens* (New York: Harper & Row, 1985).

A Boeotian mother gives her
daughter a cooking lesson.
(*Courtesy, Museum of Fine
Arts, Boston*)

eties it is the matrons and other older women who are the most vigilant
defenders of orthodoxy and the status quo. It may be the men who
actually enforce the laws, both written and unwritten, that limit wom-
en's activities and restrain their behavior but it is usually the mature
women of the community who insist that they do so. This is certainly
true in the modern Greek village and there is literary evidence to suggest
that the situation was the same in ancient Athens.

It was acknowledged that Spartan women had far more freedom
than those of other cities, and women of all the Dorian Greek settlements
seem to have had the right to own and dispose of property in their own
right. Spartan traditions held that the emancipated and outspoken
woman could best encourage the ambitious, spur on the sluggard, and
shame fools and cowards. Spartan women attended all contests to cheer
on the winners and mock the losers, and they themselves were trained
in athletic courage and endurance. The savage fortitude of the Spartan
female was legendary; thus as late as 275 B.C., King Pyrrhus of Epirus,
with a crack mercenary army at his back, hesitated to attack ramparts
defended only by Spartan women, children, and old men.

Like all her sisters, Timaea, wife of King Agis of Sparta, knew it
was the duty of Spartan women to breed brave and sturdy children,
even to the point of extending connubial privileges beyond the family
circle. It so happened that an earthquake had convinced the superstitious Agis that he ought not sleep with his wife. Unfortunately for him,
at that very time the Athenian exile Alcibiades (a man whose grace,

charm, and beauty were legendary) took refuge at Sparta. When Agis was away on campaign, Timaea decided that the handsome renegade was indeed a fit sire for Spartan kings, although her husband was later puzzled enough to check a calendar and to disown his unexpected son.[5]

Spartan society, like that described by Homer, stressed warrior virtues, and as we have seen, more respect was accorded women who were the daily companions of warriors. The same can be said of Macedonian women, and it may be because of their influence, in the wake of the conquests of Alexander, that Hellenistic cities extended the rights of equality in property owning and most business dealings to women as a matter of course. It would appear that in succeeding centuries, Greek women rose far above their limited and suppressed roles in Periclean Athens.

Travelers and Resident Aliens

During the age of the polis, the preoccupation with allegiance and the insistence that every person must have a city were underscored by the regulations that governed casual visitors and resident aliens. Most suspicious of all was the state of Sparta, which allowed only short and highly supervised visits and entirely prohibited residence by foreigners.

At one time, Thebes also had a reputation for hostility to aliens, as did many other states with a fragile power structure. Plato and Aristotle both echo what seems to be a polis-bred fear that strangers will make local citizens dissatisfied with their leaders or other aspects of their way of life.

Athens, whose laws we know the best, seems to have occupied a middle ground. Several times during the sixth century the rights of citizenship were evidently extended to foreign residents; but by the middle of the fifth century, a reaction set in and citizenship was limited to those who could prove that *both* parents were citizens. The resident aliens—known as *metics*[6]—had a definite legal status. Their names were on file in the Athenian equivalent of the War Office, understandably so, because the primary duty owed by the metic to Athens was military service during time of war. The second duty was to pay taxes, at a higher rate than that levied on citizens. Otherwise, metics were subject to the same observance and protection of the laws as any citizen. They could own all kinds of property except real estate, enter into

---

[5] See the story in Xenophon *Hellenica* 3. 3. 1 and Plutarch *Agesilaus* 3.
[6] From the Greek *metoikos*, meaning literally "one who has changed his dwelling."

contracts, bring suit against citizens, and even marry into Athenian families, although resulting children would still be metics.

Foreigners visiting Athens had to register immediately with the proxenos (a person equivalent to a modern consul or chargé d'affaires) for their home city. The difference was that the Spartan proxenos in Athens, for instance, was not a Spartan, but an Athenian whose family had traditional ties of friendship with Sparta. The proxenos was the legal host of visitors during the time they were in Athens. If a visitor got into trouble, the proxenos was theoretically responsible—with the same range of reactions one would encounter from a modern consulate: the mighty would be treated with every consideration; the humble trader who got drunk and was robbed would be ignored or be given a time in which to get out of Attica.

Great mercantile centers like Corinth, Samos, or Syracuse had a far more relaxed attitude toward foreigners, for their whole livelihood depended on them. But in every city of the Greek world, a foreigner had to be prepared to answer two questions and supply proof: Where are you from? And what is your status there? For one thing, legal responsibility for all persons had to be established; more important, the slave dealers were always lurking in the background. Even citizens avoided dark alleys down by the waterfront, where kidnapping and subsequent sale into slavery were not infrequent. The best defense was to let everyone know that important people were looking out for your safety.

Farmer and Burgher: Middle-Class Attitudes

The backbone of Greek society was the yeoman class: the small free farmers. As political theorists from Aristotle to the present have realized, a proportionately large class of landowners contributes most to political stability during peacetime, and is most enthusiastically committed to its country's interests during time of war. In Greece, it was also the citizen-farmer-soldier as a class who was most responsible for demanding government by consent and equality before the law, pragmatic attitudes resulting in the abstract ideal that we call democracy.

That the majority of Greeks consisted of farmers is often obscured by the fact that our authorities are almost all urban intellectuals and are positively hostile to the rather boorish and unlettered rustic who came to town to market or to attend the assembly. In Theophrastus' *Characters*, written near the end of the fourth century B.C., we have a portrait of such a person:

> The Rustic is the sort of person who wanders into the assembly drinking wine, and keeps saying there's no sweeter perfume than thyme, and wears shoes bigger than his feet, and chatters in a loud voice. He

won't trust his friends and neighbors, but he confides in his own
servants about the most important things. And he explains to his
paid farmhands everything that went on in the assembly. He sits down
with his clothes hitched up over his knees so his privates show. And
nothing strikes his attention walking down the street, but just let him
catch sight of some cow or donkey or goat and he stands and marvels.
Snatching a snack out of the larder, he devours it in a startling manner.
And the stronger his drink the better. While no one's looking, he tries
to tumble the cook. And he feeds the animals while still eating his
own breakfast. He answers the door himself. Taking a coin from someone, he bites it, finds it shortweight, and insists on changing it for
another. And if he lends someone his plow, or basket or sickle or
sack, he lies awake all night worrying about it. Coming into town he
asks everyone he meets: how much is leather? and salt fish? and
immediately goes on to say that he's on his way to get his hair cut.
And he sings in the bath, and pounds nails into his boots.

With a few exceptions, we would have to say that Theophrastus'
standards are snobbish and condescending, but the Athenian city
dweller no doubt agreed on the boorishness of all these traits. A century
earlier the comic playwrights used the peasant as a stock figure of fun,
whether he was a poor tiller of rocky soil like Dicaeopolis in the *Acharnians* or a rich peasant like Strepsiades in the *Clouds*, who laments his
marriage to a city-bred aristocrat:

The matchmaker ought to be cursed who got me to marry your mother.
Me a happy clod, unwashed, unkempt, lying around teeming with
honey and sheep and olive cake. And then a hayseed like me had to
go and marry the niece of Megacles Jr. from the city, proud and luxury-
loving like the rest of her family. We married and went to bed together,
me stinking of wine, brine, and sheepdip, her all perfume and saffron
and passionate kisses.

Ridiculed and despised, the *agroikos*, or rustic, was just as typical
of the Greek as the witty and sophisticated urbanite, and in the long
run rather more influential. Politically, the farmer always played a
decisive role. The bulk of the earliest citizen armies was made up of
the *hoplite* class. Hoplites, or infantrymen, were by legal definition
property owners whose income allowed them to furnish a suit of armor,
a shield, and weapons. In the typical Greek state, the majority of the
land was owned by small individual farmers. Because they also doubled
as the army during times of emergency, it is easy to see how various
forms of government by popular consent developed throughout the
Greek world. But if a large farmer-soldier class encouraged participatory
democracy, it also contributed a strong conservative element to such
democracy. Although the contrast between honest, steadfast farmer and
fickle urban poor was overdrawn by Plato and his followers, such a
contrast nevertheless existed:

The best population is an agricultural one, thus it is useful to create a democracy where everyone lives by farming or stock raising. For one thing, they do not have much property and are always busy, so that they rarely attend the assembly. . . . They rather enjoy working for themselves instead of playing politics and holding office, for office holders get little in the way of income.

Aristotle *The Politics* 6, 1318b

Greek farmers were loyal and stubborn patriots. Townspeople might have voted for war in the assembly, but farmers were the ones who went out to fight. During the Peloponnesian War, by far the greatest burden was borne by the farmers of the Attic countryside. Evacuated from their fields and crammed behind the impregnable walls of the city of Athens, they had to watch their crops being burned and century-old olive trees being destroyed each year by a numerically superior Spartan army. These displaced citizens from the rural districts of Attica had had little to do with making the war, nor is it likely that they understood the complicated reasons of state leading to the outbreak of hostilities. Now moved to the city for protection, they could easily have forced a reevaluation of war policy—but there is never a hint of such a thing. It was this unflagging and unquestioning loyalty of the yeoman class that made it possible for Athens to endure for ten years until an armistice could be concluded on favorable terms.

The farmer was suspicious of change. There is a fragile balance between success and disaster in the business of growing crops, and farmers everywhere have always resisted innovation. The old ways work to a known extent; who wants to experiment with new crops or new methods, and perhaps risk the loss of an entire year's work? It is said that Greece's greatest statesman during the War of Liberation (1820–1829) was able to introduce the potato to Greece only by making the possession and cultivation of potatoes illegal, thus combating the Greek farmers' conservatism with their even stronger love of contraband.

The farming classes understood imperfectly, if at all, the relationship between mercantile prices in the city and farm income. They did recognize, however, that all the clever plans and programs of the city politicians—no matter what their intended result—inevitably led to lower prices for farmers' crops and higher prices for things they had to buy. This failure of communication could and did lead to civil strife in states where the farmers were too often ignored. But some legislators realized the existence of economic interest groups centuries before Aristotle. By the beginning of the fifth century, Attica had been divided into three districts for the purpose of representation on the Council of Five Hundred. These were the City, the Coast, and the Interior; thus, roughly two-thirds of the councillors at any one time were from rural districts. This undoubtedly had something to do with relative conservatism and stability of the Athenian constitution.

One aspect of the Greek farmer's life would be surprising to Americans. American farmers live in houses in the middle of their fields; the nearest village is only a place to go for supplies or to make business deals or for entertainment. But from the very beginning, Greek farmers have preferred to live together in villages, no matter how small, and to go out to their fields during the day. A Greek farmer would wake at daybreak, dunk a piece of yesterday's bread into a bowl of wine for breakfast, and get about the day's work. This would be onerous only during certain times of the year: when ground had to be prepared for crops or when the harvest had to be got in. In a land like Greece, where little or no rain falls from June through September, there is little to do during the summer and winter months except to see that animals are fed and watered, and to keep birds from eating the maturing grain or fruit. As harvest time grew near, the Greek farmer, or at least part of his family, would actually go out and live in the fields where the crucial crop was growing and becoming potentially more precious every day.

Literary testimony, which is almost completely limited to the works of the Athenian comic poets, gives one a bewildering view of the farmer's life. On the one hand, we are told of the miserable, harsh, dirty environment and the back-breaking labor necessary just to stay alive— circumstances that naturally would produce crude, ignorant, and bestial human beings.

On the other hand, we find the benefits and simple pleasures of rural life sung with no less fervor. Peasants had the best of everything to eat and drink; they were hemmed in nowhere and had the sweet air of the countryside to breathe. Above all, their simple and honest life was contrasted with the frenzied pace and corruption of the city.

Both pictures are true, of course. Preparing Greek soil for sowing could be back-breaking toil, as any modern visitor can imagine, stumbling across fields replete with rocks, thistles, and here and there a bit of thin, tan, sandy soil. Olives and grapes needed careful attention, the latter particularly if vines were to bear the maximum amount of fruit. It is true that a mud brick cottage in a landscape where water is precious was not likely to be the most sanitary of dwellings; nor would its inhabitants escape notice as they came into town on a hot day, mingling with city folk in clean woolens and redolent of perfumed oil.

But once in town, the peasants either forgot their hardships or boasted about them. Unlike timid city dwellers in rented houses with nothing to call their own, the peasants were independent and self-reliant. If they smelled of garlic and manure, these were also evidence that the fields were productive and that they lived off the fat of the land. And if their country accents were laughed at in the assembly, at least their words were honest and expressive of old virtues.

Conservatism, simplicity, stability, and patriotism have been hailed as peasant virtues throughout human history, often by romantics who have never been outside a city in their lives. But the idealist can be disillusioned by some of the harsher aspects of farm life. Peasants are cruel. One is very close to essentials on a small farm. Peasants are always doing unpleasant things to animals—shearing them, branding them, taking their infants, butchering some, castrating others, forcing some to copulate, carrying them to market slung upside-down from poles. Farm children know by the age of four both how life is made and how it is ended. Some aspects of tenderness, generosity, and humanitarianism they may dismiss scornfully as squeamishness or effete luxuries that one of the soil cannot afford.

Part of peasant conservatism may with justice be branded as simple narrow-mindedness, of which the most noticeable aspect is anti-intellectualism. The broad plains of Boeotia, for instance, were notorious for producing swine rather than wit. A dubious tale by a Boeotian historian claimed that Herodotus himself had been expelled from Thebes because of Theban *agroikia* and *misologia* (hatred of learning). Boeotia produced few writers, and of the most distinguished, Pindar and Plutarch spent little time at home, whereas Hesiod was himself a most typical farmer—dour, puritanical, and superstitious.

A contrast has been implied between town and country dwellers in Greece during the age of the polis. But it was actually a mild contrast when one thinks of the disparate lives of farmer and worker in industrial Europe. With the exception of a few cities like Miletus and Corinth, which had long histories as commercial centers, most Greek urbanites were still quite close to the soil. Even when towns grew into real cities, many of their inhabitants still traveled out to bits of farmland every day. In Athens, for instance, the city walls enclosed roughly ten square miles of territory, but only two small areas were heavily built up into what we would consider urban congestion: a district under the Acropolis and the waterfront area of Piraeus. Elsewhere, small clusters of houses alternated with farmland, which continued to be cultivated from antiquity right up to the twentieth century. The burghers of Greece, therefore, may have spent much of their time at urban pursuits and expressed contempt for the rustic peasant, but not many of them were very far removed from agricultural backgrounds themselves.

Something of the political history of the Greek bourgeoisie has already been discussed. In some states like Megara or Argos, for instance, a growing urban middle class was repressed by the landowning aristocracy, leading to revolution and a precipitous acquisition of power by the burghers. Because they usually confiscated the lands of the nobles and became great landowners themselves, one could expect a repetition of this sort of class warfare every generation or so. Elsewhere, as in Athens, nobles and commons had reached an accommodation that continued to be respected except under extraordinary conditions.

Typical burghers were small businessmen or skilled laborers who quite probably owned land and expected it to supplement their income. They would be up at first light, just like farmers, for the same meager breakfast and spend the morning at their place of work. Noontime brought the important meal of the day followed by the inevitable siesta, which still divides the business day into two parts all over the eastern Mediterranean. An ambitious person or a busy worker would return to work in the later afternoon; those more casually employed might decide to take the rest of the day off for a trip to a gymnasium or public bath. Both exercise and ablutions were secondary diversions; the real purpose of such establishments was to provide a place for citizens to congregate and talk. In fact, businessmen could easily excuse long hours of leisure by claiming—with justice—that much of their business was accomplished at the bath or wrestling court: old customers were encountered, new ones cultivated, deals were initiated or concluded, and a wealth of information changed hands.

Because a great deal of literature and oratory was addressed to a bourgeois audience, we know something of bourgeois attitudes, at least in Athens, which was typical of the Greek city-state with a large middle class.

The Greek burgher was an intuitive Social Darwinist. He distrusted the poor because poverty seemed to him a direct result of some defect of character—stupidity, sloth, or meanness of spirit. He respected the status and authority of the aristocracy in theory but could be quick to anger at any lapse on the part of some specific aristocrat. Wealth and privilege were thought to bear with them added responsibility, and the severity of middle-class juries toward leaders who had gone astray was legendary.

Like his rural counterpart, the burgher was suspicious of novelty. The *Clouds* of Aristophanes attempted to play on the distrust felt by the average Athenian toward the Sophists (see below, pp. 108–109). He was also a religious bigot and was just as willing to punish unorthodoxy with death as any zealot in the blood-flecked history of Christianity. Consider the late fifth century B.C. at Athens. About 438, the scientist Anaxagoras was prosecuted for teaching astronomy and a law was passed to make study of the heavens illegal. At the same time, Pericles' consort Aspasia was attacked for "impiety." In 415, a number of prominent Athenians were executed for mocking the Eleusinian mysteries in a private home. The city also offered a substantial reward all over the Greek world for the return, alive or dead, of Diagoras the Atheist, who had revealed some of the mysteries and made fun of them. A few years later, in Syracuse, with disaster threatening, the general Nicias held up a crucial withdrawal because of an eclipse of the moon. The result was the total loss of the largest expeditionary force in Athenian history—in spite of the fact that Greek astronomers already knew the exact cause of lunar eclipses.

It is a curious fact that in the birthplace of democracy, the average Greek never became egalitarian, possibly because of the compelling conviction on the part of all individual Greeks that they were on their way up in the world. Poverty might have been a condition in the classical Greek world, but it was never an attitude: poor people considered their situation merely a temporary one, due to hard luck or a malicious god, soon to be reversed. "To confess oneself poor we do not consider shameful," said Pericles, "but it is much worse for one not to exert himself to escape poverty." Every small farmer planned eventually to acquire the fields of his neighbors and ride around them on a white horse before an admiring audience of grateful tenants. The businessman in town, no matter how tawdry his shop or abyssal his debts, looked to the day when he would corner the market, drive his rivals into bankruptcy, donate a grove of plane trees to the city, and invite his entire deme to the banquet of the century. For the ambition of every Greek was to be like Cimon: "to get money so he could spend it, and to spend it on increasing his prestige."

In the *Knights* of Aristophanes, the playwright makes fun of persons "in trade" who aspired to political leadership. There existed a peculiar prejudice against making money with one's hands. It was shared by a huge audience of Athenians, all of whom were in trade or made a living with their hands but firmly intended some day to live off their investments and estates, wear linen and perfume, dine off golden plates to the accompaniment of silken laughter, and throw coins to children in the streets.

A century after Aristophanes, at the zenith of the democracy in Athens, we find the orator Demosthenes attacking his rival because of the low origin of his parents. No doubt two-thirds of his audience came from origins just as low or lower. No matter. Both Aristophanes and Demosthenes knew the deepest convictions of the Athenians. For as far as mental attitude was concerned, there were no poor or even persons of average means in Athens: they were all destined to enormous wealth, although temporarily in straitened conditions. This kind of optimism, no matter how idiotic, or snobbish, or even vicious, helps to explain the resiliency of the Greeks and their ability to bounce back after defeat and disillusion.

Eventually, of course, in many cities, because of economic depression or poor distribution of goods and labor, the poor began to get poorer and the rich richer. And eventually, when ordinary Greeks became convinced that they were being cheated of their destiny not because of divine disfavor but because of human injustice, scythes and axes would come out from behind doors and blood would flow in the streets and the rich would pay for their vanity and avarice—often amid scenes of disgusting cruelty, for brutality lay very close to the surface in the Greek world.

The Restless Intellect

As we have seen (pp. 35–36), the first Greek philosophers had begun to question the influence of the gods on the affairs of humans. While they offered a wide range of doctrines, they all more or less agreed that mortals were capable of rational inquiry into the nature of the world they occupied and could even determine their own destiny. In the fifth century B.C., this atmosphere of intellectual liberation became not only popular but commercialized. Always quick to sense economic opportunity, Greeks who had philosophic training, or who could persuade their listeners that they had, began to set themselves up as teachers of various fields of secular knowledge. Although they specialized in many different subjects, the basic premise behind their teaching was the same: that men were capable of self-improvement through education and that such education would make them more successful. Acceptance of these ideas seems a foregone conclusion to us, but in the ancient world it was revolutionary. For if there is one theme that pervades the mythological traditions not only of the Greeks but of all other early societies in the Mediterranean and Middle East, it is this: that the Golden Age lay in the past; that gods and heroes had already done everything exciting and important long ago and that the world was now the abode of a lesser breed of mortals, who lived out their lives according to the whims of higher powers. But the new wave of teachers, or Sophists (from the Greek word for wisdom), offered the idea of human progress through one's own efforts. This concept, coupled with a growing tendency to treat the ancient deeds of gods and heroes as literature rather than history, gave the sophists rapid popularity, and because in the mid-fifth century Greek world everything novel and interesting seemed to be going on in Athens, the sophists naturally migrated there in the largest numbers.

Some Sophists taught difficult subjects like mathematics, astronomy, and physics and presumably encouraged knowledge as an end in itself. But the most popular Sophists concentrated on teaching the art of persuasion, or rhetoric. Through their arts, they promised, the lowliest man on the street could learn to speak in the assembly and the law courts, confound his opponents, and reap all the financial benefits of public life. Since in the courts, and in politics in general, there were always two or more sides to every question, these teachers of rhetoric offered to teach people how to win any argument, on either side. Some Greeks were offended by suggestion of the logical impossibility that there might be two equal and opposite answers to one question. This feeling of unease, however, was simply part of a larger unanswered question that was inevitable in the changing intellectual environment: if the gods do not in fact rule the destiny of mortals, and if mortals can seek success by their own means, why should these means be moral and just ones? This was the question that Socrates of Athens lived— and died—trying to answer.

Socrates was born in 469 and was executed in 399. His life thus spanned the rise of Athens, her greatness and her disastrous defeat by Sparta. Born into a middle class family, he started life, some said, as a stone mason, but soon gave up all interests except inquiry into the right conduct of life. To this inquiry he brought a swift intelligence, great good humor, stubborn determination, and unshakeable moral and intellectual honesty. Believing, like most Greeks, that all knowledge was innate in humans' minds, he began to try to extract this knowledge by his famous question-and-answer method. He soon attracted a loyal audience of young men, mostly of good family, but including even slaves, whom he encouraged to debate the most fundamental concepts about human behavior in an attempt to define guides for ethical conduct. These inquiries generally began with searching questions into traditional assumptions that everyone took for granted and tended to demonstrate that these assumptions were rooted more in custom and prejudice than in logic. Next Socrates would lead his audience into developing more precise definitions of things like piety, justice, good, and evil. He never went so far as to actually formulate rules of conduct, believing that by giving his followers the habits of rigorous questioning and logical thought processes he was creating a mentality that could perceive right conduct under all conditions.

Socrates was a familiar figure in Athens, but most of the general populace never bothered to find out what he was talking about and thought of him as simply another Sophist, with a headful of strange ideas. For those who became involved with Socrates, however, there was no neutral ground. The young men with whom he spent so much time developed a fanatic loyalty for their teacher, while those political leaders whose ability and judgment he questioned seethed with fury. It was the inevitable conflict between these two groups that brought Socrates to grief. The Socratic method, unfortunately, liberated the intellect at a faster rate than it developed intelligence and judgment. Many of the spoiled young men who adored Socrates were enchanted by his withering criticism of their elders and the Athenian establishment of the day but failed to follow Socrates in the far more difficult task of inquiry into creative alternatives. Most of these young men also affected an ill-disguised admiration for Sparta and things Spartan—and this in the middle of the Peloponnesian War! Through most of the war, Athenian tolerance for free speech kept Socrates out of trouble and on more than one occasion he demonstrated his courage and fortitude in the front lines. But after the war, with Athens at the mercy of Sparta, some of his enemies brought him to trial on trumped-up charges of corrupting the young. Socrates' defense was more notable for honesty than for appeasement of a hostile middle-class jury and he was condemned to death by drinking hemlock. Scholars and philosophers ever since have discussed the irony of the first great moral philosopher being executed by the first great democracy. The problem is an intricate and difficult one; unfortunately, many writers of both ancient and modern times have taken the easy way out by blaming the institution of democracy itself—as if no other form of government had ever put a philosopher to death.

Socrates never got around to discussing moral philosophy in terms of actual situations. Both he and other philosophers were more concerned with methods of perceiving right conduct than with rules of ethics per se. Curiously, it is in Greek tragedy that we find the most searching analysis of actual moral dilemmas. Tragedy had its origins in the various local festivals of the god Dionysus, celebrated all over the Greek world. By the beginning of the fifth century at Athens the celebration took the form of tragic dramas presented in competition over several days of the festival. Rivalry between playwrights and producers was spirited, for the winners were held in great honor. The first playwright whose works survive was Aeschylus (525–456 B.C.), who was most influential in establishing the form of the tragic drama as we know it. In Aeschylus' plays, gods and legendary figures were portrayed in human form and the plots were concerned with the most fundamental moral dilemmas confronting humankind. In the *Prometheus Bound,* for instance, it is the basic conflict between raw power (as represented by Zeus) and wisdom (Prometheus). Zeus had punished Prometheus savagely for placing his wisdom at the disposal of mortals. In the *Oresteia* trilogy we are observers of the downfall of arrogant pride, the punishment of adultery, murder, and matricide, and the awesome moral conflicts that ensue when mortals become enmeshed in the struggle between destiny and moral obligation.

If Athenians left the theater emotionally wrung dry, it was not just because of the provocative themes of the plays they had just seen. It was the genius of Aeschylus, the majestic verse in which he clothed his themes, and the surprising twists in familiar legends that made early Attic tragedy such an inspiring spectacle, provided models for rivals to emulate, and gave the audience more than enough in the way of moral philosophy for contemplation and discussion.

If Aeschylus was the master of austere simplicity, his younger contemporary Sophocles (496–406) was unrivaled in the complexities of his dramas. Subplots, however, only momentarily distract one from the central moral problem which must be solved or it will destroy everyone involved in it (usually the latter). In the *Antigone*, we see the struggle between what Antigone feels is her moral duty and Creon's concern for law and order in the state. The conflict itself is not insoluble; it is the personalities of the two characters that make it so.

Perhaps most interesting to modern audiences is the playwright Euripides (485–406). While Aeschylus and Sophocles showed individuals locked in conflict, Euripides was fascinated by the struggles that take place within the soul of one character. Medea became insane with rage when her husband Jason deserted her and she planned not only to kill her rival but her own children as well (a twist in the old legend which Euripides invented himself). But when it came right down to the act, her resolve weakened and in one of the most gripping soliloquies in all theater she debates with herself whether to go through with the awful deed.

During the later fifth century, tastes were changing. Euripides also wrote melodramas, with all ending happily. If some of the plots and characterizations are puzzling to critics, it is perhaps because acting and direction had assumed more importance than in the days of Aeschylus; we need to see the plays actually performed. Aeschylus, Sophocles, and Euripides wrote hundreds of plays and their contemporary rivals wrote hundreds more. It is therefore depressing to realize that of the entire legacy of Greek tragedy, only thirty-three plays survive, seven apiece from Aeschylus and Sophocles and nineteen from Euripides. We have to accept the judgment of antiquity that these were the geniuses of tragedy and hope that what we have were their masterpieces.

In the wake of Socrates' execution, one of his disciples resolved to carry on his work to continue the Socratic search for knowledge and virtue. In 387, the Athenian aristocrat Plato founded the Academy on the rolling plain to the northwest of the city walls of Athens. Plato intended the institution to be a training ground for young men from all over Greece who would immerse themselves in the Socratic search and hopefully return to their homes to teach others. It was at the Academy that Plato's philosophy began to emerge in the form of Socratic dialogues, which portrayed Socrates in his usual practice of interrogating persons famed for their wisdom and demonstrating that their so-called expert knowledge was illusory. In his later works, the dialogue form was changed to offer more in the way of positive doctrine, but Plato never really produced a philosophic system like the earlier natural philosophers. Like his teacher Socrates, Plato seemed to have been more concerned with the way men perceive knowledge, a pursuit to which the formulation of doctrinal principles was incidental. In his early work at least, Plato seems to have believed that his main task was to get people to think clearly and define precisely what they were talking about. Believing that mathematics was the "queen of sciences" because of its exactness of expression, he tried to bring this same precision to

Wealthy young aristocrats loved to attend *symposia*, or drinking parties, where they could display both their cultural achievements and their capacity for wine. (*Courtesy, Ella Riegel Memorial Museum, Bryn Mawr College*)

language, and therefore may be seen as the founder of linguistic philosophy. But he was certainly more than this. Plato's superb skill and style made him perhaps the most talented writer of antiquity. He could present an idea with grace, charm, and humor, leading his audience with relentless (if not faultless) logic to a foregone conclusion. If he is to be criticized, it is for attempting to treat the world as a set of ideals capable of being understood and realized. He has been accused both in antiquity and in modern times of refusing to deal with the reality of human fallibility and with practical solutions to human problems.

A different approach to some of these problems was formulated by one of Plato's students. Aristotle of Stagira (in Macedon) had come as a young man to the Academy. When Plato died in 347, Aristotle expected to be chosen his successor. When he was passed over, he founded his own school, which turned away from the rather rarified concerns of the Academy to an ambitious task that might have seemed impossible to a lesser mind. What Aristotle sought to do was to organize the entire sum of human knowledge of his day into fields and subfields and to inject some discipline in what had been a disorganized search for wisdom. Resisting the usual Greek impatience with research and the tendency to formulate first principles on the basis of intuition and guesswork, Aristotle forced his students to collect evidence about a certain subject until they could honestly say that they possessed all the available data. Only then did he start to sort out his information and attempt to generalize. For the *Politics*, for instance, Aristotle and his students collected 158 different constitutions of Greek and foreign states. After the job of analyzing all this data was completed, Aristotle

Athenian youths at play in the gymnasium. One can only guess at the nature of this game. (*Ashmolean Museum, Oxford*)

began to divide political forms into subtopics: monarchy, aristocracy, democracy, and so forth.

If Aristotle had a fault, it was trying to force something as irrational as human political behavior into too rigid a structure. Furthermore, in his scientific works he was hampered by the total lack of apparatus with which to measure and experiment; in a scientific field, mere visual observation is not enough. Nevertheless, Aristotle was perhaps the most learned man of antiquity, and his *method* of organizing and disseminating knowledge—if not the content—has been little changed to the present day.

The fourth century B.C. may have been one of diplomatic failure and political decline in the Greek world, but Plato and Aristotle adequately demonstrate that the ferocious intelligence and insatiable appetite for knowledge of the Greeks was never keener.

Classical Epilogue: The Rise of the Individual

During the decade of the 470s in Athens, the young Pericles appeared as an actor in a play by Sophocles (who himself served as general thirty years later), Cimon became the scourge of the Persians as the leading military figure of the city, and Melesias, the greatest wrestler of his day, retired from the ring and began to train a succession of Olympic winners. All these men—actor, general, athlete—were nobles; all were amateurs.[7] No one thought it the least surprising that a statesman should

---

[7] Athletes, however, had never been "amateurs" in the modern sense, i.e., receiving no remuneration. Victors in the Olympic and other games received prizes worth as much as three years' income. Ancient Greek "amateur" athletics is a modern myth.

A young Greek warrior sculpted in bronze portrays the ideal young male: beauty, strength, grace, . . . and a place in the front line of battle. (*Archivi Alinari/ Art Resource, N.Y.*)

excel at a number of other activities. In fact, Themistocles was thought rather one-sided because he could not sing and play the lyre.

A century later, the picture had changed. Generals were now rugged professionals, experts not only at strategy and tactics, but in the recruiting of mercenaries and the delicate maneuvering required to pry military appropriations out of reluctant civilian assemblies. A general need not even be a citizen of the polis that contracted his services. Actors and athletes had become professionalized as well. World-famous actors belonged to troupes that went from city to city with no particular attachments and no particular loyalties except to appreciative audiences and a fat share of the gate. And victories in the great Games—the Olympic, Isthmian, Pythian, and Nemean—had become so prestigious that cities no longer left the competition up to fate and a handful of talented aristocrats' sons. Husky farm boys, swift street urchins, tough juveniles from the waterfront were all actively recruited by the state and then fed, sheltered, and trained at state expense in order to bring home first prizes in the *stadion* (about 200 meters) and the *pancration* (a sort of no-holds-barred fight). There is a fourth-century statue of a pancratist in the Museum at Delphi; with his powerful build and expression of complacent insolence, no one could mistake him for anything but a professional athlete.

The fourth century saw a general movement from the farm to the city. Whereas the rate of urbanization has been exaggerated by some scholars, there is no doubt that the numbers of farmers available for military service dwindled. At the same time, city folk were becoming reluctant to spend part of every year campaigning. Aside from the fact that one might get hurt (a contingency often felt more poignantly by the sheltered and comfortable urbanite), the city dweller did not have a convenient three-month period of leisure during the summer, like the farmer between harvests. So it was not unusual for the civilians of a Greek polis with a grudge against a neighbor to gather in the assembly and authorize the council to hire a Boeotian general, Cretan archers, and Thracian troops, which would invade the offending neighbor, massacre a few shepherds, burn the city's crops, and thus bring it to its senses (or send it off looking for its own hired army).

Mercenary warfare made it possible for almost any state to become a world power overnight. Jason of Pherae, a minor despot from Thessaly with only a troop of respectable cavalry, supplemented his forces with hired infantry and stood on the brink of dominating Greece when he was assassinated by a private enemy in the year 370 B.C. Tiny Phocis, which consisted of a very little bit of river valley and a great deal of uninhabitable mountain range, seized the temple treasures of Delphi and was thus able to hire a mercenary army that held off the best armaments of Greece for five years until King Philip of Macedon came on the scene. Maussolus of Caria ruled all of southwest Asia Minor with hired troops. And poor Sparta, reduced to third-rate status as a military power in Greece, allowed her kings to rent themselves and the Spartan army to the highest bidder—Persian satraps, Egyptians, and the like.

The fourth-century philosophers deplored the growing professionalism. To them it seemed a symptom of malaise and decline that common citizens should be so intent on material gain and so insensitive to the honor of the polis that they should hire others to fight for them. The sentiments of Plato, Isocrates, Aristotle, and their disciples have been echoed right up until the present generation by classical scholars who see a kind of decline of the Greek spirit going on after the Peloponnesian War. But it should be the task of the historian to attempt first to define what was going on and then to decide what sort of decline was involved.

This kind of professionalism simply illustrates a psychological trend afoot in fourth-century Greece: average citizens were becoming more interested in their own welfare than in that of the polis. And they were beginning to discover that they themselves were the best persons to look after that welfare. This can be called simple selfishness; it can also be seen as a growing spirit of individualism replacing an outworn reliance on the polis as a security blanket, despite the soothing promises of priests and orators. In another sense, we can say that an age of faith was being replaced by one of cynicism.

The point is that a loss of faith should be explained, and one apparent explanation is the two-pronged attack taking place on the once inviolable body of tribal wisdom throughout the age of the polis. Tribal wisdom had once made things perfectly clear to the citizen of the early fifth century—let us say, to the audiences that heard the tragedies of Aeschylus. It consisted of an amalgam of beliefs about the interaction of humans, gods, and fate. Any one of these beliefs could be easily illustrated by citing the correct passage from Homer with appropriate commentary by a learned Homeric interpreter. All people were allotted a certain path in life, a path that could lead to good fortune or terminate abruptly in disaster. Catastrophe could be avoided by a pious observance of religious duties as they had been laid down by centuries of tradition. And a petitioner might gingerly pray for some benefit or advantage in life—gingerly, because the gods were fond of jokes and might well give a man some obscene variation on what he had really wanted.

But by the middle of the fourth century B.C., blind faith in tribal wisdom had eroded before philosophy, which denied divine intervention in natural processes, and sophism, which taught that humans could improve their own lives. In addition, the sophistic sponsorship of reason as a guide to conduct was powerfully supported during the late fifth century by the sheer weight of historical experience:

> I returned, and saw under the sun, that the race is not to the swift, nor the battle to the strong, neither yet bread to the wise, nor yet riches to men of understanding, nor yet favor to men of skill; but time and chance happeneth to them all.

So said the author of *Ecclesiastes*, whose skeptical essay, by delightful misadventure, has crept into an anthology otherwise chiefly noted for moral uplift and tales of mayhem. This theory of history, although expounded in the late third century B.C., might well have been shared by the Greeks in the wake of the Peloponnesian War. They had seen the wicked prosper and the good perish. War, famine, and pestilence had wiped out old and young, rich and poor, kind and selfish as a scythe mows hay. Temples had been looted and destroyed, yet the

looters remained wealthy and untouched by any kind of divine vengeance. The only person who seemed to have gained from the war was
the hated king of Persia, who was now able to dictate the foreign policy
of Greek states by the judicious application of financial blackmail.

The common citizen usually had a simple and direct response to
this new interpretation of history. If the gods neither rewarded nor
punished, and if loyalty to the ideal of the polis meant only that one
must go out with the army and risk getting killed or maimed, then it
was time to look after one's own interests. Politically, this meant that
average citizens began to take less interest in the government of their
city and in what had been an almost fanatic insistence on autonomy.
The fourth century saw on one hand the beginnings of federalism as
groups of poleis gave up some of their sovereignty and formed leagues;
on the other hand, the disinterest of the ordinary person often made it
easier for tyrants or oligarchs to assume political control.

Economically, the entrepreneur began, for the first time, to look
outside the polis for economic opportunities and overseas investments.
During the Hellenistic period, the trading firm with a board of directors
drawn from half a dozen states was a common phenomenon; such
ventures had their origins in the fourth century.

Spiritually, the new self-directed attitudes led to an increasing
popularity for various cults that had no ties to the state and no state-
appointed clergy. These cults, most of them vaguely oriental in myth
and ritual, offered a mystical and a far more personal religious experience to the individual initiates.

In one sense, the new individualism and opportunism were only
extensions of the rather blatant selfishness and exclusiveness of the
poleis themselves. A very few wise statesmen of the fourth century
deplored the endless bickering of the cities and pointed out the need
for Greek unity, in some cases actually proposing a sort of United States
of Greece. Perhaps typically, it was also proposed that such a union
might best be launched by starting a national war against Persia. But
such were the jealousies, suspicions, and rampant hatreds of the city-
states and such were the old scores that lay unsettled, the unreclaimed
territory stolen by neighbors, the border disputes on one hand and
outraged sovereignty on the other, that no all-embracing union seemed
possible—until Philip of Macedon and his son Alexander imposed
unity and order from above, in a way no one had quite expected.

There is no reason to regret the gradual disappearance of the independent polis. In an expanding economy and a society that was
becoming sophisticated and cosmopolitan, the ideal of the polis was a
luxury the Greeks could no longer afford. Although the city-state had
declined in a political sense, in so doing it freed the spirit of its inhabitants. The broadened social and economic horizons of the Hellenistic era were to prove a dramatic contrast to the narrowness of the
world enclosed by the walls of the polis.

SUGGESTIONS FOR FURTHER READING

The comedies of Aristophanes are a mirror of all classes of Athenian society, although modern opinion is divided on the degree of distortion present. See Victor Ehrenberg, *The People of Aristophanes* (New York: Schocken Books, 1962). Theophrastus' *Characters* is a unique collection of caricatures by a contemporary. There are many easily available translations of Plato's works; four dialogues concerning the trial and death of Socrates are found in Hugh Tredennick, ed., *The Last Days of Socrates* (New York: Penguin, 1959). A large collection of ancient sources on slavery will be found translated in Thomas Wiedemann, ed., *Greek and Roman Slavery* (Baltimore: Johns Hopkins University Press, 1981); see also M. I. Finley, *Ancient Slavery and Modern Ideology* (New York: Penguin, 1980). The status of women in the ancient Greek world is a complex subject, just now beginning to get the attention it deserves in books such as Sarah Pomeroy's *Goddesses, Whores, Wives, and Slaves* (New York: Schocken, 1975) and Eva Cantarella's *Pandora's Daughters* (Baltimore: Johns Hopkins University Press, 1987). See the collection of sources in Mary R. Lefkowitz and Maureen B. Fant, eds., *Women's Life in Greece and Rome* (Baltimore: Johns Hopkins University Press, 1982). P. Walcot's *Greek Peasants, Ancient and Modern* (Manchester University Press, 1970) demonstrates the surprising survival of rural Greek values in a traditional society. No book has ever given a better description of what it is like to grow up in a traditional Greek village than Nicholas Gage's *Eleni* (New York: Ballantine, 1984). A valuable collection of ancient testimony is translated in M. Austin and P. Vidal-Naquet, *Economic and Social History of Ancient Greece, An Introduction* (London: Batsford, 1977).

6 Some Greek People

AT SOME POINT in the study of past civilizations, it is useful to turn from generalizations about large masses of people and to focus instead on the lives of a few interesting individuals. This chapter describes the lives and careers of a farmer, a politician, a doctor, two *hetairai* (the Greek version of the "oldest profession"), and a sea captain. Through their stories we gain a more personal perspective of the times in which they lived.

The Farmer: Hesiod

On the north shore of the Corinthian Gulf, the range of hills called Helicon rises steeply from the narrow coastal plain. A few miles up the valley at the foot of Helicon lay the tiny hamlet of Ascra, to which, sometime in the late eighth century, came a merchant from the Aeolian coast of Asia Minor, weary of seafaring and even wearier of the poor rewards of his trade. Here in Ascra the merchant managed to acquire a piece of farmland, and when he died, the land was divided between his two sons, Perses and Hesiod. The young men disputed the resulting division—a common occurrence in the Greek world—and took their quarrel before the council of local nobles, the *basileis*. But Perses had the forethought to dispense bribes among these notables, so they awarded him the largest and most fertile share of the property.

Perses proceeded to squander his inheritance, but Hesiod labored long hours to make his small farm earn him a living. Then one day, as he was watching his sheep on the slopes of Helicon, he had a transcendent experience. Those lovely ladies the Muses appeared to him, gave him a staff of laurel, and breathed into him the spirit of poetry, "that he might sing of the things that shall be and the things that have been."

Blessed with the divine talent given to him by the Muses, Hesiod now became a professional bard, traveling around the Greek world to enter verse competitons at the funeral games of great men and similar events. But at some point he took the time to address a long poem to his brother Perses, advising him to be diligent and explaining to the wastrel in detail how his farm ought to be managed. This poem, *Works and Days*, is not only a unique literary creation, it is also a treasury of everyday practical wisdom about farming in the Greek world and, as such, is a remarkable contrast to the contemporary Homeric epic with its grand themes and demigod heroes. Central to *Works and Days* is the annual farmer's calendar in which the seasons were announced by the rising and setting of constellations and by the seasonal behavior of birds and other animals. This section is introduced by a passage thought by the ancient Greeks to have been Hesiod's own favorite:

> When the Pleiades, the daughters of Atlas, are rising
> Begin the harvest—and the plowing when they set.
> For forty nights and days they are hidden
> But appear again as the year comes round
> And the iron sickle is first sharpened.
> This is the law of the fields, for those by the sea
> Dwelling, or who have woody glens and rich lands
> Far from the stormy deep.
> Strip to sow, strip to plow,
> Strip to reap when all things are in season.

The Pleiades rise in the eastern sky just before sunrise in early May when a hot sun and longer days have turned the grain golden and ready for harvest. By the beginning of November, they set just before dawn when the rainy season has started, moistening the sun-baked ground and softening it for the plow. After this brief description of the beginning and end of the farmer's year, Hesiod went on to summarize the

Fall was the season for planting, as depicted on this black figure plate. (*Antikenmuseum, Staatliche Museen Preussischer Kulturbesitz, Berlin*)

duties of the good farmer season by season. Lines 383–615 of *Works and Days* can be paraphrased as follows:

When the summer heat is ended and Sirius is in the sky most of the night (October), cut wood for wagons, plows, and other implements. Wood cut at this time (as the trees are beginning to go dormant for the winter) is drier and less liable to worm damage.

When the voice of the crane is heard overhead (early November), begin to plow and sow your grain with a boy following behind to cover the seed (this was also the date of the Thesmophoria at Athens, when married women performed the ceremonies honoring the fertility of earth and living things). Also plow fallow land in the springtime and break it up again in the summer (to plow the weeds under; as early as Hesiod, Greeks well understood the importance of rotating their fields to avoid depleting the soil).

Hesiod cautioned against late sowing: If you wait until the solstice (December 21) to sow, you will reap sitting down (that is, because the grain will be so short), unless when the cuckoo is heard (March) it should rain steadily enough to fill a cow's hoofprint (a risky proceeding; 100-year rainfall tables for Greece show a mean of about one and a half inches of rain for March—far less than what would be needed for the immature crop),

During the winter, the farmer had no regular tasks as land needed no care until the grain began to sprout in early February. But Hesiod warned his brother: Don't waste your time hanging around the smithy in winter (a convenient and warm place for villagers to congregate and socialize). The wise man works on his house while he has the leisure.

Spring comes early in the Mediterranean world: sixty days after the solstice (that is, February 21), when Arcturus is rising at dusk and just before the swallows return, prune your grapevines. (In northern Europe, vines are pruned as soon as the first frosts of winter have made them go dormant. But it rarely gets that cold in Greece, therefore the vines were pruned—and still are today—in late winter just before the new growth begins.)

When the snails begin to climb the plants and the Pleiades appear (May), then sharpen sickles and get the harvest in.

But when the artichokes go to flower and the cicada sings in a tree (June), that is the time to sit in the shade of a tree and relax. This time of year women are wanton, but unfortunately men are weak from the heat.

When Orion rises and the sheaves of grain are well dried (July), winnow your grain on a threshing floor in a windy place; then store the grain in jars and bring in the straw for draft animals.

When Orion and Sirius are overhead at night and Arcturus is rising at dawn (September) then harvest your grapes and make wine, the gift of Dionysus. But when Orion and the Pleiades are setting, it is time to plow again.

Life has changed very little on the small Greek farm today. Farmers still plow their tiny fields behind a horse or ox and consider about half an acre a day a job well done. They still harvest by hand in late spring when one can see whole families around a circular threshing floor on the windy side of a hill pitching the grain into the air so the chaff and straw will blow away, leaving the heavier kernels of wheat or barley to fall back into the growing mounds on the floor. The modern Greek word for threshing floor—aloni—is the same as the word used by Hesiod, and rural Greeks still call the month of July alonaris—the month of threshing. Agricultural scientists deplore the inefficient use of land, divided as it is into so many small plots. But Hesiod would agree with the intuitive response of the small farmer: such land division is socially useful; a man has as much land as he can work himself with his family. He is virtually self-sufficient, working only for himself and the future of those who depend on him, neither lured into unwise expense by easy credit nor crushed by debt.

Given the satisfaction and the sense of fulfillment of the successful farmer, which Hesiod certainly was, it is curious that *Works and Days* is characterized throughout by the most gloomy and pessimistic tone. The town of Ascra is "wretched in winter, miserable in summer, good at no time." Although most foreigners find the Greek winter mild and the summer, if hot, at least devoid of the sultry humidity of other climates, Hesiod claimed that the winds of winter strip the flesh from your bones and that the summer sun is fierce and cruel. The poet also believed that the human race had undergone a steady decline from a previous golden age:

> For now is the race of iron. Neither by day
> Do men cease from toil and sorrow, nor by night
> From wasting away. The Gods will send sore cares.

Given Hesiod's own success in life and the admiration he won from his fellow Greeks during his own lifetime, we must assume that his tone of discouraged resignation was more a question of artistic style than personal outlook. Again, his complaints of endless labor do not quite ring true as we know from his own poem that he had servants— slave boys and girls and hired hands—to do the actual plowing.

In later years, Hesiod went to Delphi and there Apollo told him to avoid the grove of Nemean Zeus. Thinking that the famous Nemea in the Peloponnesus was meant, Hesiod carefully avoided the entire peninsula. But he should have known that the god's words always had a hidden meaning. He went to visit friends on the north shore of the Corinthian Gulf, not far from Delphi, not knowing that the whole area was known as the precinct of Nemean Zeus. There he was suspected of seducing the daughter of his hosts and was lynched by her younger relatives. They tried to conceal the murder by throwing his body into the sea, but on the third day dolphins brought the corpse back to dry land and the killers were found out. Certain later writers described a tradition that named a companion of Hesiod as the real seducer, but others noted that the seduced girl later gave birth to the lyric poet Stesichorus, seeming to show that the gift of the Muses could be inherited. The true story of Hesiod's death will never be known. But we have his art, and that is enough.

The Demagogue: Cleon of Athens

The regime of Pericles in Athens might have been a government of the people and for the people, but it remained a government operated by an elite circle of aristocrats. By 508, a coalition of the noble houses of

Athens had expelled the tyranny and provided the city with a democratic constitution that guaranteed the legal and constitutional equality of all citizens including the right of the popular assembly to make all laws and rule on all policy. Nevertheless, for half a century the commoners of Attica were content to be guided by aristocratic leaders; the only political contention was between the supporters of one or another statesman from a noble house. It is true that the faction led by Pericles had been responsible, by mid-century, for liberalizing the constitution still further, creating control boards staffed by commoners and removing property qualifications for office. But Pericles was himself a noble of impeccable family background, and the men with whom he surrounded himself were also aristocrats.

By the decade of the 430s, there was grumbling in the streets of Athens over the continuing aristocratic monopoly of high office. The needs of an Aegean Empire had created an economic boom at Athens, particularly among those businesses that catered to the military and naval establishments and to the building trades. This boom had in turn brought into being a new class of wealthy people who had made their money in trade. Such a person was Cleon the tanner. We know almost nothing about his background[1] except that he came from the deme Kydathenaion, right in the heart of the city on the north slope of the Acropolis, a stone's throw from the agora. He was typical of this new class, which had acquired riches and now wished political power as well.

When Aristophanes in the *Knights* scornfully named the succession of "tradesmen" who had followed Pericles as the leaders of the people, he makes two things clear. First, the trades named are those of a sheep dealer, an oakum merchant, and a dealer in hides (who is Cleon, of course, thinly disguised as "Paphlagon," a crude and vulgar bully). Mutton, wool and fleeces, oakum for ropes and caulking ships, and leather—that ancient equivalent of almost everything we use plastics and rubber for today—these were products in the highest demand; thus an astute dealer in these commodities could have become as wealthy as any great landowner. The second most obvious implication of that passage of Aristophanes is that such wealthy tradesmen were looked down on when they aspired to political office or influence. No one objected to a person's becoming wealthy; but the idea that an uneducated and vulgar craftsman or tradesman might actually rise and address the popular assembly continued to be offensive to a large segment of the Athenian people for a long time—even to a sizable proportion of those who were themselves born of humble origins.

---

[1] His father is said to have owned a workshop of slave tanners.

But Cleon and those like him were not exactly insensitive to popular opinion either, and in 438 B.C. they thought they had a perfect issue with which to topple Pericles. Like so many other aristocrats, Pericles was vitally interested in all the new intellectual currents associated with the Sophists. His closest advisor was the astronomer Anaxagoras and his consort was the beautiful Aspasia (see pp. 131–135) who dared to talk philosophy with men as an equal. While maintaining a cold and austere front before good Athenian citizens, Pericles was capable of spending hours discussing the most absurd points of morality with an agnostic like Protagoras, or any other foreigner with a head full of learning.

It is a curious fact that Athens, like so many other societies, began to suffer some of the classic symptoms of bourgeois intolerance as its democracy became broader based. Cleon evidently realized that it might be possible to associate Pericles with all the popular misconceptions about the Sophists: they were almost all foreigners; they had very dubious views about the gods; they were able to disguise all manner of wickedness by volleys of logic complex enough to make one's head hurt. He therefore arranged for a series of indictments to be brought against Pericles and his friends, indictments that seriously embarrassed the statesman, although his political influence remained strong enough to blunt the attacks and to get most of his friends off.

When the Peloponnesian War broke out in the spring of 431, Cleon found another issue. Assailing Pericles' cautious attitude toward land warfare as cowardice, he and his friends raised a clamor in Athens for a more adventurous use of the infantry. A year and a half later, after several disastrous Athenian setbacks, Cleon's party was successful in having Pericles deposed for a short time, although the Athenians soon realized they could not do without him and thus reelected him. Political power was not a matter of being elected to office in Athens. The most influential politicians were those who could sway the assembly and the juries and who had attained a kind of unofficial status as popular leaders. We know little more about Cleon's early career than that by 427 he had achieved this status.

But in 429, Pericles died of the plague. Because no aristocrat was competent to replace him as a popular leader, Cleon now for the first time had an opportunity to seek political primacy for himself. The contrast was astonishing. Contemptuous of the dignified bearing and the fine phrases of the aristocracy, Cleon was the first political leader to address the people in the language of the streets, the docks, and the marketplace. He clowned around on the speaker's stand, spat, scratched, and was openly scornful of the style of the Athenian elite.

The Athenian public was amused, but not entirely convinced by the platform antics of Cleon. He was more insidiously effective with his use of the law courts to attack his enemies. His supporters lined up early in the morning to pack the juries; a false accusation against a person of noble family, combined with a raucous denunciation of aristocratic wealth, style, and privilege, was generally sufficient to cripple a potential enemy. Even more damaging were accusations of being soft on Sparta, which were particularly effective during the bitterness of the Peloponnesian War, and like all such accusations, virtually unanswerable.

The Athenian establishment was aghast at the antics of Cleon. Two literary men who both suffered at his hands have left us the most memorable picture of the demagogue. Thucydides presents him as a ruthless and power-mad rabble-rouser, cruel and crafty. He is shown proposing the slaughter of the entire male population of two cities that had revolted from Athens. He also purposely prolonged the war because it kept him in power. Vulgarity and buffoonery seemed to follow him around even when the most serious matters were at stake.

In 424, the Athenians managed to trap over 400 Spartans on the island of Sphacteria off the western Peloponnesus. Sparta sued for peace, but Cleon persuaded the assembly to impose impossible terms. When the ensuing siege seemed to be taking too long, Cleon attacked the general Nicias:

> Taunting him, he said it would be easy, if the generals were real men, to sail there with a proper force and capture those on the island; this was what he would do, if he were in command. When the Athenians began to clamor at Cleon, asking him why he didn't go himself, if it looked so easy to him, Nicias faced his accuser and told him he was free to take any force he wished and make the attempt himself.
>
> Thucydides 4. 28–29

Cleon became alarmed and tried to back down, but the crowd was now infected with the humor of the situation and became more and more unruly, insisting that the super-patriot should become a general. But in the end, Nicias' attempt to embarrass Cleon failed, partly because of Cleon's insistence on direct action and partly because of the military skill of his colleagues. The island of Sphacteria was taken by assault, and Cleon triumphantly returned to Athens with 292 surviving Spartans in chains.

Aristophanes' *Knights* was first performed shortly after this episode. We see the Athenian people characterized by Demos, a senile and flattery-prone fool. His two slaves, Nicias and Demosthenes, are outraged because they had just baked a beautiful cake (that is, the Spartans on Sphacteria) for their master, when his new slave Paphlagon (that is, Cleon) stole it and gave it to Demos, passing it off as his own. In this play, the Knights—the noble young men of Athens—finally defeat Paphlagon by finding an even greater rogue to be their champion. In the *Wasps*, we find a chorus of elderly and penurious jurymen who look to Cleon to find rich gentlemen on whom they can take out their resentment.

Following the Sphacteria campaign the Spartans began negotiating for an end to the war. Cleon's enemies accused him of sabotaging the negotiations because it was the war that kept him in power. Whatever the truth of this accusation, both Cleon and the foremost Spartan general were killed in the same battle two years later in northern Greece and shortly afterwards an armistice was concluded.

Cleon spent his life trying to rouse and exploit class warfare for his own ends. Thanks to the usual moderation of the Athenian public, he was not successful; but his extremism did in fact help to create organized oligarchic opposition, which blamed not just Cleon, but the whole idea of democracy as a system that permitted Cleons to thrive. Cleon thus, in his own way, helped to set the stage for the Thirty Tyrants and their attempt to destroy the democracy.

On the other hand, Cleon's career did serve to open Athenian government to broader-based representation. Never again was a narrow class of nobles to monopolize public affairs. Although the aristocracy continued to occupy favored positions in government right down to the end of the fourth century, there was now a steady influx of commoners with fresh ideas and fresh perspectives. If sometimes they lowered the overall tone of public debate, they increased its vigor and made it more responsive to popular opinion.

The Doctor: Ctesias of Cnidus

Although Greek science was often crippled by a characteristic excess of theory, the field of medicine enjoyed a more practical or clinical approach, tending to apply remedies on the basis of what had worked in the past. The most illustrious school of medicine was on the island of Cos, where the great Hippocrates practiced during the fifth century; he and his disciples claimed descent from the patron god of medicine, Asclepius. Just a three-hour sail from Cos is the city of Cnidus, situated at the end of a long peninsula of Asia Minor. Another branch of the Sons of Asclepius had moved here and had also produced many renowned doctors.

Ctesias of Cnidus completed his medical training here sometime during the late fifth century. But he had little chance to make a name for himself as a doctor in the Greek world because he fell into Persian hands in about 415 and was hauled off to the interior of the Persian Empire. To some the future might have looked bleak, but Ctesias was a born survivor equipped with cunning, energy, and ambition, and he was not the sort to pine away as a common slave. We know nothing of the details of his advancement through the intricacies of the Persian hierarchy, but in 404, when Artaxerxes II succeeded his father on the Persian throne, Ctesias was court physician, entrusted with the well-being of the king, his wife, and his children, and had become a special favorite of the crafty and vicious queen mother Parysatis.

One of the most memorable events of the classical period was the attempt of Artaxerxes' younger brother Cyrus to usurp the Persian throne with the aid of an army of 10,000 Greek mercenaries—an attempt secretly encouraged by his mother Parysatis. At the battle of Cunaxa near Babylon in 401, the Greeks carried all before them on their part of the line, but wasted their energies in a useless pursuit. Meanwhile, Cyrus had gotten himself killed in a foolish, headlong assault on his brother, thus effectively ending the revolt. In the aftermath, the Greek force was tricked into surrendering its leaders, but the main body was able to escape and make its way back to the sea through the heart of a hostile Persian Empire.[2] King Artaxerxes eventually executed the Greek generals and otherwise rewarded or punished members of his own court for their participation in the events.

In all the excitement, Ctesias was everywhere. He attended the king during the battle and successfully treated his wounds. During the following weeks, he acted as the queen mother's emissary, making sure the Greek generals were comfortable and well fed. Parysatis did her best to get them freed, but in this she was unable to sway her son, who thought it intolerable that foreigners should march to the heart of the Persian Empire and escape unscathed. The argument deepened the existing hatred between the king's mother and his wife Stateira—a rivalry for loyalty and affection closely and eagerly observed by Ctesias, whose description of the eventual outcome was quoted by Plutarch in his *Life* of Artaxerxes:

> The two women had begun again to visit each other and to eat together but though they had thus far relaxed their former habits of jealousy and variance, still, out of fear and as a matter of caution, they always ate of the same dishes and of the same parts of them. Now there is a small Persian bird, inside of which no excrement is found, only a mass of fat, so that they suppose the little creatures live upon air and dew. It is called *rhyntaces*. Ctesias affirms that Parysatis, cutting a bird of this kind into two pieces with a knife one side of which had been smeared with poison, the other side being clear of it, ate the untouched and wholesome part herself, and gave Stateira that which was thus infected.

Stateira died in agony, but Artaxerxes was still too afraid of his mother to do any more than rack her servants.

---

[2] A story brilliantly told in the *Anabasis* of Xenophon, one of the most notable surviving works of Greek literature.

It was perhaps during this exciting period that Ctesias came to the conclusion reached by many doctors after him: that fame and fortune were to be obtained no less by writing books than by healing. After all, he had been the king's physician for years; no one in the world was privy to as many secrets, scandals, and intrigues of the Persian court. In addition, he had had the opportunity to collect information about the Persian Empire from Persian sources, and he knew that with his credentials he would be an instant success in Greek literary circles. There was only one problem—how was he to end his employment with Artaxerxes? All Persian subjects were considered slaves of the king, and Ctesias knew only too well how painfully the lives of those considered unfaithful could end (and he has left us a number of disgusting descriptions).

The eventual solution was typical of the wily Greek doctor. A messenger came from Cyprus with the information that an Athenian exile wished to help Artaxerxes in his war with Sparta. Ctesias managed to intercept the message and forged into it an express request that Artaxerxes send Ctesias back to the coast to act as liaison. Thus did the doctor end his long sojourn and begin a new career as historian of the Persian Empire.

Regretfully, Ctesias' many years of intrigue amidst the labyrinthine corruptions of the Persian court had made him rather indifferent to truth and accuracy. He began his history with a vicious attack on Herodotus for having filled his work with lies, but it takes little reading to determine who is guilty of distortion. Old Persian inscriptions, for instance, show that where the two writers are describing the same events, Herodotus is almost always right, Ctesias almost always wrong. And there is adequate evidence of the Persian Wars to show that Ctesias thought minor details unimportant: the campaigns of 480 and 479 are muddled together, a eunuch is sent to sack Delphi, Cretan archers prevent Xerxes from building a causeway to the island of Salamis, and a host of other inaccuracies and absurdities.

With the exception of the Persian Wars, the *Persica* of Ctesias is almost entirely about the court of the Persian kings,[3] and what a court it was! Not a year passed without plot and counterplot between court eunuchs and the innumerable relatives of the royal house. Kings or heirs apparent were assassinated and their deaths cruelly avenged. And what cruelty! Crucifixion and impalement were everyday occurrences, noses and tongues were cut off, eyes put out, molten brass poured in ears, men flayed alive. We learn rather casually why the court physi-

---

[3] Unfortunately, Ctesias' work exists only in the form of a short summary by a Byzantine scholar and a number of citations and quotations by later authors. Plutarch's *Artaxerxes* is largely drawn from Ctesias.

cian's job happened to be vacant. Ctesias' recent predecessor, Apollonides of Cos, had seduced the king's daughter (after convincing her that sex was the only cure for a malady of the womb). When caught, he was tortured for two months and then buried alive. No doubt Ctesias exercised a certain amount of discretion in his relations with the king's ladies.

Ctesias also wrote a work on India—without ever having been there. One reads about some of the same wonders reported by Herodotus, like gold-guarding griffins, but also a host of new marvels: men who live to be 200 years old with white hair that turns black as they age; sheep and goats as large as asses; and asses larger than horses (with horns). There is never thunder or lightning in India, we are told, and there are no pigs, trees are made of metal, and elephant sperm turns to amber.

In all honesty, it must be admitted that Ctesias knew his audience. Long afterward, in the Hellenistic period, when countless Greeks had been to India, people who had traveled all over the country wrote books about it, repeating some of Ctesias' tales, and making up further wonders themselves. This does not mean that the Greek reading public was unduly credulous—they merely appreciated fine stories, and Ctesias accommodated them, whether it was stories about India or Persia they wanted. Incidentally, a few small citations of his medical writings still exist, and they show him to be a perfectly sober and unspectacular practitioner:

> During the times of my father and grandfather, no doctor prescribed hellebore [an herbal heart stimulant]. For they did not understand its strength, the dosage, or how often it should be given. And if anyone did in fact give hellebore he advised the patient to make his will, as if he were about to undergo some great peril. Most of those who drank it choked to death; only a few survived. But today the drug seems to be most safe.

We do not know if Ctesias continued his medical career once he returned to Greek lands, or if he decided that writing sensational literature was more remunerative. But he was not the first doctor to make a good thing out of being a court physician, nor was he to be the last.

One other form of medicine deserves mention because it continued to rival the active and rational practice of the art throughout antiquity. At Epidaurus in the Argolid and at other famous sanctuaries of the god Asclepius, patients went in to sleep in the inner sanctuary, where the god appeared to them in their sleep and either cured them or told them how they might be cured. One of the most remarkable survivals from antiquity is a group of inscriptions from Epidaurus that are testimonials to the effectiveness of cures bestowed by the god at the local shrine. We note a high incidence of gall or kidney stones:

Euphanes of Epidaurus, a child. He lay down to sleep, having the stone. And to him the God appeared standing forth, and said, "what will you give me if I make you well?" The boy said, "ten knuckle-bones." The God laughed and said he would end his illness. And when a day passed he came forth well.

A man had a stone in his member. He had a dream. He seemed to be making love to a beautiful boy. Having an emission in his sleep, he passed the stone and the next day came forth with it in his hand.

Sometimes rich men would come from hundreds of miles away for minor reasons:

Heraeus of Mytilene. He had no hair on his head, but his chin was completely covered with hair. Being ashamed because others laughed at him he went in to sleep. And the God smearing a drug on his head made him have hair.

At other times the hopelessness of a case could lead a man to forsake a great medical center elsewhere in hopes of a divine cure:

A——crates of Cnidus, for his eyes. In a battle he was struck by a spear through both eyes and was blind, and went around with the spear point still stuck in his face. Coming in and sleeping he saw a vision. It seemed that the God pulled out the missile and put pupils back inside his eyelids. A day later he came out well.

The Hetairai: Aspasia and Neaira

The cities of Ionia enjoyed a great commercial renaissance after their liberation in the Persian Wars. Miletus, which had been utterly destroyed by the Persian sack of 494, was no exception and had begun a rapid climb toward her old primacy. By the middle of the fifth century, Miletus was paying a tribute of five talents annually to the Athenian imperial treasury, an assessment that indicates a large and prosperous state.

About 470 or so, a girl was born to the wife of a citizen of Miletus named Axiochus. This girl, named Aspasia, was eventually to become the most famous prostitute in Greek history. Because in most Greek cities it was illegal for free women to turn professional, it is probable that at an early age, her pious parents dedicated her to a temple of Aphrodite for training as a devotee of the goddess—in short, a temple prostitute. This was a perfectly legitimate way of getting rid of expensive and unwanted girl children, who had to be fed and whose dowries might cost a whole year's income. Dedication as a priestess relieved the family of the expense, brought honor on them for their gift to the goddess, and of course avoided the cruel alternative of exposure.

Pericles' mistress Aspasia, as depicted in this Roman copy of what may have been a fifth-century original. (*Hirmer Fotoarchiv*)

Temple prostitution was actually a form of slavery. We must assume that sometime during her early career, Aspasia gained her freedom (perhaps buying it herself, perhaps receiving it as a gift from an admiring patron) and went into private practice. Endowed with both brains and beauty, she became a great success and was on intimate terms with some of the most prominent citizens of Miletus.

In 448, the Athenian people authorized enormous expenditures for the adornment of the city with temples, porticoes, and other public buildings. There was a sudden wave of immigration to Athens as experts in the building trades—architects, engineers, artists, masons, and others—poured into the city from all over the Greek world. It was probably during this period that Aspasia moved to Athens, no doubt believing that the fastest growing city in Greece offered opportunities in all fields.

Here she set herself up with a number of younger women in a house of assignation. Such institutions were quite popular in a society

Artists enjoyed portraying the
homely face and unheroic
physique of the great philosopher Socrates. (*Reproduced
by Courtesy of the Trustees of
the British Museum*)

that did not otherwise permit free association between the sexes, and
we know a great deal about them, particularly from the much later
Alexandrian pedant and dilettante, Athenaeus, who collected all the
stories. These show that as in so many other business enterprises, the
Greeks did their best to avoid crass commercialism. There are many
fetching tales about the love affairs—some of them semipermanent—
between courtesans and the smart set of Athenian gentlemen.

The house of Aspasia was known all over the Greek world not only
for the beauty of her girls, but for the fame of her customers and the
high level of the conversation that went on. Here came statesmen, playwrights, generals, and now and then a funny little man with a squashed-
in face and pug nose named Socrates, who was one of Aspasia's favorites

133

and who insisted on talking about the most unusual subjects. One fateful day the great Pericles caught sight of Aspasia. With the directness typical of the man, he divorced his wife—a rich and noble lady—and took Aspasia as his mistress. Such a union could never become a legal marriage by Athenian law because only citizens could marry and produce citizen children, but Pericles remained loyal to Aspasia until he died. We do not know when the association began, but she bore him a son, also named Pericles, sometime before 441.

With the union, Aspasia's influence and fame increased and became in fact the focus of hostile comment in Athens, where growing democratization brought with it some of the more unwelcome bourgeois attitudes: anti-intellectualism, puritanism, fear of foreigners, and a deep distrust of intelligence in women. We see echoes of such gossip in the fragments of the comic poets who called her the new Omphale (who had once made Heracles wear women's clothes) and Deianeira (the wife of Heracles, who accidentally caused his death). The point of such comment is obvious. Even more vicious was the comic poet Cratinus who styled Aspasia as "Pericles' Hera, born of buggery, the dog-eyed whore," a passage that truly attests the freedom of speech available at Athens. One comic poet even went beyond satirical attacks and indicted Aspasia outright in the law courts for procuring free women for Pericles' use.

More serious were the attacks on Aspasia for meddling in politics. One rumor had it that Aspasia was the one who helped Pericles perfect his persuasive rhetoric. On this basis, much later, Plato wrote the dialogue *Menexenus*, which professes to contain a funeral oration delivered by Pericles but written by Aspasia.

In 440, Athens intervened in a border dispute between Miletus and the island of Samos. Taking Miletus' side, the city unwittingly involved itself in a long and bitter war, which ended only after the loss in combat of an unexpectedly large number of young Athenian men—"like losing the spring out of the year," Pericles said at their funeral rites. Inevitably, it was said that the Milesian Aspasia had talked Pericles into taking her city's part in the conflict, which otherwise could have been avoided.

Even after Pericles' death, gossip of this sort went on, gossip that Aristophanes parodied in his play the *Acharnians*, produced in 425 after six long years of war:

> Some drunken young dandies went to Megara
> And stole the whore, Simaetha.
> But the Megarians, maddened by grief, in return,
> Stole two whores from Aspasia.
> And thus because of three sluts, there burst out
> The start of war for all Greeks.
> For then, enraged, the Olympian Pericles
> Thundered and lightninged and threw Greece into turmoil. . . .

Such accusations appear cruel and slanderous to us. But there was another side of the Athenian temperament. During the first onslaught of the disastrous plague at the beginning of the war, Pericles lost both his legitimate sons by his previous wife. Therefore, appearing before the Athenian assembly, he humbly asked them to take pity on a man deprived of legal heirs. Always moved by personal tragedy, they proceeded to confer citizenship upon Aspasia's son, who later served the state both as treasurer and as a general.

After the death of Pericles in 429, Aspasia remained active in politics. She evidently became the companion of a rich wool merchant named Lysicles who was, like Cleon, one of the first of the nonnoble commercial class to try for political leadership. Once again the comic poets had a field day, claiming that such an untutored tradesman, who could once talk only about sheep, wool, and fleeces, had suddenly become a master rhetorician because of Aspasia's training. When Lysicles died fighting as a general in Asia Minor, our sources are silent and we know nothing more about this remarkable woman, one of the few Greek women to break down the barriers of masculine prejudice to become a person not only of beauty and grace, but power and influence as well.

Sometime in the early fourth century, a former slave woman named Nicarete decided to go into business. She began to buy little slave girls and train them for an eventual career as prostitutes. As these girls reached puberty, she began to sell their services, passing them off as her daughters because freeborn girls brought a higher fee than run-of-the-mill slave prostitutes. Eventually she sold all the girls to various patrons, but two of them remained with her when she moved to a friend's house in Athens, where the older girl, Metaneira, would be available for the orator Lysias, who had fallen in love with her. The younger girl, Neaira, had already begun to sleep with men for money, although she was not yet fifteen.

Neaira turned out to be the best investment of all the girls and Nicarete moved with her to Corinth, a prosperous city full of wealthy merchants and travelers. Here, two of Neaira's regular clients grew tired of paying large fees to her "mother," so they bought her outright from Nicarete for 3,000 drachmas.[4] This was a happy arrangement for a while, but then the two young men decided to get married to respectable Corinthian maidens. They also wanted to avoid the embarrassment of having their former concubine working the streets or the brothels of Corinth, so they agreed to sell her her freedom on very generous terms. Neaira went around to many of her former lovers and managed to raise

---

[4] One can see from the table on p. 69 that, even allowing for inflation, this was a substantial price for a slave.

part of the price. But she collected the largest sum from an Athenian playboy named Phrynion, who was famous for his wild and dissolute life. In return she agreed to go off to Athens with him and ply her trade no more in Corinth. In Athens, Neaira enjoyed the *dolce vita* for a time. The two spent much of their time at parties where the rich and bored young men of Athens tended to drink too much and where the conviviality often degenerated into sexual orgies. When the wealthy general Chabrias won a chariot race in Delphi in 373 B.C., he gave a victory party at his seaside villa south of Athens. It was a memorable affair: everyone got drunk, and when Phrynion and most of the other guests had fallen asleep, Neaira became particularly generous with her favors, even permitting some of Chabrias' household slaves to enjoy her.

But Neaira grew tired of Phrynion and the next year ran off to neighboring Megara, taking with her not only her clothing and jewelry but her serving girls and everything they could carry from Phrynion's house. She worked at her profession for two years in Megara, becoming more and more dissatisfied, for the Megareans were notoriously tight-fisted and few wealthy travelers passed through the town. Then one day she was visited by an Athenian named Stephanus, a petty crook who made a living hanging around the courts bringing suits for citizens who wished to remain anonymous. After making love with Stephanus, Neaira poured out all her complaints about the hardships that had befallen her: she was legally unable to work in Corinth and Athens was dangerous for her because of the violent temper of Phrynion, whom she had robbed and deserted.

Stephanus saw an opportunity to acquire a beautiful hetaira without spending a drachma for her services, plus a regular income from procuring clients for her, so he boasted that no one could ever take her away from him. Neaira then moved back to Athens with her goods, her maidservants, and her three children—a daughter named Phano and two sons. There life was not exactly as Stephanus had advertised, for he put her up in a miserable little hovel and her former owner Phrynion soon found out she was back in town and started making trouble. Stephanus, however, was now claiming that Neaira was not only a free woman but his wife, and he posted bond as surety for his claims. The situation was serious. In Athens, the penalty for falsely claiming citizenship was to be sold into slavery, and this suited no one. So Neaira persuaded Stephanus and Phrynion to make a deal: that they should share both her body and her upkeep, sleeping with her every other day and making new arrangements only upon mutual agreement. Now more secure in her role as a free Athenian woman, Neaira continued to live with both men in turn, frequently dining and drinking with them and their company (a fact that was later brought out in court to prove that she must have been a hetaira, for no Athenian housewife was permitted such latitude). From time to time, she and Stephanus would swindle

Prostitutes at drinking parties were a popular theme for vase painters. (*Ronald Sheridan's Photo-Library*)

wealthy and naïve foreigners. Neaira would entice them to her room and when they were in her embrace, Stephanus would come bursting in, playing the role of a betrayed husband. Because Athenian law allowed wronged husbands to punish the adulterer in any way he chose, including death, the befuddled foreigners quickly paid the extortionate sums demanded of them.

The years passed. Phrynion seems to have dropped out of the picture and little Phano had grown up—at least she was now old enough to follow her mother's career. Stephanus managed to pass her off as a citizen's daughter and got her married, but the husband soon found out what sort of woman he had fallen in with and threw her out, neglecting, however, to return her dowry of 3,000 drachmas. To recoup, Stephanus invited a rich old admirer of Neaira to come and visit. Phano had learned her mother's tricks well. She seduced the old man, who was then "surprised" in the act by Stephanus.

But respectability beckoned. Theogenes, a man of aristocratic family and good character (but not too smart), had been chosen as King Archon for the year. As the chief religious official of the Athenians, it was the King Archon's duty to preside over the most sacred ceremonies and to administer the oath to priestesses; and his wife was supposed to preside over those Dionysiac rites from which men were excluded. As a courthouse idler, Stephanus knew Theogenes well. He not only talked his way into a job on his staff but managed to persuade him to marry Phano, passing her off as a maiden of impeccable Athenian background. In her new role, Phano, already an accomplished prostitute and the daughter of a prostitute, was admitted to the holiest rites of Athenian cults. She must have enjoyed the irony in administering the priestesses' oath, an oath that read in part: "My life is holy and I am pure and undefiled by anything impure or by intercourse with men."

But now not only Phano but her mother Neaira got into trouble. The Council of the Areopagus, defenders of the law and religious law in particular, discovered just who had been presiding over their sacred rites. They would have punished Theogenes severely, but he managed to convince them that he had been deceived and to prove his good faith, he went home and threw Phano out into the street. Stephanus had made many enemies in his day and now a pair of them saw an opportunity to ruin him permanently. It was against the law for an Athenian citizen to live with an alien woman of any kind as husband and wife; an alien passing herself off as a citizen could be sold into slavery if found guilty. These enemies of Stephanus brought an indictment against Neaira and had a professional orator write them a long speech for the prosecution.[5] This speech has come down to us among the orations of Demosthenes (although most scholars do not believe he wrote it), and we learn of the lively careers of Neaira and Phano from the full description of their activities in this indictment.

In summing up, the speaker asked the members of the jury how they could possibly face their own wives and daughters—modest and respectable Athenian women—and tell them they had acquitted this notorious and shameful pair of alien prostitutes. If all the arguments, proofs, and affidavits submitted by the prosecution had stood up to cross examination, the two women would undoubtedly have been found guilty and sentenced to slavery. Unfortunately, we do not know the outcome of the case—as with most of the law cases for which we have the prosecution's speech only. If it looked as if things were going badly, Neaira and her daughter would undoubtedly have packed up their belongings and left town to practice their profession elsewhere.

Many people would tend to agree with the speaker for the prosecution in condemning these two women for selling their bodies to all applicants and for the other deceptions they practiced on the unsuspecting. One must remember, however, that for an alien woman with no protector and no money, there was virtually no other career open. Furthermore, prostitution existed because men demanded the services of prostitutes, including young children. From the perspective of Neaira and Phano, it was no doubt better to become a freewoman and practice prostitution than to remain a slave and endure it.

---

[5] There was no "district attorney" in Athens. Even criminal cases had to be prosecuted by private citizens.

The Explorer: Pytheas of Massalia

The small town of Phocaea on the coast of Asia Minor was one of the champion colonizers of the archaic period. The area dominated by Phocaean colonies was the western Mediterranean, including southern France and Spain; the city of Massalia (the modern Marseilles) eventually became the largest and wealthiest of these, taking advantage of its superb harbor near the mouth of the Rhone River. Down the river came Gallic merchants with trade goods from the interior. From Massalia, ships went west to buy silver and tin in Spain, and east to take all these commodities to the Greeks of the eastern Mediterranean. Massalian navigators had a reputation the length of the Greek world for their expert sailing and adventurous nature. Only jealous guarding of the Straits of Gibraltar by the Carthaginians kept the Massaliotes from venturing out into the Atlantic to negotiate for tin and other valuable goods at their source.

    Sailors of the Aegean have always been able to ignore the science of navigation. As a glance at a map will show, one is never out of sight of land. Furthermore, predominantly clear skies, predictable winds,

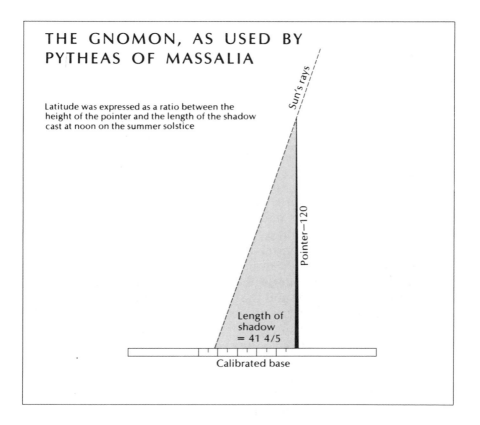

THE GNOMON, AS USED BY PYTHEAS OF MASSALIA

Latitude was expressed as a ratio between the height of the pointer and the length of the shadow cast at noon on the summer solstice

Sun's rays

Pointer—120

Length of
shadow
= 41 4/5

Calibrated base

The Greek merchant vessel was swift and seaworthy. A recent full-size replica outperformed modern yachts of the same size in downwind sailing trials. (*The British Museum*)

and a lack of tides or currents make any kind of sophisticated reckoning unnecessary. But the sailors of the western Mediterranean were far more likely to be blown out of sight of land by storms. Therefore, some kind of rudimentary art of finding one's position when surrounded by a featureless expanse of water became a matter of lively interest to them. The first person we know by name who managed to combine practical navigation with theoretical mathematics was Pytheas, a sea captain of Massalia.

In the work of Pytheas we can see how far the science had progressed by the end of the fourth century B.C. It had long been recognized that the earth was spherical, and it was taken for granted that the sun, moon, and stars rotated around the earth. Because the position of the sun is crucial to any system of navigation, the earliest experts had devoted a great deal of study to its orbit. It was known that the path of the sun passed twenty-four degrees north of the equator on the summer solstice (about June 21) and the same distance south on the winter solstice (about December 21).

If you know where the sun is supposed to be at any time, it follows that you ought to be able to calculate your own position relative to the sun and measured in terms of degrees north or south of the equator, or what we call latitude. By Pytheas' day, navigators had developed the gnomon (Herodotus wrote that it was introduced from Babylon), which measured the relationship of a shadow to the vertical pointer

THE FROZEN SEA

THULE?

Orkneys?

(SCOTLAND)

IERNE
(IRELAND)

DENMARK

Amber Isles

BRETTANICE
(BRITAIN)

N

Ushant

English Channel

CELTICE
(FRANCE)

Massalia

(SPAIN)

0   500
Miles

Straits of
Gibraltar

THE PROBABLE ROUTE OF
PYTHEAS OF MASSALIA

that cast the shadow, like a sundial. With this primitive instrument, the ancient navigators performed calculations that seem marvelous to anyone who has tried to use a modern sextant on the deck of a pitching boat at sea.

Using the gnomon, Pytheas established the latitude of Massalia as 43°11', which is remarkably close to the true figure of 43°18' (an error of about eight miles). His observation of the North Star was also accurate: he was able to state that true north actually lies somewhere within a square formed by the North Star and three others. It is probable that he also made a connection between the phases of the moon and the tides, although this piece of information, transmitted as it was by a landlubber, does not make any particular sense as it stands.[6]

These bits of information show that Pytheas was a skilled observer and had a solid grasp of navigational theory. But what has really caught

---

[6] Pytheas' book, On the Ocean, has not survived. Only citation by later authors still exists to give us an idea of the original scope of the work.

the imagination of all historians of exploration was the amazing journey he made into totally uncharted waters sometime near the end of the fourth century B.C., a journey that has established him as one of the world's greatest explorers, ranking with Columbus or Magellan. Moreover, he returned from this voyage with a wealth of geographical observations that formed the basis of the map of northern Europe from his day to the later Middle Ages.

In some unknown fashion, Pytheas was able to escape the Carthaginian blockade at the Straits of Gibraltar. He then sailed north along the coasts of Spain and France until he reached the Breton peninsula and the island of Ushant. Crossing over to Cornwall, he made special note of the tin mines, which has led many to believe that the tin trade was one of the more immediate objectives of his journey.

Because Pytheas described the shape of Britain and estimated its circumference, it is generally agreed that he circumnavigated the island. In the course of this voyage, he collected both scientific and cultural information. At four points somewhere between Brittany and the Orkneys, he determined the lengths of the longest day as sixteen, seventeen, eighteen, and nineteen hours—observations that mathematicians two hundred years later were able to convert into degrees of latitude. Pytheas and his crew ventured into the interior where, like good inquisitive Greeks, they studied the customs of the inhabitants. These lived indoors in log houses most of the time, stored grain underground because of the cold, and fought their infrequent wars from chariots, just like the Greeks of an older time.

In northern Scotland, the natives told Pytheas about the place "where the sun goes to sleep" and where there were only two or three hours of night during the summer solstice. This was probably a reference to the phenomenon of the sun dipping briefly below the horizon during the arctic summer. Even farther north was the legendary "island" of Thule, where the sun shone all night long, the natives threshed their grain indoors because of the wet and made their wine out of honey (that is, mead). But it was evidently not summer when Pytheas and his men ventured north in search of Thule, for he reported that his ship came to a place in the sea where air, water, and ice united into one element and prevented him from going any farther.

Sailing south along the west coast of Britain, he once more entered the English Channel and proceeded eastward, probably to Denmark, or maybe even into the Baltic, where he reported the existence of an island where amber was found in great quantities. This may have been another of the objectives of his voyage, for amber was highly prized for suppositious magical and medicinal properties back in Greece.

Pytheas finally returned from the far reaches of the northern European continent to Massalia, where he completed his major work, *On the Ocean*. His reward was to have his research treated with scorn and disbelief by some of the most elegant Greek writers of the next four centuries. For one thing, the fashion of travel writers was to collect stories of marvels, not scientific data. Therefore, Pytheas was taken for a charlatan because he tried to make his stories about Britain and Thule credible by mixing in astronomical observations. Also, it was reasoned by armchair theorists back in Greece that the farther north one went, the colder it got. It was cold enough in northern Macedonia and Thrace, they said; just to look at a map was enough to convince any intelligent person that life in northern Britain must be impossible because of the cold. Curiously, this type of criticism persisted even after Caesar had marched all over southern England.

Pytheas' account of Thule, in fact, was doubted by many scholars right up to the twentieth century. It was then that arctic explorers like Fridtjof Nansen and Vilhjalmur Stefansson recognized in Pytheas a kindred spirit, explained how his descriptions might apply to Iceland or Norway, and even identified the strange mixture of air, ice, and water as a not infrequent phenomenon of the arctic sea when a dense fog coincides with the onset of slush ice.

Although the voyage undertaken by Pytheas rarely led him out of sight of land, it was nevertheless as adventurous as any other undertaken by the great explorers of history. Not only were the regions penetrated by Pytheas and his men totally unknown to the Greeks, they are also subject to some of the worst weather in the world. The Mediterranean can be stormy, but at least it is generally warm and almost devoid of tides and currents. Pytheas ventured into a wilderness of mountainous and frigid gray seas punctuated with black rocks, where bitterly cold winds blow unceasingly, even during the summer. On the west coast of Scotland, powerful currents create whirlpools of maelstrom proportions, and tidal variations along the indented coast are as much as forty feet. The Pentland Firth, between the northernmost promontory of Scotland and the Orkney Islands, is one of the nastiest places in the world, particularly when a four-knot current sweeping west meets a howling nor'wester. Pytheas is reported to have seen seas running over a hundred feet high, and although quite a few feet can be attributed to good Greek exaggeration, modern observers can attest that the size of the waves at such times is truly awesome.

It was from this wholly unpromising vantage that Pytheas and his crew set out into the open sea to venture even farther in search of Thule. When they finally ran into fog and ice, we can hardly blame them for turning back. We can only sympathize with them because their voyage was so little appreciated in subsequent centuries, when only a few mathematicians and mapmakers treasured the data they brought back with them. Pytheas is reported to have been a man of modest private means, without the support of his city. So although he received no fanfare, his exploration is as great an accomplishment in its own way as was the far more famous journey in the opposite direction, undertaken at just about the same time by Alexander, son of Philip, the young king of Macedon.

SUGGESTIONS FOR FURTHER READING

Evidence for Hesiod may be found in his own *Works and Days*, less reliably in the anonymous biographical tradition found in later writers. For Cleon, see Aristophanes, *Wasps, Knights*; Thucydides 2–5; and F. J. Frost, "Pericles, Thucydides and Athenian Politics before the War," *Historia* 13 (1964) 385–399. There is little on Ctesias in English; what remains of his work in the original may be found in the basic collection by Felix Jacoby, *Die Fragmente der Griechischen Historiker*, part 3C (Leiden: Brill, 1958). A major portion of his history appears in French translation in R. Henry, *Ctesias La Perse, L'Inde* (Brussels: Office de publicité, 1947). Also see the appraisal by T. S. Brown, *The Greek Historians* (Lexington, Mass.: D. C. Heath, 1973), pp. 77–106. For Aspasia, Plutarch's *Pericles* 24 is the fullest ancient reference. The careers of Neaira and Phano are known from the Demosthenic speech for the prosecution, *Orat.* 59, *Against Neaira*. For Pytheas, the remaining fragments have been collected in the original languages by H. J. Mette in *Pytheas von Massalia* (Berlin: De Gruyter, 1952). See also M. Cary and E. Warmington, *The Ancient Explorers* (Baltimore: Penguin Books, 1963), pp. 47–56, and D. R. Dicks, *The Fragments of Hipparchus* (London: Athlone Press, 1960), p. 178 ff. Sketches of some other Greek individuals will be found in Robert Kebric, *Greek People* (Mountain View, Calif.: Mayfield, 1989).

7 The Hellenistic World

DESPITE THE convenient use of terms like "Dark Age" and "Age of the Polis," there are actually very few moments at any time in history when one can say that one era has finished and another has started. But the lifetime of Alexander the Great does mark one such dividing line. Although much of the social and economic identity of the Hellenistic world was already detectable in the decades before his conquest of the Persian Empire, it was that conquest, and above all the manic genius of the man expressed in conquest, that acted as a catalyst, accelerated change, and made even contemporaries realize that nothing would ever be the same again.

It is still necessary to justify time and energy spent on the Hellenistic era. Too many textbooks of Greek history end with Alexander or devote only an epilogue to the two centuries between his accession and the beginning of Roman domination. The very word *Hellenistic* is a nineteenth-century invention made necessary by the European rediscovery and growing appreciation of Greek history after Alexander. Until that time, very few scholars or educators had been particularly interested in the Greeks once they had lost political independence. It was felt that with the death of Demosthenes and Aristotle in 322 B.C. and the ascendancy of coarse Macedonians to the ruling power all over the Greek world, some sort of purity had gone out of Greek life and the Greek ideal had lost its purpose.

Actually, the last three centuries B.C. saw the emergence of a society in which Greek values and Greek culture were eagerly adopted by certain elements within the subject populations of Anatolians, Syrians, Jews, Egyptians, and others. This cosmopolitan society impressed and instructed the Romans and finally admitted them to the mixture as well. Much of what the Romans left as a legacy to the Western world was learned from Hellenistic models. Furthermore, it was the Hellenistic world with its Greek and Semitic influences that so decisively shaped and spread early Christianity.

The Conquests of Alexander the Great

Alexander crossed the Hellespont from Europe to Asia in the spring of 334. He was 22 years old and his prospects were not particularly hopeful: he was attacking the most powerful, extensive, and wealthy empire in the world. He left behind him a Greek world seething with resentment over subjection by Macedonians and ready to revolt at his first false step. He intended to take control of the shores of the eastern Mediterranean, but he had virtually no navy. His meager supplies were sufficient to maintain his army in the field for at most a month.

He solved the first problem with a swift victory over Persian cavalry at the Granicus River in northwest Asia Minor, thus gaining control over the rich revenues of the Ionian coast and its hinterland. In November 333, he finally met the full Persian army, led by King Darius III, on the northern Phoenician coast. Although heavily outnumbered, the Macedonians routed Darius, who fled ignobly on a borrowed horse. A successful siege of the Phoenician stronghold of Tyre delivered the rest of the Levant into Alexander's hands and he proceeded to Egypt, where the populace greeted him as a worthy successor of the Pharaohs. In January 331, he ordered his architects to begin constructing his intended capital Alexandria just west of the Nile Delta (see pp. 157–161).

Meanwhile Darius was back in Persia, raising an even greater army and claiming that the terrain of the Phoenician coast had prevented his forces from defeating Alexander. The young Macedonian king disposed of this dubious claim by marching directly into the heart of Mesopotamia. There on the broad plains east of the Tigris River on the first day of October 331, Alexander's army routed a Persian force perhaps ten times as large. The Persian and Bactrian cavalry on the flanks fought bravely but Alexander concentrated his attack on the center of the Persian front, where King Darius was stationed. In the confusion and dust the massive Persian numbers were only an encumbrance, preventing maneuver and reinforcement of threatened positions. Once again Darius fled, leaving his army no reason to continue the fight. In one day Alexander had won title to an empire that had once stretched from Egypt and the Mediterranean to the plains of central Asia and the broad valleys of northern India.

Having mopped up the last pockets of resistance in the Iranian heartland, Alexander left for the East, chasing the remnants of the Bactrian cavalry, which had headed for home, taking with them the fugitive king Darius. Alexander soon overtook them, only to find Darius murdered and the Bactrian leaders raising a rebellion in their rugged homeland—modern Afghanistan and the plains east of the Caspian Sea. From 330 to 327 Alexander wandered the northeastern limits of his domain, subduing rebellious tribes and founding cities on the Greek pattern as future administrative centers. In summer 327, his forces descended into the Indus River Valley of northwest India, defeated the local rulers in a great battle (where the Macedonian infantry had to hold their line against elephants), and then proceeded eastward once more. It seems strange that Alexander expended so much time and effort on these remote eastern lands, which would in fact revert to local rule soon after his death. But it is probable that he was unaware of the huge extent of eastern Asia, including China and Siberia. He may have thought that a conquest of India would complete his control of the known eastern world, leaving him free to return and subdue Africa and Europe. His weary troops mutinied, however, and compelled him to return to Mesopotamia in late 325. Two years later, on a sultry day in June, the great conqueror, weakened by old wounds and a long bout of drinking, died of some unknown illness by the waters of Babylon. Only 33 years old, he had compiled a string of brilliant military victories that would never be equaled, considering the variety of his opponents, the odds against which he consistently fought, and the vast territorial range of his conquests.

Although they displayed genuine grief, Alexander's generals undoubtedly also had the eventual fate of this empire on their minds. These gentlemen were all ferocious veterans of hard-fought campaigns, all of them brilliant strategists, and all of them proud, ambitious, and none too convinced that Alexander's imperial throne could be held in trust for his heirs.[1] It was the wars of these generals and of their sons after them that kept the world in an uproar for another fifty years.

---

[1] During his eastern campaigns Alexander had married a Bactrian princess named Roxane. At his death she was pregnant with his son, the unfortunate Alexander IV, who was murdered, together with his mother and half-brother, in 310 by the Macedonian regent Cassander.

The Political Settlement, 323–272 B.C.

The first of the generals to realize the opportunities inherent in the situation and to disregard any sentimental attachment to the ideal of a united empire was Alexander's boyhood companion, trusted friend, and able lieutenant, Ptolemy, son of Lagos, a member of the Macedonian nobility. Ptolemy gained possession of the corpse of Alexander and with his own loyal troops descended swiftly from Babylon to the valley of the Nile. The other generals made one abortive attempt to dispossess him of Egypt; after their failure, the rule of Ptolemy and his successors over the land of the Pharaohs was not seriously threatened again for centuries, although the first Ptolemy's brilliance and ability were not to be matched until the last of the line, Cleopatra the Great.

For a time, the fiction of Alexander's empire was kept alive by his former general staff. But while they paid lip service to the ideal, they carefully maneuvered themselves into the strongest possible positions in various parts of Greece and the Near East. As a handful of these ruthless Macedonian barons competed to see who would "liberate" the cities of Greece, one of Ptolemy's lieutenants, Seleucus by name, made a successful descent on Babylon in 311 and captured the imperial treasure stored there. He was equally successful in laying claim to that part of Alexander's domain which had once constituted the heartland of the Persian Empire: the Iranian plateau, the rich teeming cities of Mesopotamia, and the coast of Syria-Palestine. Seleucus and his descendants were to rule this patchwork of nations, tribes, and cities until it was brought under Roman rule by Pompey the Great in 62 B.C.

The fate of Greece and the Aegean coasts was not so quickly settled. Here, in 310, the forces of the major players were too evenly balanced. Cassander, son of Alexander's regent, controlled Macedon and as many of the Greek cities as he could garrison. A tough, old, one-eyed general named Antigonus based his operations on the cities of Asia Minor and on control of the seas, aided by his brilliant but erratic son Demetrius, "Besieger of Cities." The shrewdly competent Lysimachus had seized Thrace and the Hellespontine regions and stood poised in excellent position to move in any direction when someone faltered or proved less than vigilant.

In 307, Antigonus and Demetrius "liberated" Athens. A few years later, their forces had grown so alarmingly that the balance of power was threatened. Ptolemy, Seleucus, Cassander, and Lysimachus united to meet the threat, and in 301, on the battlefield of Ipsus, in Asia Minor, Antigonus the One-eyed died fighting the coalition; his mercenary troops were dispersed—or went over to the victors—and his son Demetrius was lucky to escape with an intact fleet and a few cities still loyal.

Half a dozen years later, the seemingly absurd working of Chance (who became a full-fledged goddess in the unstable world of Alex-

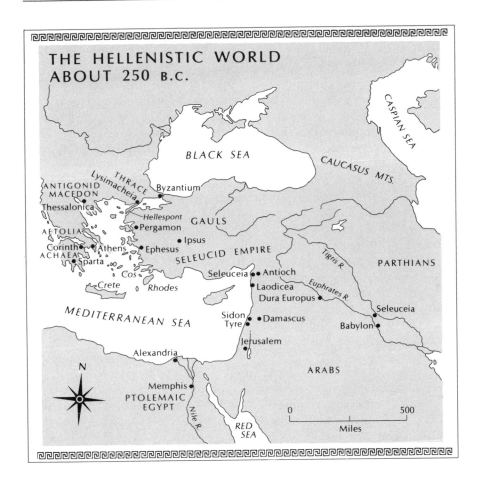

THE HELLENISTIC WORLD
ABOUT 250 B.C.

ander's successors) delivered the kingdom of Macedon into Demetrius' hands, and his armies increased once more. His sovereignty over mainland Greece thus seemed unchallengeable, and the whole Greek world awaited his preparations to reconquer Alexander's empire. If anyone seemed suited to inherit the mantle of the Conqueror, it was Demetrius. Nobly handsome, gifted, brilliant in war, he far surpassed Alexander in his capacity for good-natured enjoyment of the pleasures of life once the campaign was over.[2] His mercenary troops were amazingly loyal and would follow him anywhere, even when their pay was months in arrears. But he completely failed to measure up to Alexander's achievements in one respect: he was almost pathologically unable to consolidate, to administer, or to organize his winnings for constructive purposes. He was, in short, unfit to rule civilians.

---

[2] The details are preserved in Plutarch's *Life of Demetrius.*

During the decade of the 290s, another young general was beginning to rival Demetrius in his military skill, his charisma with hired troops, and—it must be admitted—his incompetence to govern peaceful territories. This was the young king Pyrrhus of Epirus from the mountainous northwest corner of the Greek world—an almost Homeric figure from out of the past: huge, red-haired, courageous, good-humored, generous. Like Demetrius, he followed some archaic code of knight-errantry, whereas the majority of Alexander's other generals were doing their best to master the arts of Greek statecraft and bureaucracy.

From 295 to 285, Demetrius kept the Aegean in a state of flux, but in 285 he was captured by Seleucus and penned up on an island, where he soon drank himself to death. With Demetrius dead and Pyrrhus off on a wild venture in Italy, the Greek world seemed ready to settle down and enjoy comparative stability. But the vacuum was filled with new quarrels; Lysimachus and Seleucus were both killed in unduly ambitious quests for empire; and once more Chance rivaled the human capacity for mischief by introducing an entirely new dimension. The blow fell in 279.

Down through the Balkans, across the plains of Thrace came an enormous army of Gauls, inspired by God-knows-what disturbances at home or hope of gain abroad. At first they swept all before them. Macedon lay in anarchy and the Greek cities in the grip of terror; even Delphi in its mountain fastness was threatened and was rescued only at the last moment. Having happily reduced everything to a chaotic state, the Gauls crossed over the Hellespont in 278 and carved themselves an empire in the interior of Asia Minor, where they were content to collect tribute from neighboring Greek cities for the next generation. The only beneficiary was the son of Demetrius, Antigonus Gonatas, who had inherited his father's capacity for being in the right place at the right time. The weary Macedonian citizenry invited him to be monarch (276–239), and he responded by giving them thirty-eight years of competent rule. His descendants governed Macedon and much of Greece for another century.[3]

These three dynasties—Ptolemies in Egypt, Seleucids in the Near East, Antigonids on the Greek mainland—were the three primary axes of power all through the Hellenistic world from about 275 to 146. Although they fought from time to time amongst themselves and their borders fluctuated, these dynasties and the lands they ruled reached a rather stable configuration; neither war nor revolution was to be the devastating force it had been to the generation after Alexander's death.

---

[3] In an absurd climax to a wild career, Pyrrhus of Epirus was killed in 272 B.C. while attempting a raid on the city of Argos. His murderer was an old lady who dropped a tile on his head from the rooftop of a building that overlooked the street fighting.

The Ptolemies and their Greek entourage never represented more than a small fraction of the enormous Egyptian population, and they made every effort to accommodate Egyptian traditions and beliefs, as illustrated by this head of a Ptolemy in the guise of an Egyptian Pharaoh. (*Brussels, Royal Museum of Art & History*)

In the century to come, Hellenistic kingship as a political institution would become the predominant form of government in the Western world, and the imperial systems of these kings would become models for the Romans to follow.

Egypt Under the Ptolemies

For over 3,000 years, the inhabitants of the Nile Valley had lived in very much the same way, their lives dictated by one overwhelming factor, the Nile River. Each year, about the middle of July, the Nile began to rise. As it receded, it left behind a thick new layer of rich muck. The peasants of the Nile Valley needed only to trample in seed grain; the sun shone without interruption, irrigation was easy, and two or three harvests could be won from the constantly refreshed soil with a minimum of effort.

From the earliest times, powerful individuals had recognized that the land along the banks of the Nile was too valuable to be entrusted haphazardly to anyone who chose to farm it. All the land of Egypt, therefore, and the bodies of its inhabitants as well, were held to be the property of the god-king, the Pharaoh. Temporary title to some land was assigned by the royal household to priests and nobles; the lands of all were worked by the Egyptian peasantry whose status was half serf, half tenant.

Every year, peasants sowed new crops, tended them to the extent necessary, and at harvest time, turned over the required quota to their landlord, whether a noble, a high priest, or Pharaoh himself. All details of acreage under cultivation, irrigation systems, planting, and harvest were under the supervision of a tightly organized bureaucracy that was able to calculate to a handful the amount of grain every plot ought to produce. Not only grain, but livestock as well were owed to the ultimate landlord, the Pharaoh.

The rigidly authoritarian social structure of Egypt was made possible by the world-renowned docility of the Egyptian peasant who took it for granted that Pharaoh was the son of God and held it to be only natural for Pharaoh to own the Nile Valley and to do with its inhabitants as he wished. We know that Egyptian peasants complained from time to time about unjust exactments or unrealistic quotas, or grumbled about haughty and arbitrary tax collectors; but the system itself was never questioned and seemed to all Egyptians of whatever station to be as permanent and unchanging as the Nile itself.

Such a rich land and such remarkably placid and hard-working inhabitants could not fail to attract attention from neighbors, particularly when the vigor of native Pharaohs began to flag. After 945 B.C., Libyans, Ethiopians, and Assyrians in succession became masters of the land. A native dynasty undertook a revival from 663 to 525, but in that year, the Persian Empire swallowed Egypt with minimal difficulty and, except for a brief period in the fourth century, exercised control until the triumphant entry of Alexander the Great in 332.

The foreign masters of Egypt never considered tampering with the Egyptian economy or the well-established bureaucracy that made that economy work. All that was necessary to grasp the reins and enjoy the fruits of Egypt was to come to a satisfactory accommodation with the Egyptian priesthoods and to put one's own officials in charge of the tax-collecting apparatus. As long as the gods of Egypt were served, as long as priests and nobles were allowed to retain nominal honors, incomes, and lands, whoever was master of the Nile Valley could enjoy the enormous revenues of what had once been the royal lands of Egypt.

In his invasion of Egypt, as in so many other ventures, Alexander planned to outstrip his predecessors in every way. The first absolute necessity was to reach an accord with the gods who ruled the Nile Valley. The most recent Persian conquerors had plundered the Egyptian temples in an excess of monotheistic zeal. Alexander, with the usual Greek assumption that gods were universal, entered fully and sincerely into Egyptian religious life, restored the power of the priesthoods, and subsequently was recognized by the priests—and therefore by all Egypt—as the legitimate successor to the Pharaohs. Egyptian hieroglyphic inscriptions name him with all the panoply accorded an Amenhotep or Rameses. The story was widely put about that the conqueror was in fact a son of the Egyptian god Ammon who had visited Alexander's mother while Philip was away on campaign—a story that Alexander himself seems to have believed.

The second necessity was to build an administrative headquarters where Alexander's deputies could rule Egypt while living in as Greek a setting as possible. For this purpose, the city of Alexandria was laid out along the sands of the Mediterranean on the western edge of the Nile Delta. It was to the infant capital of Alexandria that Ptolemy came in 322 to bury his friend and commander in a spot where his magnificent tomb would serve to enhance the legitimacy of Macedonian rule. Immediately, Ptolemy showed that he had fully understood Alexander's genius for organizing and consolidating new conquests. Egypt would give its new ruler obedience and wealth; it was up to Ptolemy to use these gifts constructively.

Throughout the Greek world the word went out: Ptolemy needed Greeks of every sort—clerks, accountants, masons, engineers, artists, doctors, actors, scholars, and of course, able-bodied men to serve in his army. Ptolemy intended that the Egyptian economic system should continue as before, staffed at the lowest bureaucratic levels by Egyptians, but that at a certain point, every channel of authority, every chain of command should become Greek, or Macedonian, and continue to the upper levels where an entirely Graeco-Macedonian elite would exist and operate in an artificially created Greek world, a thin veneer riding upon and wholly insulated from the great mass of Egyptian peasants.

The Ptolemies, just like previous conquerors, intended that the land of the Nile should become a gigantic revenue-producing machine; but no earlier rulers had labored so fanatically and incessantly to make the machine so ruthlessly efficient. Through the centuries of Ptolemaic rule, an army of bureaucrats worked to record every transaction, every impost, every grain of wheat due to the crown, every fraction of the more than 200 taxes that could be levied on the foreign and native population. In the course of time, file cabinets had to be emptied to make room for more records; the used papyri were dumped in rubbish heaps out in the desert, soon to be covered and preserved by the shifting sands. Thousands of fragments from old Ptolemaic wastebaskets have been recovered, and these have made it possible for modern scholars to reconstruct a detailed picture of an ancient economy in operation.

Most of the Egyptian farmland was owned outright by the crown, and the rest of it was tightly controlled. The royal land was tilled by royal peasants. Each planting season they were issued seed grain to plant, and each harvest they were expected to turn over a certain percentage of the crop to the rent collectors. On the village level, these financial officials were themselves Egyptians who could read and write Greek. A number of villages formed larger districts, called *topoi;* these in turn were divided among the major provinces of Egypt, called *nomoi.* In general, all officials above the village level were Greek or Macedonian.

The land of Egypt not directly owned by the crown was parceled out to worthy recipients on a more or less permanent leasehold system. The various Egyptian priesthoods were allowed to retain the use of wide temple lands because it was considered an absolute necessity to keep the native religious establishment complaisant; nevertheless, temple lands were taxed like any others. The Ptolemies also let out choice real estate to the high Greek and Macedonian officials as a form of incentive above and beyond mere salary. Finally, thousands of small tracts were awarded to mercenary soldiers who were thus lured into Ptolemaic service (the idea of arming native Egyptians was long resisted; when finally tried, it proved a mistake). Veterans were allowed to farm this land tax-free as long as one member of the family in each generation served in the army.

The millions of bushels of grain—primarily wheat and barley—harvested each year were Egypt's greatest export and financial resource. Grain harvesting along the Nile was supervised so efficiently that even after being taxed several times on its way down the Nile, after being assessed for warehouse charges, after being charged export duty, Egyptian wheat was still cheap enough to drive Sicilian or Black Sea wheat off the market in the cities of Italy and Greece.

But grain was only the largest item of the Nile Valley's agricultural bounty. Orchard crops, flax, and papyrus were also grown under royal supervision, while the Ptolemies vastly increased production of livestock, particularly sheep and pigs. Probably the second greatest revenue-producing export of Egypt was papyrus. The pith of this splendid reed was the universal writing material of the entire ancient world, and virtually every scrap was produced in Egypt where its manufacture was a royal monopoly.

Another aspect of Ptolemaic enterprise was the control of certain manufactures. The Egyptians had been skillful and conscientious craftsmen for thousands of years. Taking this quality to be no less a valuable resource than the soil of the Nile, the Ptolemies converted all the most successful industries of Egypt into royal monopolies whose revenues, after wages and other overhead, went directly into the treasury. Among these industries was the production of beer—the Egyptian national drink from time immemorial. Every drop of the millions of gallons of this beverage consumed every year was supposed to be brewed in royal breweries. Even home production for home consumption was theoretically forbidden, although we may suppose this law

received no more compliance than it deserved. Other rewarding monopolies were producing sesame and cottonseed oil for cooking, salt
manufacture, linen weaving, operating public baths, and refining various highly prized scents and perfumes such as myrrh and
frankincense.

A third rigorously exploited source of revenue was from trade—
primarily foreign trade. Egypt produced for export a surplus of grain,
papyrus, linen, ivory, cosmetics, various kinds of cut stone, drugs and
cosmetics, and a wide variety of manufactured articles famed all over
the Mediterranean world for the beauty and precision of Egyptian crafts-
manship. Every item exported by the entrepreneurs of Alexandria and
Naucratis was taxed up to a dozen or so times: compulsory warehouse
charges, export duty, lading charges, and so forth until the price was
possibly doubled or trebled.

The same was true of imports. Vital necessities to Egypt were timber
in a treeless land; various metals, of which iron and copper were the
most important; horses; and to some extent, slaves. The large Greek
community was also responsible for a number of imports, insisting as
it did on an abundant supply of wine instead of the local beer, and
olive oil instead of the ubiquitous Egyptian vegetable seed oil. Neither
vines nor olive trees ever did well in Egyptian soil. The Ptolemies were
fully in accord with such parochial tastes for they enabled the tax
collectors to saddle these imports with as much as a 300 percent duty.

The sort of economy the rulers enjoyed is called by modern economists a command economy, meaning that every phase of the economy
is under state control, from production quotas to artificially rigged wage
and price controls. Such systems have, in the past, been referred to less
accurately as "state socialism," which obscures the meaning by introducing a concept of political ideology. None of the Ptolemies ever
displayed the slightest interest in political ideology; their economic
system was entirely a pragmatic one, devised to exact the greatest
amount of revenue possible from the Nile Valley.

Command economies have had little success in the modern world,
whether based on political ideology or not; there are generally far too
many unpredictable factors involved in any aspect of a complex modern
economy to make it subject to rigid state control of any kind. But the
Ptolemaic command economy worked for two important reasons. First
one could predict that every year the Nile would overflow its banks
and deposit new soil, which would once more bear one or two or even
three bumper crops. Second, the economy was based on the existence
of several million Egyptian peasants who were in effect slaves, who
would work every year just as hard in a docile and uncomplaining
fashion as they had worked for thousands of years, and who never
dreamed that any other existence was possible or even preferable. Some
of the later Ptolemies, forced to the wall by the expenses of foreign war,

made the mistake of pressing the peasantry too hard, which led to native revolt; but for the most part, the Egyptian peasantry was as predictable as a finely tuned machine.

If the Ptolemies brought to the Greek world the concept of a controlled economy, they also vastly increased the Greek notion of the responsibilities the state owed to its citizens. The idea of the welfare state was probably a direct result of the fact that the first Ptolemy had to recruit his entire government and army from elsewhere. The Greeks who responded were promised various benefits, and after a while, these began to be taken for granted. Municipalities throughout the Hellenistic world began to assume the responsibility for public education, providing funds for school buildings and sometimes even the teacher's stipend. The government also spent a great deal of money on internal improvements like roads, canals, irrigation systems, and reclamation of land from desert or marsh. Much of this sort of public work was directly subsidized by tolls or imposts on those benefited or was accomplished in part by a corvée. But a substantial amount of what we would call research and development—for example, experimenting with hybrid crops to increase yield or resist disease—must be viewed as an intangible investment for the future with no immediate financial return.

By far the most startling new institution created by the Ptolemies was the Museum of Alexandria and its adjunct the Library, which were innovations in that they were wholly subsidized by the state. The Macedonian kings in the past, perhaps smarting under the usual Greek notion that Macedonians were unlettered barbarians, had for centuries adorned their courts with the most fashionable Greek poets, philosophers, and actors and rewarded them with royal honoraria. But Ptolemy's creations went far beyond anything envisioned by previous Macedonian patrons of the arts.

The Museum was actually part of the palace complex. Here lived and worked world-famous scholars invited to carry on their research, to engage in learned discourse, and in general to make Alexandria the new capital of Greek scholarship. The Museum was not a university in the modern sense, for the resident scholars gave no regular courses of instruction, but they did attract disciples from all over the Greek world who worked under them and sometimes succeeded them after their death or retirement. The primary duty of the Alexandrian scholars was to continue to produce works of literature or scholarly research in order to keep their names renowned all over the world and thus increase the fame of the Museum—in short, the theoretical duty of university professors today. And just like the universities of today, the Museum produced far more in the way of scholarship than it did *belles lettres;* this was a limitation of one sort, nevertheless fine work was produced during the last three centuries B.C., particularly in the fields of science and literary criticism.

The Library of Alexandria was an essential part of the Museum, designed to be the world's first complete collection of published works and to serve the needs both of the Museum fellows and of numerous visiting scholars, artists, and literati who converged on Alexandria. Begun perhaps in the 280s, by the first century B.C. the Library contained over 700,000 works and remained the largest and most impressive library in the ancient world even in Roman times.

Alexandria, the Hellenistic City

> The impresario city, the perfection of Hellas,
> In every art and science most wise.
>
> C. P. Cavafy, *The Glory of the Ptolemies*

From the beginning, Alexandria was a work of mortals rather than gods. The streets were laid out on a grid plan and temples were situated in the most practical place, just like the market, theater, and gymnasium. The most famous structures of Alexandria—the Museum and Library and the Lighthouse—were secular. To the Museum and Library came scholars from all over the Greek world to enhance the reputation of the Ptolemies as patrons of wisdom, arts, and sciences. Another famous structure—the enormous Pharos—could be seen from far out

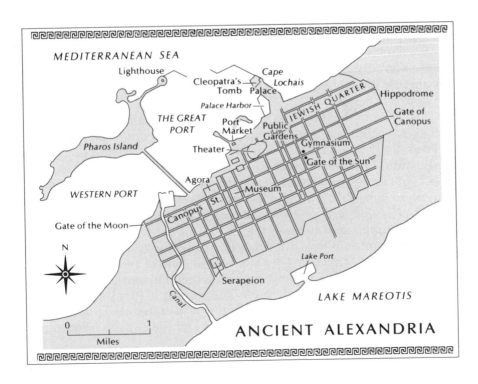

at sea. This lighthouse, with its beacon four hundred feet above the ground, warned mariners of the coastal shallows. Even the most famous religious structure, the Sarapeion, housed a man-made cult created for the Alexandrian Greeks by theological pedants, as if urban planners had been set loose in the City of God. The god Sarapis combined Hellenic and Egyptian attributes intended to appeal to Alexandrians and other Greeks as well, and his temple, the Sarapeion, was listed as one of the wonders of the world.

Alexandria was planned as an administrative center from which Greeks and Macedonians could rule Egypt. It was always more European than Egyptian—in Africa, but not of it. Here was fresh water, limestone for building, and a continual cool breeze blowing from the Mediterranean creating a climate more like the Aegean than the rest of the Nile Valley. It became, as planned, the bureaucratic nerve center of the Ptolemaic Empire, but it was much more. It was the first Greek megalopolis—a world-city where anyone could live without the bothersome constraints of the polis: political loyalty, military obligations, traditional social status. Here anyone could rise to wealth and fame, or seek out utter anonymity with no questions asked. Here opportunity and oblivion walked hand in hand, available to all.

Alexandria was also the first city where anyone could become a Greek, regardless of ethnic origin. From its very start, the city attracted residents from all over the eastern Mediterranean: Phoenicians, Jews, Babylonians, Arabs, Syrians. The more pious Jews founded a quarter and stayed in it, keeping their faith and their customs, but the young and adventurous joined youths from a hundred other races in taking Greek names and mastering the Greek language, for this way lay advancement. By the time of Cleopatra, it would have been impossible to unravel the ethnic background of an average Alexandrian—even if anyone had cared.

The city of the Ptolemies was only the first of the many Hellenistic Greek megalopoleis that sprang up throughout the former empire of Alexander in outright imitation of the conqueror's creation. Seleucus built Antioch on the Orontes River in northern Syria and Seleuceia on the Tigris, a day's journey away from old Babylon. When Seleuceia did not seem to be filling up satisfactorily, the king forcibly removed part of Babylon's population to his new city. By mid-third century, Pergamon in Phrygia had become the capital of an Anatolian empire and had a museum and library that nearly rivaled those of Alexandria. Even the cities of old Greece were copying the style of the super-cities and opening their gates (and sometimes even their citizenship rolls) to newcomers. The great mercantile centers like Corinth, Rhodes, and Smyrna were first but were soon joined by some of the formerly most exclusive and chauvinistic cities, including Athens and even Sparta where money itself had once been illegal.

Cleopatra the Great, last of
the Ptolemaic rulers of Egypt.
(*Reproduced by Courtesy of
the Trustees of the British
Museum*)

The promise of the Hellenistic super-cities was irresistible to idealists. The megalopolis offered to Greeks and Hellenized Orientals opportunities that had never existed in the tribal community or the city-state, where social mobility depended on the correct ancestry or the proper credentials of citizenship. Many of the ministers and commanders of the Ptolemies and Seleucids had risen from obscure origins and their cities served as magnets attracting those who sought similar eminence.

But a classical meritocracy of this type was a two-way street. Both the tribal society of archaic Greece and the classical city-state were concerned social units that provided buffers against failure. Weakness, inefficiency, mediocrity, and a languid pace were tolerated by these older, more sensitive, and more rigidly structured groups—in fact, they were taken for granted. Tribe and community took care of their own, just as the family protected its simpleton and fed and sheltered its old and infirm. In the old tribal community, members could not starve or go homeless for it was the sacred duty of their closest relatives to provide food and shelter. This was a duty enforced by the tribal ethic, for a child or elder of the tribe who suffered through neglect was a pollution on the whole tribe and an offense to the gods. As tribal community gradually evolved into city-state, this duty was absorbed by the city, which provided welfare to orphans, subsidies to the poor and disabled, and defined legal responsibility for the care of the elderly. In Athens, even beasts of burden that had spent their lives working on public projects were supported at state expense after their working life was over.

159

But in the Hellenistic megalopolis, all people were liberated individuals—organisms competing for the free energy of the system in the classical Darwinian sense. For every clever young person who rose to the top of this "tyranny of talent," there were perhaps dozens who were unable to compete and thus sank into crushing poverty in the permanent slums that became as characteristic a part of the new cities as their libraries and museums. If rulers gave food to the poor and free education to the young, these were merely public services performed as impersonally as collecting the garbage. These services gave the recipients no true sense of belonging to a community but were designed primarily to maintain good order in the city and provide a minimum of training for future potential civil servants.

It is no surprise that Hellenistic cities were the birthplaces of a number of associations that offered the poor, the hopeless, and the alienated an opportunity to rejoin a community in at least a symbolic sense. Guilds of artisans appeared, although the purposes of these were patently more social than economic. The proliferation of burial associations must be interpreted as a yearning for the old tribal tradition that assured all members of proper burial rites and a certain amount of care for widows and dependents. Of great importance were the mystery religions that grew up in Hellenistic cities and soon numbered their adherents in the millions. For those who needed spiritual consolation, these new cults offered the advantages of older, more traditional societies. The communion of initiates with a god or cult figure gave the lonely city dweller a consciousness of belonging to a community once more, whether it was the Solar City or the family of fellow Christians.

For adventurous soldiers, politicians, bureaucrats, entrepreneurs—and even criminals—Alexandria offered a playing field for competitive energies. By coming to the megalopolis, these immigrants demonstrated that they had outgrown their dependence on a sense of kinship and community with fellow citizens. They were the spiritual ancestors of generations of gifted individualists ever after, from the Greeks who pulled the strings behind scenes in the Roman Empire, to the energetic expatriate Greek entrepreneurs scattered throughout the world today.

It is perhaps symbolic that Alexandria is practically without horizons: on all sides, ocean, lagoon, and desert recede into the featureless distance as if impressing on the strong and clever that here are no obstacles or barriers to ambition. But we must imagine that the vast majority who came to Alexandria never realized their dreams and came to despair for closer horizons, horizons they could touch like the familiar mountains that ringed old homelands in the distant Aegean world. Guilds, associations, and religions therefore can be viewed as attempts to recreate tribal and civic environments in the heart of the megalopolis. The astounding success of Christianity, which was largely a phenomenon of urban slums, shows, as we should expect, that Christianity was simply more successful than other cults in giving spiritual rebirth to tribal and civic consciousness—a new consciousness of belonging to the brotherhood of man and the city of God.

The Empire of the Seleucids

The problems of the Seleucids were as manifold as the advantages of the Ptolemies. Viewing the extent of the terrain over which they attempted to extend their rule and the variety of the peoples they attempted to govern, one is surprised not at their eventual failure, but at the fact that they succeeded in haphazard fashion for so long.

The unmanageable size of Alexander's oriental empire was recognized by the first Seleucus, who agreed in 310 to give northwestern India back to its native dynasts in return for 500 elephants of war. Then, between 250 and 225 B.C., a central Asian people called the Parthians managed to dislodge the Seleucids from much of old Persia and Media. Meanwhile, in northwestern Asia Minor, the descendants of some very minor deputies created a dynasty that was to rule Pergamon for the next century and a half and turn it into an empire that made up in power and prestige what it lacked in size.

Even the remaining territories were too much for the Seleucids. As if local uprisings and continual border warfare with the Ptolemies were not enough, the descendants of the first Seleucus showed an almost Persian talent for trying to usurp the throne and territories of the rightful heir. Only the reign of an unusually gifted monarch like Antiochus III (223–187) managed to keep the empire together. But he made the mistake, late in his career, of challenging the power of Rome. His successor further wasted the energies of the empire by a quixotic attempt to force the worship of his graven image upon the Jews; this produced the inevitable revolt, led by Judas Maccabeus and his sons, which tied down major portions of his army and ended in the eventual loss of Judaea as part of the empire.

For the century following the death of Antiochus III in 187, the Romans were content to meddle in Seleucid politics only enough to keep the entire empire weak and in a continual state of dynastic turmoil. But the resulting power vacuum only proved inviting for Asiatic neighbors, and the Romans eventually carved much of the old Seleucid Empire into provinces.

Depressing as the political and dynastic history of the Seleucid Empire may be, the territories it included contributed in a number of ways to creating a cosmopolitan society—a fusion of East and West—that in the long run was more influential than Ptolemaic society in determining the future course of Graeco-Roman civilization. It was here, for the six centuries following the death of Alexander, that the seemingly eternal barrier between Europe and Asia broke down, resulting in a mutually beneficial mingling of energies and intellects.

Asia Minor contained the most varied assortment of cities, tribes, and nations. Along the coasts and up the river valleys of the western and southern coasts were old Greek cities that had themselves once merged with the indigenous population of Phrygians, Lydians, Lycians, Cilicians, and others. The Seleucids competed endlessly with the Ptolemies for the allegiance of some of these cities, particularly those along the southern coast, promising to restore the cities' freedom and autonomy. That this was merely a propaganda ploy is adequately demonstrated by the restrictions imposed on Greek cities securely bound to the Seleucid throne. Although these cities retained the right to elect or choose their own magistrates and in general live by their old laws and customs, the Seleucid monarch or his deputy on the scene could always exercise a veto power. The cities were denied the right to an independent foreign policy and were subject to a variety of taxes and imposts. Highly encouraged by the state were the ruler cults, which sprang up in all the cities to honor a deified Seleucus or Antiochus, complete with temples, priesthoods, and annual games.

Less is known about the interior of Asia Minor, which consists of a number of higher plateaus separated from the coastal valleys by mountain ranges. It is likely that most of the land of the interior was accounted royal land—that is, it belonged to the monarch himself and was worked by the Anatolian peasantry under the supervision of local barons appointed by the court. But in no way did either the exploitation or supervision of this land come anywhere close to the preoccupation of the Ptolemies with their Egyptian domain. Communication in the interior of Asia Minor was difficult enough to allow the local satraps to be a law unto themselves. Northern and eastern Asia Minor remained in the hands of native dynasts. These areas had escaped the attention of Alexander on his way east and had successfully resisted the attempts of the successors to bring them under Macedonian rule; by the late second century, the growing kingdoms of Pontus and Armenia had divided the territory into spheres of interest.

In the eastern provinces, the Seleucids continued the process of Hellenizing started by Alexander. Because there were no Greek foundations on which to build, Seleucus and his son Antiochus had to start from scratch. Two typical Hellenistic settlements were Seleuceia and Dura Europus. Seleuceia was about fifty miles north of Babylon, which it gradually replaced as the economic and cultural hub of Mesopotamia. The city was intended to be the Seleucids' eastern capital: the inland terminal for trade coming from the cities of the Mediterranean coast on one hand, and on the other hand, the western end of the great silk route, which had been established centuries earlier across the plains

of Iran and Bactria to the Pamir foothills and thence across the roof of
the world to western China. That the road remained in operation despite
political amputation of the Seleucid eastern provinces by the Parthians
is shown by the discovery of second century B.C. Greek trade goods in
Mongolia.

Seleuceia must have been a bewildering mixture of races, languages, and peoples with Greek bureaucrats and Macedonian soldiery
supervising a mob of Asiatics coming and going in all directions: barges
coming up the Tigris from the Persian Gulf bearing goods from India,
camel caravans from the central Asian steppe, Syrian and Phoenician
traders from the coast, and Arabs in from the desert to buy horses, or
steal them. These all mingled with a native Babylonian population, part
of which had been forcibly transplanted from the ancient city of Babylon for no other purpose than to fill out the new settlement of Seleuceia and give it some body. Here also a community of scholars
emerged, differing from the Alexandrians in that most of them, while
taking Greek names and writing in Greek, were Babylonians by birth.
Among these were Berossus, who wrote the history of Babylonia from
the flood, and Seleucus "the astronomer," one of the so-called Chal-
daeans, who had developed the art of what is actually astrology to the
highest point it was to reach until the Renaissance.

Dura Europus, on the middle Euphrates, was located strategically
to protect and control traffic coming down the river roads and across
the desert from Damascus. Built according to the latest theories of town
planning with a gridwork of broad streets, it was populated first by
military colonists, probably Macedonians, but soon filled up with local
population from the surrounding countryside. Organized like a Greek
polis, with marketplace, theater, acropolis, temple of Zeus, and a written constitution, it soon became as much a blend of east and west as
Seleuceia; excavations have revealed temples belonging to Babylonian
deities sharing the same street front with Greek temples.

The political and economic center of gravity of the Seleucid Empire
remained at Antioch, on the Orontes, named for Seleucus' son, Antiochus. From here the Seleucids attempted to rule their broad empire,
relying on the old Persian roads that connected them with Mesopotamia, and the two new seaports of Seleuceia and Laodicea serving sea
traffic to the west. The overwhelming majority of the population here
was Syrian and Phoenician, peoples accustomed for centuries to being
ruled by others and asking only that their rulers preserve favorable
conditions for commerce and trade. Here also, the Seleucid rulers introduced the largest Graeco-Macedonian element as they competed
with the Ptolemies in recruiting clerks and accountants, courtiers and
mercenaries from old Greece. The result, both in the newly constructed
Greek cities and in the older Syrian and Phoenician settlements, which
received a significant number of Greek immigrants, was a remarkable

blend of Greek and Semitic cultures. The most common feature of this fusion was the adoption of Greek names, dress, and customs by Phoenicians and Syrians, accompanied by the universal use of Greek as a second language.

It is impossible to guess at the extent of intermarriage between the Greek and Macedonian soldiery and functionaries, and the Syro-Phoenician women. We must assume that there was a great deal because the Greeks—with a few exceptions like Aristotle—had neither racial prejudice nor available women of their own kind. The local population, for their part, no doubt viewed a marriage connection with the ruling elite as a good way to get ahead. Hellenized Orientals or half-Greeks attended Greek theaters in Antioch, Laodicea, or Aradus. They worshiped in Greek temples and took part in Greek games. Naturally enough, the continuing personnel demands of the Seleucid bureaucracy ensured that such adequately Hellenized Orientals would be given every opportunity to enter government service. By about 100 B.C., it would have been as difficult to unravel the racial background of an Antiochene as it would have been to identify that of an Alexandrian. That such blending of populations did nothing to hinder continuing intellectual development was conclusively demonstrated by such Graeco-Semitic literary figures as the philosopher-polymath Posidonius, the poet Meleager of Gadara, St. Paul, the authors of the Gospels, and that most stylish humorist of the Roman period, Lucian of Samosata.

But if the great cities of the Syrian seaboard did become Hellenized, they remained Greek islands in a sea of Syrian peasant villages. The proportion of native farmers to the Greek elite was not nearly as overwhelming as in Egypt, but the Semitic subculture of the Seleucid Near Eastern Empire still remained the most enduring element; many centuries later, in the wake of the Arab invasions, it was this subculture that gradually overwhelmed the remaining Greek institutions.

Old Greece: Macedon and the New Federalism

Diogenes the Cynic greeted the new age by asking to be buried face down when he died. "Because," he said, "in a little while, what is down will be up." This must have echoed the sentiments of many of the inhabitants of old Greece during the half century following the death of Alexander, when they found that the world was changing more rapidly than they could adjust.

The three greatest factors of change were the wars of the Successors, emigration to the new Hellenistic settlements of the Orient, and economic instability caused by a sudden influx of new wealth. Until the downfall of Demetrius in 289, the cities of the Greek mainland were subjected intermittently to the attempts of one or another of the Ma-

Sleeping Eros, a masterpiece of Hellenistic kitsch from the island of Rhodes. (*The Metropolitan Museum of Art, Rogers Fund, 1943*)

cedonian generals to "liberate" them. The mere presence of an army of 20,000 or so, plus cavalry, elephants, and a swarm of camp followers was enough to impoverish the countryside of a small state, even if the army were friendly. When such a mob was allowed or encouraged to plunder, the results were catastrophic. Where agriculture was marginal, land could go out of cultivation permanently. And a city unlucky enough to choose the wrong side could find its walls razed, its statesmen executed, and its surviving population sold into slavery.

The great wave of Greeks who emigrated to the new Hellenistic kingdoms in the Orient helped to relieve the overpopulation that had become a problem in much of Greece by the end of the fourth century. But such relief was not an unmixed blessing. The emigrants, after all, tended to be vigorous, energetic, and ambitious young men, alive to a world of new opportunities, unafraid of the novelties a strange land might produce. The loss of such a population at just the time fortitude and imagination were needed at home to face the altered conditions of the new age must be interpreted as a net loss to the Greek mainland.

In the same fashion, the expansion of the economy was not equally advantageous to all. The gold and silver of the Persian treasuries had been minted into millions of new coins by Alexander and his successors; this currency was distributed to armies and in the form of gifts and subsidies to friendly cities and individuals. Naturally enough, distribution of the new money was uneven, flowing first into the hands of the entrepreneurial classes in the cities—merchants, bankers, con-

165

tractors, shopkeepers, and of course, tavern owners and prostitutes. In many fields, production could not keep up with the demands of the new wealthy classes; thus prices inevitably soared, helping to bring about a new wave of prosperity, particularly among the working classes and the business communities of the bigger cities like Athens and Corinth. But higher prices also tended to impoverish persons on fixed incomes, such as the inhabitants of small towns and farmers, none of whom were able to share the proceeds of the new economy. The result was a growing gap between rich and poor.

The existence of enormous fortunes on one hand and pauperization on the other could not fail to have political consequences. Broadly based democracy, where it had existed in the poleis of classical Greece, was a tenuous thing requiring the existence of a large middle class, which also served as the army in time of war. The citizenry of many cities had become unused to military service during the fourth century, preferring to raise the money for mercenary troops when they were required. The presence of professional soldiers all over the Greek world in the aftermath of the Successors' wars made it rather simple for anyone who had enough money and ambition to hire mercenaries, bring them secretly into his city a few at a time in civilian dress, and then swiftly seize power. Once in control, such a man could continue to pay his troops by exacting money from his new subjects. It is against this background that we must see the new rivals for control of the Greek cities.

Alexander had intended to govern Greece through a Panhellenic League, a patently fictitious federation of Greek states cowed by military might and forced to operate as a rubber stamp for any decree Alexander might choose to issue. Succeeding kings of Macedon could never spare armies large enough to exercise outright dominion of all mainland Greece and therefore had to be content with mastery of three strategic fortresses. The strongholds of Demetrias and Chalcis controlled the land and sea routes north and south through central Greece; the thousand-foot crag of the Acrocorinthus acted as the gateway to the Peloponnesus and kept Corinth under Macedonian control. Meanwhile, a small but stalwart Macedonian garrison occupied part of the Piraeus in Athens down to the late third century. Although they could not ensure the political primacy of the pro-Macedonian party in town, these troops effectively kept Athens neutral throughout the century.

Elsewhere in southern Greece, the Macedonian monarchs either purchased the loyalty of local tyrants or helped a pro-Macedonian party stay in power with the aid of a small garrison in the town citadel. The result was the almost complete disappearance of the autonomous and democratic polis, which had once so thoroughly typified the classical period. Even in Athens, which retained a core of democratic institutions, the franchise was usually limited to property owners, while all over Greece, a growing mass of poor found themselves deprived of political resources.

In this statue of an old woman coming from market we see the greater realism of the Hellenistic artist. (*The Metropolitan Museum of Art, Rogers Fund, 1909*)

The third century in old Greece was thus characterized on the one hand by the forces called forth to rally the Greek cities against Macedonian suzerainty, and on the other by demands for social justice on the part of the poor, demands that gradually hardened into an ideological front during the course of the century. The former movement is most notable for the growth of the first true confederacies of Greek states in which no one state acted as leader, but all member states acted in concert to determine policy and to carry it out.

Such a confederacy was begun in Aetolia, a backwater of northwestern Greece, whose inhabitants lived in tiny villages or mountain cantons, pasturing sheep and goats or living by casual brigandage. There was no suspicion of Greek intellect or civilized arts in Aetolia; nevertheless, this region was first to succeed where other Greeks had failed in a federalist experiment. The Aetolian League was little heard of until the Gallic invasion of 279, when an Aetolian army helped repel a Gallic war party from Delphi. In the wake of the prestige thus won, the Aetolians opened their league to any other state that could be induced (or forced) to join, and by the end of the third century, their territories stretched in an unbroken line from the Adriatic to the Aegean.

Cities that joined the Aetolian League retained sovereignty of a sort, being expected to follow the lead of the league only in war and diplomacy, and in granting *isopolity*—mutual citizenship—to citizens of any other city in the league. The representative council and the popular assembly met twice a year to elect officers and decide questions of policy. The council was apportioned on the basis of the number of troops a city supplied to the federal army; the popular assembly was open to any citizen of a league city.

The constitution of the Aetolian League was in theory eminently fair and democratic, and effectively prevented any one state from dominating the others. Unfortunately, the league used its stability primarily to build a military machine that was used to plunder neighboring states with no regard for treaties or an existing state of peace. It was finally annihilated by the Romans in 167, to no one's regret.

More in the Greek tradition of responsible and constructive statesmanship was the Achaean League. Beginning as an obscure federation of eleven tiny city-states in a backward corner of the northern Peloponnesus, the Achaean League became an Aegean power of the first rank, due mainly to the work of one man. Aratus of Sicyon was a full-fledged neurotic, obsessed by haunting insecurities, hatred of tyranny (to which his father had fallen victim), and a fanatic belief in himself as a person of destiny. An egotist of the caliber of Aratus could not fail to capture the imagination of fellow Greeks who still believed in the old Hellenic ideals of freedom and autonomy.

In 246, Aratus managed to oust the tyrant of his home town of Sicyon by a superbly executed night raid. Guerrilla exploits, in fact, were always his strong point: darkness and stealth brought out his superb tactical talents and a penchant for intricate planning. But more than once, in the bright light of day, Aratus inexplicably lost his nerve at the crucial moment in a pitched battle—a fact that contemporaries commented on wonderingly. Aratus brought Sicyon into the Achaean League, thus bringing the infant federation to the attention of all Greeks as a force to which lovers of freedom everywhere might rally. In 243, he pulled off his master coup and captured the Macedonian-occupied citadel on the Acrocorinthus, which had never before been taken by force. Once more the feat was accomplished by moonlight, accompanied by remarkable intrigue and daring.[4] The subsequent entrance

---

[4] This episode is well described by Plutarch in his *Life of Aratus*.

of mighty Corinth into the Achaean League made it an overnight success; afterward, cities everywhere in the Peloponnesus vied with each other in throwing out their tyrants and joining the league crusade against Macedonian domination.

The Achaean League possessed a constitution very like the Aetolian except that it forced member cities to remodel their governments to eliminate tyranny. The chief executive was a general elected to a one-year term, while a representative council discussed and ruled on matters of policy. The general could not succeed himself in consecutive terms of office, but Aratus usually managed to be elected general every other year. The league was successful in creating political stability and peace in the Peloponnesus for over a generation and in staving off the attacks of Macedon and the Aetolian League. Its principal failure was an internal one due to its inability to deal with the problems of a growing class of poor in each one of its cities.

Unlike the Hellenistic monarchies, the cities of old Greece, with a stubborn faith in the old polis tradition of self-sufficiency, refused to recognize any responsibility for the welfare of the poorer citizens. By the middle of the third century, this neglect resulted in the existence of second- or even third-generation poor in every city of Greece and of tenant farmers in the countryside. For the first time in Greek history, a class-consciousness began to spread from city to city—a recognition among the poverty-stricken that they existed as a class, and the suspicion that they had become prisoners of their status because of the injustice of the propertied classes. Everywhere slogans—those harbingers of ideology—began to appear, the most common being "cancellation of debts" and "redistribution of land." Nevertheless, fears that the poor and dispossessed might unite under a common cause were scoffed at until suddenly, in 227, the news struck Greece like a thunderbolt: Sparta had undergone a social revolution, had redistributed land, had freed and armed slaves, was preaching a purification and purging of Spartan society in a revival of the old Lycurgan code, and was inviting all the cities of the Achaean League to join in its reforms.

All this had been the work of one man, King Cleomenes of Sparta, who had secretly planned a coup to overthrow opposition within the Spartan government and then ruthlessly exterminated adherents of the old regime.[5] For several years, the new-style Spartan army was successful everywhere and seemed on the brink of recapturing its old dominion of the entire Peloponnesus. There was even strong sentiment within the Achaean League to elect Cleomenes to the annual generalship if he would agree to bring Sparta into the league.

---

[5] See pp. 199–203 for a sketch of the life and career of Cleomenes.

Dread of social revolution and fears for his own personal primacy drove Aratus to the wall. He finally took the only possible way out: he turned to his most hated enemy, King Antigonus Doson of Macedon, and offered to turn Corinth back over to a Macedonian garrison if he would bring his army south and end the Spartan threat. Aratus has been condemned as a traitor to the Hellenic spirit both by contemporaries and by subsequent generations, but he was able to find enough supporters among the terrified property owners of the Achaean League who viewed the Macedonians as a lesser threat than a Spartan king preaching the overthrow of the propertied classes.

In 222, the Macedonians joined forces with the army of the Achaean League and marched on Sparta. The Spartans fought bravely but to no avail against superior numbers. Cleomenes was forced to flee and the Achaean League, although giving up Corinth, regained its leadership of the Peloponnesus for another seventy years. At some time near the end of the third century, one of the Achaean generals became the father of a boy named Polybius. This youth was to become the best of the later Greek historians; most notably, although a Greek patriot and a high-ranking Achaean politician in his early career, he was the first to realize that the leadership of the Mediterranean world had somehow slipped from Greek hands and had passed to a new empire rising in the West.

SUGGESTIONS FOR FURTHER READING

There is no connected historical narrative concerning the Hellenistic period by any ancient historian until we reach 220 B.C., when Polybius' history begins. The selections in Ian Scott-Kilvert, ed., Polybius, The Rise of the Roman Empire (New York: Penguin, 1979) include much of the history of the Hellenistic world in the third century. Plutarch's Lives of Eumenes, Demetrius, Pyrrhus, Agis, Cleomenes, Aratus, and Philopoemen are based on older Greek literature, now lost, and have therefore become major historical sources, although the author intended these biographies for moral instruction. M. M. Austin, ed., The Hellenistic World from Alexander to the Roman Conquest (New York: Cambridge University Press, 1981) is a valuable and extensive collection of ancient literary sources and documents in translation. Two recent books on Alexander the Great are Robin Lane Fox, The Search for Alexander (Boston: Little, Brown, 1980), copiously illustrated with photographs of Alexander's eastern domains, and A. B. Bosworth, Conquest and Empire (New York: Cambridge University Press, 1989), which is well documented and authoritative. Peter Green's From Alexander to Actium (Berkeley and Los Angeles: University of California Press, 1990) now supersedes other one-volume histories of the Hellenistic era.

8 The Greek World Under Roman Rule

Dᴜʀɪɴɢ ʜɪꜱ lifetime (ca. 200–118 B.C.), the historian Polybius saw the Romans proclaim the freedom of all Greeks, then shortly afterwards make a mockery of such freedom, eventually destroying it entirely. In spite of this course of events, when Polybius began to write his history he had become an eager champion of Roman destiny and saw expressed in Rome's conquests the inevitable workings of historical logic.

Taken to Rome as a hostage in 167, Polybius was fortunate enough to find a place in the entourage of Scipio Aemilianus, a leading states-man and general of his day who included among his many other qual-ities a love of learning and an appreciation of Hellenism. Polybius thus began to see the Greeks from a Roman standpoint: petty, short-sighted, selfish Greek politicians had squandered the greatness of Hellas in frivolous quarrels and arrogant quests for primacy; it was better that Romans rule and allow Greeks to pursue their true talents, which lay in philosophy and the arts. It is hard to argue with this interpretation when one considers the perspective from which Romans viewed Greek history.

This superb bronze statue of a young jockey and magnificent mount was recovered from the sea off Cape Artemision, on the island of Euboea. (*National Museum of Athens*)

First of all, we must remember that regardless of what *we* know about the origins of Rome and the Romans, all educated Romans of the second century B.C. knew as a fact that they were the descendants of the Trojans, and that the Greeks were the descendants of those fierce Achaeans who had utterly sacked Troy and scattered the refugees to the winds. Their traditions held that the first Roman constitution was modeled on laws brought back from fifth-century Athens. They had heard of the great and glorious military exploits of the Greeks and Macedonians, from the battle of Marathon to the conquests of Alexander, and the first Hellenistic army they had encountered—that of King Pyrrhus—had been driven off only after shocking casualties. Later they conquered Sicily and found those Greeks not particularly formidable in battle; but simple Roman soldiers marveled at Greek works of art and architecture and felt themselves small before the civilization these works implied. The first Roman historians wrote in Greek, believing it the language of culture. But with the Greek homeland and the Greek East, the great mass of Romans had as yet no acquaintance.

Then in 200 B.C., the first of many Greek embassies arrived on the banks of the Tiber, begging the Roman Senate for help against the attacks of King Philip V of Macedon. The Romans were unable to resist an appeal for military aid; thus they eventually sent an expedition that made Philip sue for peace. At the Isthmian Games in Corinth during the summer of 196 B.C., the Roman herald announced that henceforth

the Greek cities were to be free of Macedonian domination—a decla-
ration greeted with such thunderous applause that we are told birds
flying overhead fell dead from the very sound. It was a magnificent
gesture. Unfortunately, the Romans soon found that they had inherited
the role of arbiter of every Greek quarrel from that moment on, whether
significant or petty. Almost immediately the Aegean coasts were threatened again, this time by King Antiochus III of the Seleucid Empire.
Once more Greeks ventured to Rome to plead for Roman military assistance. Once more the Romans crossed the Adriatic, and by 188 had
reduced Antiochus to suppliant status.

   One can hardly blame the Romans for becoming contemptuous of
the Greeks in the following decades. The descendants of Achilles and
Odysseus turned out to be petulant, complaining, treacherous, unreliable, and seemingly incapable of governing themselves. To the Romans' credit, they attempted to keep their involvement in Greek affairs
to a minimum; that such a policy of partial interference was doomed
to failure is well known by readers of the twentieth century who have
seen enough examples to realize that any intervention at all in another
country's affairs usually leads to total commitment. In 146, Macedon
was finally made into a Roman province complete with Roman governor
and garrison. The cities of Greece were spared outright annexation but
became tributary and were subject to the orders of the governor of
Macedon. Finally, the Greek mainland became the province of Achaea
in the imperial reorganization under Augustus.

   From the beginning of the second century on, the small empire of
Pergamon made a very good thing out of being Rome's most loyal friend
and ally in the East. With the gradual eclipse of the Seleucids, Pergamon
prospered, gaining control of most of western Asia Minor. In 133, when
King Attalus III died without heirs, he took the surprising step of leaving
his kingdom to Rome in his will. The legacy was accepted and converted
to the province of Asia. Its prosperity unfortunately made it a special
attraction for the exploitation of Roman tax collectors.

   The rest of the Near East remained in the hands of the last Seleucids,
crippled and ineffectual because of continual Roman tampering and
the resultant dynastic disputes. But the beginning of the first century
saw the rise of King Mithridates of Pontus, who took advantage of wide
social discontent and an almost racial hatred of Italians to sponsor an
uprising against Rome throughout Asia Minor. By 88 B.C., Mithridates'
armies had crossed over to Greece and were greeted by many cities as
a champion against Roman domination. But the king's oriental levies
were no match for the Roman legions that eventually appeared. Athens
passed under the control of radicals who insisted on holding out against
the Romans; when the city was taken in 86, it was savagely plundered
and took over a century to recover. In the meantime, the rest of Greece
and Asia Minor were once more made safe for Italian businessmen and

tax collectors, having been thoroughly looted to pay for Greek misconceptions about Roman determination and obduracy.

Mithridates continued to threaten Roman interests in the East, and eventually Pompey was sent to create some kind of stability. The result was the division of much of the old Seleucid Empire into Roman provinces. Only Egypt remained sovereign in the eastern Mediterranean, and in the aftermath of the Roman civil wars (49–31 B.C.), the land of the Ptolemies was conquered and made a personal possession of the young man whom the Senate chose to call Augustus. The year 31 B.C. is conventionally taken to signal the end of the Roman Republic and the beginning of the Roman Empire; for the Greeks, as well as for the rest of the world, the results would be momentous.

Greece in the Roman Empire: The Economy

The land of Greece and the coasts of the Aegean can be economically self-sufficient only so long as they are not forced to compete with more favored parts of the Mediterranean. For centuries before the Roman

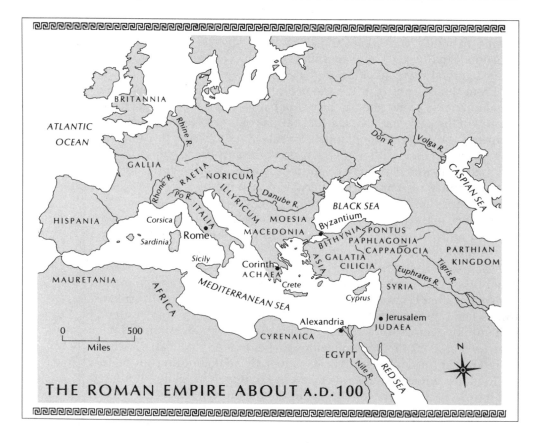

THE ROMAN EMPIRE ABOUT A.D. 100

domination, the major cities of the Aegean basin had had to import a major portion of their food, and a balance of trade had been maintained only so long as these cities were able to capture a fair share of the world market with quality exports. The resources of the Greek world do not consist of agricultural surpluses, or minerals, precious or otherwise, off whose proceeds a placid and complacent population can subsist. The greatest resource of Greece, in all ages including the present, has been the Greek people, characteristically industrious, aggressive, keenly intelligent, and alive to the necessity of living by their wits. When the political supremacy of Rome was accompanied by a usurpation of the formerly Greek markets, there were two far-reaching consequences. First, the economy of Greece became a matter to be determined by Roman whim; second, the Greek people spread out and overwhelmed Rome with Greek culture and Greek lifestyle.

The social and economic history of the Greek world under Roman rule can easily be divided into two distinct stages. During the first century of Roman rule, approximately 146–31 B.C., the ruling power was theoretically the Roman Republic: the Senate and People of Rome. The drawbacks of Roman imperial administration under the republic are best left to a book of Roman history; here it suffices to say that imperial administration barely existed under the republic. It was generally believed that the state had no responsibility for the welfare of its subjects, and that matters of administration, taxation, and so forth were not the concerns of gentlemen and statesmen but ought to be farmed out to private enterprise. As a result, the Greek cities suffered no less than the rest of the Roman provinces from the exactions of tax contractors, who had bought the right to collect taxes.[1]

The Roman Senate, naturally conservative and accustomed to the elitist and paternalistic city governments of Italian *municipia*, also forced the Greek cities to modify their constitutions to a point approaching oligarchy. The natural consequence was that a pro-Roman oligarchic faction and an anti-Roman democratic faction developed all over the Greek world. Thus, the poorer classes were losing all voice and were being forced to contribute the greatest amount to the tax bill at the very same time that the Greek economy was suffering because of Italian competition. If the process had continued for very long, a severe economic depression might have resulted.

In fact, because the Roman civil wars were fought largely in and around the Balkan Peninsula, the result for Greece was not depression but outright catastrophe. Every Roman legion that crossed and recrossed the Greek mountains seeking out rival Roman armies to slaughter had to be supported by a Greek population that, in many places, was reduced

---

[1] The classic example of provincial misadministration is described by Cicero in his attack on Verres, who in three years of governing Sicily had nearly gutted the island.

to a condition of slavery. The young Plutarch had heard his grandfather speak of the days when Antony conscripted the entire manpower of Chaeronea to carry grain from the plains of their homeland across the mountains to the sea. A Roman army might appear at any moment before the walls of a Greek city anywhere on the coasts of the Aegean and demand enough money to pay the troops. When a victorious Augustus announced the end of civil war and the beginning of the principate, surviving Greeks everywhere sighed with relief. By then it mattered little to the mauled and pauperized spectators who had won the battle for dominion. All they wanted was a moment to draw a breath and an opportunity to rebuild some kind of life in peace.

This Augustus gave them. Both he and his adoptive parent Julius Caesar had learned and appreciated the lessons of Hellenistic kingship. Provinces and subjects were to be treated as a responsibility of the ruler, not as a cow to be milked dry and then neglected. The nations and peoples under Roman rule were to be encouraged to become self-sufficient where possible, and they were to be subsidized where absolutely necessary. Several decades later, the court poet Virgil could say with some truth about the ideal of imperial Rome:

> Others will hammer bronzes into life
> More softly, no doubt, carve from marble
> Better likenesses, prove more eloquent
> In courts, map out the pathways of the sky,
> Forecast better the risings of the stars.
> You must remember, Roman, how to rule
> The nations under your command. Your arts
> Will be these: to impose the ways of peace,
> To spare the conquered and beat down the proud.
>
> Aeneid 6. 847 ff.[2]

The peace imposed by Augustus, which was to last for two centuries, went far to restore conditions of prosperity all over the Mediterranean world; but in old Greece, prosperity was selective. The great cities where a lot of imperial business was done, like Athens, Ephesus, Argos, or Corinth (rebuilt by Julius Caesar in 44 B.C.), or which became capitals of world trade, like Patras or Rhodes, shared in the general prosperity. But they grew at the expense of the surrounding countryside. Megara, lying midway between Athens and Corinth, lost all reason for existence as anything more than a barren and grubby farm town. Even later public works subsidized by the emperors did nothing to encourage a viable economy, as a visitor of the second century A.D. reported. A good illustration of gradual decay is given us by a philos-

---

[2] J. P. Sullivan, trans.

opher of the late first century A.D. named Dio (and nicknamed Chrysostom—"golden mouth"—by contemporaries because of his rhetorical brilliance). Shipwrecked on the coast of Euboea, Dio was taken in and sheltered by a family of squatters who had taken over a beautiful estate, now deserted and overgrown like two-thirds of the surrounding land. Later, on his way back to civilization, Dio made his way to the chief city of the district, where, he said, lack of employment continued even though the population of the city was only a fraction of what it had formerly been. Block after block of the city was totally deserted, and only the very center still showed signs of the old life.

The ideal of the empire was for the cities and provinces to be self-governing and self-sufficient. They were to receive from Rome the benefits of a Roman peace, Roman law, and protection, and thus grow prosperous enough to pay taxes back into the imperial treasury. Over much of the Greek world, the reality was far different. Here cities faced bankruptcy; their walls, roads, and buildings fell into disrepair, and they were able to do nothing to support a growing mass of paupers who demanded some kind of subsistence. Both Greek and Roman contemporaries were bewildered by the situation, some seeing a loss of moral fiber as the cause of the depressing conditions, others believing that the favor of the gods had gone elsewhere. From our perspective, we can see that the decline of the Aegean basin was inevitable because the great arteries of world trade now bypassed the Greek homeland, and the huge fleets of merchantmen now sailed directly from Alexandria or Syria to Rome. The Roman peace created a Mediterranean-wide economy; as prosperity made prices rise from Spain to Syria, the backwaters of the empire had to suffer.

The emperors, in good pragmatic Roman fashion, lost no sleep over moral or spiritual decay but dealt simply with the symptoms of the economic depression. One of our best examples is the province of Bithynia in Asia Minor where the emperor Trajan sent his troubleshooter, Pliny, to bring some kind of order into the administration and do what he could to make the economy viable. The copious correspondence between Pliny and Trajan has survived and gives a detailed picture of the day-to-day decisions an imperial administrator encountered.

Pliny to the emperor Trajan:

> The town of Sinope, Sir, is in need of a water supply. I think there is plenty of good water which could be brought from a source sixteen miles away, though there is a doubtful area of marshy ground stretching for more than a mile from the spring. For the moment I have only given orders for a survey to be made to find out whether the ground can support the weight of an aqueduct. This will not cost much, and I will guarantee that there will be no lack of funds so long as you, Sir, will approve a scheme so conducive to the health and amenities of this very thirsty city.

Trajan to Pliny:

> See that the survey you have begun is thoroughly carried out, my dear Pliny, and find out whether the ground you suspect can support the weight of an aqueduct. There can be no doubt, I think, that Sinope must be provided with a water supply, so long as the town can meet the expense out of its own resources. It will contribute a great deal to the health and happiness of the people.

Pliny *Letters* 10. 90–91[3]

Elsewhere, emperors responded with both direct and indirect relief. All taxes of a poverty-stricken area might be remitted for a certain period, and even some bills paid out of imperial funds. More common, and of more permanent value, was the initiation of public works projects, particularly by the Philhellene emperor Hadrian (117–138). Aqueducts and public buildings contributed to a city's economy; their construction provided a continuing payroll for hundreds of citizens; and the final inscription glorified the munificent emperor who had ordered the project and ensured that a grateful and loyal citizenry would remember his name. The visitor to Athens today may note that many of the graceful classical ruins that adorn the city are imperial Roman in date, and some of these were subsidized by Hadrian, who made a policy of honoring Athens as the spiritual capital of Hellas.

In the midst of poverty, there were spectacularly rich individuals. Some had acquired wealth through trade or increased it through clever speculation. Some, like the Sophists Scopelian or Polemon, had accumulated princely wealth from the fees they commanded as rhetoricians; others simply knew the paths to imperial favor. One of the most famous multimillionaires was Herodes Atticus of Athens, who showered his city with gifts and benefits; the theater he built is still in regular use. Among other anecdotes, we are told that he had a retarded son who could not learn the alphabet, so he bought twenty-four slaves the same age as his son, named them after the letters of the Greek alphabet, and gave them to the boy as constant companions. The day when the Roman state would force the wealthiest classes to contribute to the tax bill was still in the distant future, but as a matter of convention, most rich men did spend substantial amounts on their cities, and it was customary for the most prosperous citizens to make up any deficit in the tax bill. Much later, during the imperial crisis of the third century, this was naturally enough one of the first customs that was converted into a legal obligation.

Such revenues as there were in the Greek world came primarily from agriculture, the export trade, and the beginnings of that modern

---

[3] Betty Radice, ed. and trans., *The Letters of the Younger Pliny* (Baltimore: Penguin Books, 1963). Reprinted by permission of Penguin Books.

A model of the Athenian acropolis as it would have appeared in the late Roman empire. The theater in the left foreground, built by Herodes Atticus in the second century A.D., is still used for concerts and stage productions. (*Agora Excavation, American School of Classical Studies at Athens/Photo: Craig A. Mauzy*)

mainstay of the Greek economy—tourism. Although our evidence suggests that some land had gone out of cultivation because of depopulation, the most favorably endowed areas of Greece sometimes produced a surplus for export. These areas included the broad plains of Thessaly, parts of Phocis and Boeotia in northern Greece, and Laconia, Messenia, and Elis in the Peloponnesus, where greater rainfall contributed to agricultural prosperity.

Although only Thessaly seems to have grown enough grain for export, other areas regularly produced crops for the world market. Only the expensive vintage wines had retained their popularity after the science of viticulture spread to Italy and Gaul, but Greek olive oil still dominated the market and fetched such attractive prices that some producing cities enacted laws requiring processors to sell at least a certain amount locally. In volume, Phocis and Attica were the leaders, but the areas of the southern Peloponnesus, which are still famous today for quality, are mentioned by our ancient sources as well. Specialized exports noted by contemporary writers included flax and purple dye. The flax and hemp of Elis had long been famous, and the emergence of the city of Patras as the major port of western Greece considerably increased the employment of weavers of linen and other textiles. The coasts of Greece have always been a favored breeding ground for the two species of murex shell that produce the famous "Tyrian" purple. With ostentation on the increase everywhere in the Roman Empire, display of garments tinted with this most costly dye encouraged the exploitation of this industry in various places along the Aegean coasts.

Although the silver mines of Greece seem to have petered out by the imperial period, the fine marble and limestone of the peninsula and Aegean islands were exploited as never before during the first four centuries A.D. In terms of simple tonnage, quarried stone must have constituted the number one export of the province of Achaea. The demands of the Roman building industry for fine stone and marble always exceeded the supply. In addition, although our sources do not mention such a mundane subject, Roman contractors must have scoured the Aegean for cement. One thinks first and foremost of the great buildings of antiquity constructed of marble and limestone, but by far the most common method of building in the Roman Empire was with bricks and mortar. Mortar requires cement, cement is made by burning limestone in a furnace, and the Greek peninsula and islands are practically one lump of limestone of one sort or another. The cement industry must have been as ubiquitous in ancient Greece as it is today.

Harbors and shipping were not often mentioned by ancient writers, who customarily sought loftier themes. An exception is The Ship, a dialogue by Lucian, in which he described the giant grain freighter Isis, which was blown off course by a storm and had to put into Piraeus. The whole city of Athens trooped down to the waterfront to see the unaccustomed sight, for Athens was no longer the thriving commercial city of the past.

Corinth, on the other hand, retained her share of world trade. During the past decade, excavators working for the most part underwater have uncovered extensive remains of the harbor district of Kenchreai, near Corinth, revealing the outlines of a major port. There are also substantial remains of harbor works and buildings underwater at Gythion, the port of Sparta, and Asopos, to the east across the Laconian Gulf, to name just two ports as yet unexplored. The fact that the sea level has risen as much as twelve feet since classical times means that future underwater research may yield new and exciting discoveries that will make a major contribution to the study of the economic history of many coastal cities.

An often neglected aspect of the Greek economy during the Roman period is the tourist industry. The 200 years of the Pax Romana created ideal conditions for travel from one end of the empire to the other, with minimum difficulty for the more prosperous classes. Most writers of the period seem to have traveled extensively, often just because of a desire to see other parts of the world. Old Greece in particular became an attraction to wealthy Italians, Gauls, Africans, or Syrians who

The temple of Olympian Zeus in Athens was started by Peisistratus and finished by the Emperor Hadrian six and a half centuries later. (*Robert Freryck/Odyssey Productions*)

wanted to see for themselves the bay of Marathon, or the Acropolis of Athens, Delphi, Olympia, and so many other famous sites of what they also considered ancient Greek history. There is ample evidence to show that residents of such historical sites began to take a lively interest in their own antiquities, real or assumed, with a view to exploiting the tourist trade. All over Greece old monuments were dusted off, inscriptions uncovered—or sometimes even reinscribed—and old religious celebrations and pageants, which might have even gone out of use for centuries, were exhumed and observed with a maximum of enthusiasm. Plutarch noted the annual celebration of the funeral rites for the men who died at the battle of Plataea (replete with the slaughter of a black bull, somber processions, and the anointing of the gravestones with myrrh), and the ritual whipping of the boys at Sparta during initiation rites designed to prove their bravery. It does not take a cynic to wonder if these ceremonies had actually survived in full flower for six or more centuries.

Our best source for the sites most visited by the tourists in old Greece is the *Description of Greece* by the traveler Pausanias. Sometime in the later second century A.D., this writer journeyed from one end of

Greece to the other, with an eye for the antiquities still exhibited during his day. He has left us an appealing picture of a society that still took care to display its history and monuments to their best advantage. At numerous points in his narrative he mentions the local tourist guides— professionals who explained the history and purpose of all points of interest to inquisitive visitors.

It is probably impossible to guess at the contribution tourism made to the Greek economy, but it is certain that many villages prospered when they otherwise might have slumbered peacefully, content with a local subsistence economy.

Greece in the Roman Empire: The Triumph of Hellenism

> Graecia capta ferum victorem cepit et artis
> Intulit agresti Latio.
>
> Horace Epistle 2. 1. 156 f.
>
> Conquered Greece her fierce victor conquered
> And bore her arts into rustic Latium.

Astute Romans began to realize that something of this sort might be going on after a whole generation of Romans had come in contact with the Greeks of Sicily during the first Punic War (264–241 B.C.). Romans eagerly brought home not only the products of Greek civilization—statuary, pottery, dinnerware, and furniture—but also memories of a softer and more elegant way of life and an appreciation of pleasures and amusements that contrasted with the traditional Roman indifference to pain, hardship, and extremes of weather. The material benefits of Greek civilization were further publicized by the return of Roman veterans from Greece in the next two centuries with whole boatloads of loot—furniture, plate, art masterpieces, even Athenian inscriptions as conversation pieces.[4]

Roman moralists, like the elder Cato, saw the dangers in the spread of Greek civilization. Inevitably, they argued, Hellenism would corrupt and corrode the earthy and puritan Roman virtues. Greek products were bad enough; but even worse, as far as these critics were concerned, was the appearance on the banks of the Tiber of Greeks themselves—not Greeks from southern Italy, who had been around for ages and who spoke proper Latin and wore proper Italian clothes, but real Athenians

---

[4] Two shipwrecks show the diversity of objects that were on their way back to Rome as plunder from looted cities. One off the island of Antikythera was full of priceless bronze and marble statues. Another, off the African coast, contained marble blocks and columns and four Attic inscriptions. See also the sculpture shown on p. 114, which was found off Riace in southern Italy.

The author visits the wreck of a ship that once carried olive oil. The shape of the amphora dates the wreck to the first century B.C.

and Ionians. Their ambassadors attempted to deceive the august fathers of the Senate with cunning and sophistic arguments that made honest people's heads ache, and in their wake came a host of philosophers and merchants, astrologers, teachers of rhetoric, quacks, and charlatans of every variety. During the second century, indignant and super-patriotic Romans twice expelled Greek philosophy from the city of Rome. Cato himself explained to his son that the Romans would lose their empire when they began to be infected with Greek literature.

But the tide of fashion was running directly counter to such sentiment. Hellenic culture had an immediate success with Romans of all classes. Young gentlemen began to study the classics of Greek literature and philosophy as a matter of course, and by the first century B.C., any statesman who wished respectability had to have studied with one of the great Greek teachers of rhetoric and statesmanship. The influence of Greek models on Roman literature is so well known that it needs no discussion here; but in no area did Roman civilization escape remodeling at the hands of Greeks during the last two centuries B.C.

Slaves in a Roman household wait on table and perform kitchen chores. (*Art Resource/Alinari*)

The Roman general Marius, an uncouth and violent man who prided himself on his general lack of either manners or culture, said he refused to learn Greek because it was a language whose teachers were slaves. This was literally true. The number of Romans and Italians who visited the Greek East is insignificant compared to the numbers of Greeks who came or were brought to Italy during the last two centuries of the republic. Some Greeks were free and professional, from craftsmen and entertainers to august scholars like Dionysius of Halicarnassus who wrote a still extant history of Rome. But the vast majority of Greeks in Italy were, in fact, slaves. Perhaps as many as a quarter of a million Greeks were hauled off in the second century B.C. alone as prisoners of war, hostages, or the surviving population of defeated cities like Corinth. Despite the depths into which they had sunk, they generally found employment where their Hellenism was most influential: in the more favored forms of servitude as domestics, tutors, secretaries, and so forth.

Of course, not all Greeks were intellectuals or even accustomed to any sort of gracious living, but in comparison with the personnel from other Roman slave hauls—Gauls, Spaniards, or Thracians—they must have appeared so to the masters. Consequently, the shaggy Celt or the lumbering German was sent off to gladiatorial training or to work in the fields; the young shepherd from Boeotia, who might never have worked a day of his life indoors, was trained as a doorkeeper or butler so that his master could boast that his lowliest servants knew Homer by heart. Distinctions were ignored. A Greek was a Greek. Thus, by the end of the republic, the pace of Hellenization had already become quite brisk, although far more Romans learned Greek from slaves who had once been donkey drivers or tavern owners than ever attended the lectures of Panaetius or Posidonius or the other eminent scholars who educated the Roman elite.

In the wake of the Augustan settlement, the Hellenization of the Roman Empire proceeded even more swiftly aided by an atmosphere of peace, ease of travel, and, most of all, a new climate of social and economic mobility officially sponsored by Augustus during his long reign (31 B.C.–A.D. 14). First of all, hundreds of thousands of Greeks were descended from ancestors who had been brought to Italy as slaves. Many remained slaves, of course, but there are countless examples of individuals who managed to purchase their freedom or otherwise escape servile status. Greek freedmen appeared in every sort of enterprise and endeavor in the early empire. With their native gift for sensing opportunity combined with their Roman upbringing, freedmen were uniquely equipped to work their way up in the imperial civil service or serve some great Roman in a position of power and trust.[5]

The already sizable Greek population of Italy was augmented during the early empire by a wave of Greeks and Hellenized Orientals from old Greece and the Near East. These new immigrants began to move westward into Italy, Gaul, Spain, or Roman Africa, unerringly seeking out the new centers of opportunity, power, pleasure, and material gain. It was necessary only to learn some Latin and there would be a position open in the administration of some estate, great house, or imperial office.

The Roman reaction to Hellenization was peculiarly ambivalent but has left us with a number of remarkable literary portraits of Greeks in the Roman world. The ambivalence is understandable; we have the modern example of a Europe that has for centuries followed French cultural and intellectual models to the point of affectation, all the time unjustly satirizing the French as vain and frivolous, shallow, and effeminate. The same was true of Rome. Cicero and his circle were masters of Greek literature and philosophy, emperors knew all of Homer by heart and wrote their memoirs in Greek, no Roman of means owned a home ungraced by Greek works of art, and anyone with any pretensions to education learned Greek as a second language. But as fashionable as all things Greek were, it was still just as fashionable to despise the Greeks themselves as the very embodiment of knavery and deception, unworthy latter-day recipients of a civilization created by inspired ancestors of long ago.

Pallas, the emperor Claudius' freedman, was said to be the richest man in the world during his lifetime. Because of favors he was able to do for various senators in his position of influence as confidential sec-

---

[5] See the example, pp. 204–210.

retary to the emperor, the Senate voted him the insignia of a high Roman magistrate and fifteen million sesterces.[6] Pallas accepted the praetorian honors but graciously turned down the money and was content to record the decree on a monument by one of the roads leading out of Rome. Fifty years later, the monument infuriated a Roman like Pliny, normally a tolerant and generous man:

> This decree showed me how farcical and useless such honors were when they could be showered on that dirt and that filth—honors which that jailbird presumed to accept or refuse as if proclaiming for posterity an example of moderation.
>
> Pliny *Letters* 7. 29; cf. 8. 6.

The immortal *Satyricon* of Petronius gives us the classic insight into the seamiest side of the Hellenic and pseudo-Hellenic subculture of Italy. There is the enormously rich and vulgar Trimalchio, the archetypal *nouveau riche*, born a slave in the Hellenistic East, who obtained freedom and wealth by gratifying his master's appetites, and then multiplied the fortune many times by clever investments in trade. But he still invites people in off the streets for dinner, discusses his bowel movements at the table as a matter of common interest, and orders silver cups fallen from the table swept up and thrown out with the rest of the garbage. The other characters of the tale are a fine flock of degenerates and parasites who live by their wits—confidence men, pederast tutors, whoremongers, and so forth—who give formerly staid Latin Italy an exotic flavor quite unappreciated by true-born Romans of the old school.

Slightly more respectable was another familiar figure in first century A.D. Rome—the paid companion. This was a learned Greek who was hired to grace the household of some wealthy ignoramus and thereby give his employer the appearance of being a patron of philosophy. A hilarious description of the pitfalls of such an existence is drawn by the satirist Lucian in the later second century A.D. The grave, bearded scholar at first sits near the head of the table, while he is still a novelty in the household, and comes up with the appropriate classical allusions to give the whole congregation the air of philosophy and erudition. But his salary is infinitesimal, he is up from dawn till after midnight, attendant on his employer's whim, and eventually he is taken for granted. Born a free man and trained under the most illustrious scholars, he is forced to seek favor from Syrian waiters and to tip Libyan butlers in order to get enough to eat and to keep from having malicious gossip put about. He may be reduced to the most shameful sort of

---

[6] As usual, it is almost impossible to equate systems of currency; the entire estate required of a person of senatorial rank was only one million sesterces.

existence, half flatterer, half parasite, with all his books and all his acquired wisdom quite useless to him. We are told the story of one such venerable scholar in the employ of a rich old Roman lady. On a trip to the country, he was forced to share the carriage with an exquisite young man, who giggled at his every embarrassment, and with her ladyship's Maltese terrier, which gave birth to a litter of puppies in the folds of his robe.

Being a Greek Asiatic himself, Lucian was at least sympathetic. But Roman observers were unanimous in their condemnation of the Greek invasion. The classic example of anti-Greek prejudice was the attitude of the Roman poet Juvenal (ca. A.D. 50–130), an old-fashioned idealist who was nostalgic about the old Roman standards of conduct, and whose verses brought him little in the way of financial reward. He was unable to understand that social and economic mobility are valuable in any society; that only free communication, association, and exchange between *all* the members of an empire, regardless of ethnic origin, can liberate the potential energies of that empire. Juvenal remained intolerant of Greeks and Orientals whom he felt had usurped the privileges of honest Romans, and he wrote some of the most scathing criticism Greeks have ever been subjected to:

> Now let me turn to that race which goes down so well
> With our millionaires but remains my special pet aversion,
> And not mince my words. I cannot, citizens, stomach
> A Greek-struck Rome. . . .
> . . . Here's one from Sicyon,
> Another from Macedonia, two from Aegean islands—
> Andros, say, or Samos—two more from Caria,
> All of them lighting out for the City's classiest districts
> And burrowing into great houses, with a long-term plan
> For taking them over. Quick wit, unlimited nerve, a gift
> Of the gab that outsmarts a professional public speaker—
> These are their characteristics. What do you take
> That fellow's profession to be? He has brought a whole bundle
> Of personalities with him—schoolmaster, rhetorician,
> Surveyor, artist, masseur, diviner, tightrope-walker,
> Magician or quack, your versatile hungry Greekling
> Is all by turns. Tell him to fly—he's airborne . . .
> . . . Greece is a nation
> Of actors. Laugh, and they split their sides. At the sight
> Of a friend's tears, they weep too—though quite unmoved.
> If you ask for a fire in winter, the Greek puts on his cloak;
> If you say "I'm hot," he starts sweating. So you see
> We are not on an equal footing: he has the great advantage
> Of being able on all occasions, night and day,
> To take his cue, his mask, from others. He's always ready
> To throw up his hands when a friend delivers
> A really resounding belch, or pisses right on the mark,

With a splendid drumming sound from the upturned golden basin.
Besides, he holds nothing sacred, not a soul is safe
From his randy urges, the lady of the house, her
Virgin daughter, her daughter's still unbearded
Husband-to-be, her hitherto virtuous son—
And if none of these are to hand, he'll cheerfully lay
His best friend's grandmother. (Anything to ferret
Domestic secrets out, and get a hold over people.)

Satire 3. 59–62; 70–78; 100–114[7]

It is unfortunate that Romans so often accepted these clichés and saw Greeks only from this perspective, because from our vantage we can see a quite different picture. At the height of the Roman Empire, Hellenism was the one bond common to all, the catalyst, the quickening energy that suffused the air from the Thames to the Euphrates, the heritage that everyone somehow felt part of, whether Syrian merchant or Egyptian doctor or that brooding Spanish emperor, Marcus Aurelius, writing his *pensées* in the language of Plato.

Examples of the Hellenic synthesis in the Roman world are not hard to come by. The Moor Juba (50 B.C.–A.D. 23), heir to the throne of Numidia, was taken to Rome as a hostage and was later reinstalled at home as a client king. An African by birth, Roman by citizenship, he was a Greek scholar by inclination and education, and during his lifetime he turned out scores of works in Greek: a Roman history, works on grammar and literature, painting and the theater. Greek contemporaries compared him in erudition with the best scholars of Alexandria. The Jewish priest Josephus, once a general in the Jewish revolt against Rome (A.D. 66–70) who later took the Roman side, was honored with Roman citizenship and imperial favor, but wrote the history of the war in Greek in order, as he said, that the emperor's subjects might all know the true events. Favorinus, a Gaul from Arelate (the modern Arles), was a favored companion of the emperor Hadrian and was famous in his day as one of the most eminent and learned Greek writers, orators, and philosophers.

Hellenism was tolerant and adaptable. It savored and sampled everything with which it came in contact. It was able to blend with both older and newer civilizations, appropriating what it found useful and congenial, changing it subtly, and still remaining overwhelmingly Greek. For a long time, there were stringent qualifications for Roman citizenship, but all races could become Greek without test or proof of pure birth. All that was required was a Greek name and a Greek education, and any Parthian or Ethiopian or hairy northerner was taken as

---

[7] Peter Green, ed. and trans., *Juvenal, The Sixteen Satires* (Baltimore: Penguin Books, 1967). Reprinted by permission of Penguin Books.

a latter-day Hellene without further sham or artifice. In no way can the Greek influence be seen more clearly than in the metamorphosis it worked on Christianity.

The Law and the Logos: Christianity and the Greeks

It is impossible for any one, whether he be a student of history or no, to fail to notice a difference of both form and content between the Sermon on the Mount and the Nicene Creed. The Sermon on the Mount is the promulgation of a new law of conduct; it assumes beliefs rather than formulates them; the theological conceptions which underlie it belong to the ethical rather than the speculative side of theology; metaphysics are wholly absent. The Nicene Creed is a statement partly of historical facts and partly of dogmatic inferences; the metaphysical terms which it contains would probably have been unintelligible to the first disciples; ethics have no place in it. The one belongs to a world of Syrian peasants, the other to a world of Greek philosophers.

The contrast is patent. If any one thinks that it is sufficiently explained by saying that the one is a sermon and the other a creed, it must be pointed out in reply that the question why an ethical sermon stood in the forefront of the teaching of Jesus Christ, and a metaphysical creed in the forefront of the Christianity of the fourth century, is a problem which claims investigation.

Thus, in 1888, the eminent British historian Edwin Hatch began his classic, *The Influence of Greek Ideas on Christianity,* which so lucidly demonstrated the extent of the capture of the infant religion by Greek philosophy.

In historical perspective, one might see Jesus of Nazareth as merely the last in a line of Hebrew prophets who came along from time to time to purify the religion of the children of Israel. Certainly such Greek and Roman writers who had heard of him a generation later thought him to have been only the obscure founder of a particular Jewish heresy. But when the scales fell from the eyes of Paul and he set out to bring the God of Israel as a light to the Gentiles, the movement was destined for an incredible and revolutionary future, for Paul was another of those combinations of the Hellenistic East. He was Jewish by birth and a Roman citizen by adoption, but he proclaimed the new faith to crowds everywhere in the universal language of his day in order that all might understand. Therefore, the first conception of the new religion was expressed everywhere in Greek, and the rich abstractions of the language forever colored the beginnings of Christian learning. After a century or so, Greek philosophers were to administer the finishing touches.

The peoples of the Hellenistic Orient and Greece had always accepted new religions as they came along, admiring this or that myth, marveling at a spectacular sacrifice here or a promise of eternal life there. Many citizens of the eastern Roman Empire were adherents of one or more of the various mystery religions, so called because the whole fabric of the cult was revealed only to initiates. In general, the mysteries aimed at a purification through ritual, after which the initiate, freed of earthly anxieties and corruptions, could seek a mystic communion with the god himself. In some, the death of the god, or cult figure, was ritually acted out in what is often thought to be a symbolic representation of the annual death and rebirth of vegetation. In others, a sacrificial animal was represented as the flesh of the god and consumed by the worshipers who hoped thus to partake of the god's strength. To intellectuals like Plutarch, the goal of the mysteries was to share in the infinite wisdom of the god; for simple folk, we might assume that the group emotionalism and frenzy of the rituals were ends in themselves.

To naïve Anatolians and Syrians, to slaves, women, and soldiers everywhere—the vast and untutored substructure of the eastern Mediterranean—Christianity seemed a perfectly legitimate new mystery religion, with a number of advantages. It was open to all, and preached equality both on earth and in heaven, regardless of race, sex, or financial position. Unlike Sabazius or Sarapis, the cult figure was a living man; contemporaries remembered him and were transfixed by the memory. He was said to have died on the cross for the sins of all human beings— an agony well appreciated by the lower orders of a brutal society. And real miracles were taking place every day in his name: the lame leapt to their feet, the blind saw, and the very dead rose again. As the apostles traveled dusty roads throughout the empire of the Caesars bringing their ecstatic message, they had little trouble founding congregation after congregation of Syrian fishermen, Anatolian villagers, and *proletarii* in the dingy slums of Corinth, Ephesus, Antioch, Alexandria, or even Rome itself.

For more than a century, the movement spread throughout the empire with each congregation almost undisturbed in its interpretation of the dynamic new mystery. Doctrine was simple: basically all that was required was baptism (a common sacrament in other cults); salvation would follow through faith in the Son of God, and grace through direct revelation. The novelty was the ethical code preserved in the sayings of Jesus, particularly in that oration called the Sermon on the Mount. In a world of violence and greed, the meek were to be blessed and the poor in spirit were to inherit the Kingdom of Heaven. One was to love not only one's friends, but enemies as well. Those who kept to the simple life, sharing their possessions with the needy, loving all around them, secure in their faith, could not be harmed. Of course, much of this was already familiar to followers of Socrates or Epicurus. The even greater novelty was that the early Christians were willing to die for their beliefs. In the wake of the great fire in Rome in A.D. 64, most Romans would have been perfectly willing to believe Nero's claim that the Christians had spread the flames. But when the Roman mob saw the processions of captives jubilantly singing hymns of exaltation as they were torn apart, or burned alive, or nailed to crosses, they felt a sudden revulsion for human cruelty and a wonder at this new God who could so inspire the souls of slaves, women, paupers, and criminals.

The exemplary conduct of the martyrs vastly expanded the ranks of early Christians and began to bring the religion to the attention of the elite classes as well. It was probably sometime in the second century that Greek intellectuals first began to see the amazing metaphysical possibilities in the story of Christ. His mother a virgin, his father a God—certainly there was nothing new in this in the land of Zeus—but here it had actually happened before the eyes of living people. Jesus was the Son of God. But did this mean he himself was mortal or divine? If he had walked the earth as a god in mortal guise, the significance of his death on the cross vanished, for everyone knew gods could feel no pain. On the other hand, if he were mortal, how did he accomplish his miracles, and how did he eventually become divine? More than once he had mentioned the Holy Spirit. What was this Spirit? Did it rival God? And were Father and Son equal in powers?

After long and fevered arguments over points such as this, a body of doctrine began to grow up, doctrine that was all-important to the Greeks. The Jews were content with a sign, as Paul had said, but the Greeks sought wisdom; they required a formal logos of some kind. In the Greek tradition, any philosophical or religious creed required an explicit formulation of the nature of the world and a person's place in that world. At the same time, most Greek religions had little in the way of recommended ethical conduct. It was felt that the important thing was to acquire knowledge of the world, to perceive the logos in its entirety and the premises on which the whole creation was founded. Once the premises were known, Greek logic said, right conduct would follow as a matter of course.

But the Jewish faith on which Jesus had based his message was entirely the opposite. Judaism stressed adherence to the Law of Moses, which Jesus had said he had come to fulfill—actually an entire set of laws governing daily life and conduct. Knowledge of God's nature was not only unnecessary, it was forbidden. It sufficed to know that God punished people at will for infractions of His Law, or sometimes even smote the righteous, like Job. Greek philosophers could spend their lifetimes debating the nature of the logos, if they wanted; Jewish scholars devoted their waking hours to the study of the Law and the interpretation of minute points might occupy the constant attention of hundreds of scholars for generation after generation.

Religious imagery shows the tendency of the Greeks to find a common element in divine figures from all religions. This pose of the Virgin Mary (right) is virtually identical to that of Isis (left) in an earlier depiction, which is in turn based on all the mother goddess figures in Greek cults going back a thousand years and more.

Perhaps the fundamental distinction between Greek Christianity and its Jewish origins can be seen in the persons of the preacher and the prophet. In the Jewish prophetic tradition, a person filled with the spirit of the Lord would exhort the people to cast out vanity and to obey the Law. Joel had prophesied that the Lord would pour his spirit over the flesh of all mankind (Joel 2:28), and Peter believed that "the final days" of the prophecy had come to pass—that the spirit of prophecy lay upon all people (Acts 2:16 ff.). But in the Greek tradition, the most influential thinkers were those brilliant philosophers who appeared from time to time to expound a new logos or give an entirely new interpretation to an old one. It was the Greek expounder and interpreter who eventually became the Christian preacher.

In the early years of Christianity, the Jewish concept of prophecy was still the dominant theme of the religion as Peter had made clear. Jesus was the prophet of God, and the apostles were prophets of Father and Son. Behind inspired prophecy lay the experience of personal revelation, which was held by the earliest congregations to be the highest sort of religious experience, just as the pagan mystery cults believed. The concept of a highly personal, individual communion with God, although often treated as heresy, can be seen from our perspective as a fundamental recurring theme of Christianity throughout its history, finally given official doctrinal recognition by certain of the first Protestant churches.

But as the infant church began to be dominated more and more by a Hellenized elite, Greek philosophy began its struggle with revelation. The questions of fundamental importance, Greek church members would say, were the nature of God, Son, and Holy Ghost, the nature of their energies, and their relationship to mortals. It was already apparent that these questions would challenge the most brilliant intellects Greek philosophy could produce—how absurd then to believe that they could be left to the discussion of illiterate and uneducated Greek slum dwellers or Anatolian peasants. This was, of course, merely a variation of the argument used by Plato to discredit democracy. A profound distrust of personal revelation and resultant prophecy developed among these latter-day Platonic aristocrats. After all, if *anyone* could experience personal revelation with God and go around as a self-appointed prophet, how could an orderly fabric of doctrine be maintained? How could a Christian logos stand in the face of continual new revelations experienced by inspired—or simply neurotic—members of the lower orders? It was surely more logical that God should seek out chosen vessels through whom he might communicate with the rest of his children. These chosen few would be the shepherds of the Lord's flock: educated philosophers who had mastered all the literature on doctrine, who could expound the Christian logos with unassailable logic, and who could lead the less fortunate and less gifted to a closer communion with God. Thus did the Greek preacher triumph over prophecy and revelation.

By the time Christianity was recognized in the fourth century and had become the official religion of the Roman Empire, its emphasis on doctrine had become predominant. The greatest struggle of the following centuries was to enforce orthodoxy in the eastern, Greek portion of the Roman Empire, where philosophical disputation and, hence, theological disputation were so much a part of everyone's life. Muleteers and tavern wenches argued the common or disparate nature of Father and Son with no less heat than the most eminent theologians. Thorny points of doctrine evoked both stormy debates between bishops and riots in the streets of Alexandria, Antioch, and Constantinople. Such riots killed thousands of citizens who emerged from shops and tenements to do battle with the mobs going home from the hippodrome, fighting over such matters as the placement of one preposition in the liturgy.

All this was in contrast to the Latin church in the West. As East and West gradually drew apart under the onslaught of barbarian invasions in the fifth and sixth centuries, the Western church assumed the usual pragmatic Roman attitudes in its approach to Christianity. Doctrine was less important than survival, and Roman clergymen were impatient with paradoxical points of theology. In the ensuing centuries, the pastoral mission of the church was to become paramount in the Latin West and was essential in preserving some vestiges of civil authority. In the Greek East, the philosophical aspects remained fascinating, exasperating, gloriously satisfying to the soul, an eternal resource to challenge the Greek intellect and to stimulate the sort of civic disorder the Greek regarded as almost a normal pastime.

This does not mean that Greek Christians were any less pious and devoted to their faith than austere Latin puritans like Augustine or Montanist heretics who still clung to the concept of an irrational and mystic personal communion with God. Greeks merely responded to Christianity in a wholly Greek way: they could never submit to an unknowable omnipotent Oriental deity or be content with a simple and nonintellectualized faith like that of the Latin Fathers. To them, belief in Jesus Christ was both wine for the soul and meat for the intellect, and they would have had it no other way. A thousand years later, with the barbarian at the gate, and the Greek church discussing a compromise in matters of doctrine with the Roman church in return for military aid, dissenting priests let the Turks inside the walls of Constantinople, preferring Orthodoxy under foreign rule to a shameful corruption of what they considered the logical and therefore the only possible form of the Christian faith.

The Fall of Rome and the Survival of Greece

> . . . some men came from the frontier
> And said there are no longer any Barbarians.
> And now what will become of us without Barbarians?
> Those people were some kind of solution.
>
> C. P. Cavafy, *Waiting for the Barbarians*

When the emperor Constantine converted the old Greek city of Byzantium into an eastern capital of the Roman Empire in 324 and renamed it Constantinople, he completed the formal division of the empire into two major administrative areas. But a *de facto* division between Latin West and Greek East had always existed: an imaginary line that ran more or less vertically through the Adriatic Sea. Much of the West had always been populated by peasants—Gauls, Britons, and Spaniards—with a Romanized town here or an aqueduct there as the only signs that a civilizing power was present. When the money ran out and the overseers disappeared and the civilizing power fell into the hands of people who wore furs and felt most at home on horseback, the towns gradually became deserted, the aqueducts ran dry, and the countryside reverted to a peasant existence.

But in the Greek East, a highly sophisticated, literate urban society had more adequate resources on which to draw when threatened by barbarian invasion and economic depression. We sometimes read of the chaotic years of the imperial crisis of the third century, the campaigns of the fourth century, or the final overwhelming of the West in the fifth, marveling that any vestige of civilization could have survived anywhere in the empire. But during these three centuries, eminent sophists continued to draw enormous crowds in the cities of Greece and Ionia, elegant philosophers debated the relative merits of Neoplatonism and Christianity in Alexandria, and the citizens of the city of Antioch set new standards for frivolity and for the pursuit of self-gratification. While barbarian emperors hired barbarian armies to repel still other varieties of barbarians along the Rhine and Danube frontiers, the Hellenized cities were the bulwark of civilization in the East. When hard pressed, the cities could always come up with just a little more in the way of taxes in order to pay for military survival. Generation after generation, they still produced a large population of alert and ambitious citizens to serve the administrative and economic needs of a complex society. And as the darkness descended over the West, these citizens tended to shrug their shoulders and to thank various gods that they were a part of a Greek rather than Roman world.

Only in official documents did the Latin language continue to be used in the East. When the emperor Heraclius (610–641) abolished even this archaic holdover, he eliminated one of the last anomalies in what was now once more a Greek society. It was possible for learned people to look all the way back to Homer and see the civilization of Hellas as a unified whole, with the period of Roman domination only a quaint political experiment.

This continuity of Hellenism may be illustrated in a number of ways. Two contemporary historians, for instance, illustrate the persistence of classical antiquity in the East and its almost complete death in the West. Gregory of Tours (538–594) was a historian from Gaul who wrote the history of the Franks in Latin; but his Latin is barbarous and his viewpoint is that of someone looking forward to the rise of a new civilization. The Byzantine historian Procopius (ca. 500–560), on the other hand, was an authentic classical Greek. His style and his philosophy of history closely follow classical models, particularly Herodotus and Thucydides. Although nominally a Christian, his outlook is strictly that of a classical Greek humanist and rationalist. His syntax and vocabulary are consciously archaic, and only a few telltale lapses show that he could not entirely avoid the influence of the spoken language of his day. All through his work there is a careful attention to rhetorical conventions that had become mandatory centuries before—including the fatuous and contrived speeches that it seems every general must address to his troops before every battle.

The continuity of Greek civilization would be seen in even sharper relief if we had no literary sources at all and had to depend on archaeological evidence. Taking the Aegean basin as the heartland of a single culture, the archaeologist would begin from the discontinuity evident at the end of Mycenaean civilization noting that from that time on, no similar disruption, no similar revolutionary change in lifestyle presents itself in the archaeological record. The archaic villages grew and became proper poleis. Pottery styles changed gradually from generation to generation, as did architectural styles. The Persian and Peloponnesian wars left only faint marks on the landscape, and the archaeologist would be able to see no signs of the "decline" classical scholars used to talk about in tones of resignation and pity, thus excusing their unwillingness to study Greek history after Alexander. During the Hellenistic and Roman eras, depopulation would be noted at some sites, but the excavator would attribute this correctly to evolutionary changes in the economy rather than to intrusion and destruction by a new people. The only evidence of any kind of Roman influence in the Greek world would be the new and practical fashion of building ordinary buildings with bricks and mortar.

In the Roman West, the decline of classical society and the primacy of barbarian tribes is all part of the archaeological record: the deserted and plundered cities, the new lifestyles illustrated by cruder artifacts, the primitive rebuilding of toppled villas, the growth of new centers of power outside of Italy, the disappearance of currency. But in the East, there was no parallel decay, no evidence of intrusive elements. The archaeologist would note the now ubiquitous appearance of a new religious symbol—the Cross—and would see that old shrines of Aphrodite or Artemis or Athena had been converted by frugal and practical people to worship of Mary, but would observe that this was an internal change in the religious patterns of society, introduced gradually over a number of centuries without evidence of violence.

Architecture, art, and pottery styles continued to change gradually into the Byzantine period. There are signs here and there of invasions of a cruder people and gradual depopulation of seacoast areas subject to frequent attack by sea raiders, but in general, the archaeologist would feel safe in claiming that this vigorous and creative Greek society, born on the shores of the Aegean Sea a thousand or so years before Christ, had persisted and survived without a cultural break a thousand years more and then some.

SUGGESTIONS FOR FURTHER READING

The preoccupation of the ancient world with political history once more leaves us with little contemporary comment on social or economic history. A Greek impression of the Roman Empire in mid-second century A.D. is the *Roman Oration* of the Greek rhetorician Aelius Aristides, published with translation and copious commentary by J. H. Oliver (Philadelphia: American Philosophical Society, 1953). Much of the flavor of life in the Graeco-Roman world of the first two centuries A.D. can be seen in the orations of Dio Chrysostom, various works from Plutarch's *Moralia*, Pausanias' *Description of Greece*, the works of Lucian, and Philostratus' *Lives of the Sophists*. The Roman historian Livy gives a narrative account of the conquest of the Greek world in books 31–45 of his Roman history. Other Latin writers who commented on Hellenic influence and affairs include Suetonius, *On Grammarians and Rhetoricians*, Petronius, *Satyricon*, and Pliny, *Letters*, book 10. The complex relationship of Greeks and Romans and the stages by which Rome was led to intervene in Hellenistic politics are thoroughly analyzed by Erich Gruen, *The Hellenistic World and the Coming of Rome* (Berkeley and Los Angeles: University of California Press, 1984). The culture of the Greek world under Roman sway is depicted by F. E. Peters, *The Harvest of Hellenism* (New York: Simon & Schuster, 1970) and Samuel Dill's *Roman Society from Nero to Marcus Aurelius* (Cleveland: Meridian Books, 1956) which, although dated (originally published in 1904), has never been superseded. For Greek Christianity see E. Hatch, *The Influence of Greek Ideas on Christianity* (New York: Harper and Row, 1957).

9 Some More Greek People

The Revolutionary: Cleomenes of Sparta

THE PECULIAR Lycurgan system that existed for so long in Sparta depended primarily on the theoretical equality of Sparta's military aristocracy: those 5,000 or so full citizens who were the core of the most fearsome military machine of classical Greece. Supported economically by the taxes of non-Spartan inhabitants of Laconia and by the slave labor of Messenian helots, these Spartans found it easy to renounce materialism and to measure people only by their prowess in war.

The Peloponnesian War was thought to have brought the first corruption into the Lycurgan system by introducing gold and silver for the first time into Sparta and by exposing a generation of Spartans to the outside world with all its pleasures and luxuries. Skeptical Greeks were no doubt quite amused at the example set by Spartans who ventured out of their communist utopia into materialist society: when tempted by riches or vice they almost invariably succumbed. The rot was accelerated by a new law that made it possible for the first time for Spartan citizens to sell their land to whomever they wished. The loss of much territory in the fourth century and the generally depressed condition of agriculture in the years after Alexander only made the new and un-Spartan quest for material gain more vigorous.

Hellenistic Sparta, except for the survival of its peculiar dual monarchy, was like any other Hellenistic city-state on the Greek mainland. The rich were getting richer while a class of permanently poor was being increased every day from the ranks of those who had once been more fortunate—including former Spartan citizens. These impoverished Spartans, as unwilling as other Greeks to accept an inexplicable and unjust fate, now supported the two most common demands of the day—abolition of debts and redistribution of land.

In 244 B.C., a young and idealistic king came to the throne of Sparta and tried to implement this program. His ideological base was the old system of Lycurgus in which all true Spartans were equal. But his immediate purpose was to recreate an old-fashioned army of true Spartan citizens, although there remained as few as a hundred who had any land left; the rest had been dispossessed by an economic competition they did not understand. King Agis, barely out of his teens, naïvely sought to purify the state overnight simply by the force of persuasion. He was successful at abolishing debts, but, as the more cynical will understand, the people who clamor for the abolition of debts are by no means always the same who demand a redistribution of land. Agis' wealthy enemies tricked him into disillusioning the landless; when his popular support had dwindled they unceremoniously strangled him, his mother, and his grandmother and hung the bodies out in public to demonstrate the dangers of ideology to the young.

Just as unceremoniously, Agis' widow was forced to marry the young heir to the other throne of Sparta. But this was the worst mistake Agis' opponents could have made. When the embittered young woman found her new husband—several years her junior—to be both sympathetic and smart, she began a campaign of indoctrination, preaching the martyred king's dream of a purified Sparta where all were equal, strong, brave, and loyal to the ideals of Lycurgus. Until that time, Cleomenes of Sparta had not stood out among his fellows. Manly, handsome, athletic, and intelligent, he seemed to his elders to be good-natured and complaisant; in fact, if he had shown any of the crusading zeal of Agis, he would never have lived to succeed his father to the dual throne of Sparta.

By the time he ascended the throne in 237, Cleomenes had become a dedicated disciple of Agis and the Lycurgan dream. But his path to the goal of a reborn Sparta was cloaked with masterly deceit, for Cleomenes was capable of cunning and opportunism as well as idealism. For ten years he prepared with infinite care and guile. Only a very few chosen companions were allowed to share his secret plans; it was enough for him to know that a majority of the population was unhappy and would probably join a revolution, once it was started, with a good chance of success. Cleomenes' first goal was a well-trained military loyal to himself. It was easy for him to persuade the Ephors of Sparta to send him out year after year to challenge the Achaean domination of the southern Peloponnesus. During these campaigns, the majority of the Spartan army consisted of mercenaries, for few Spartans could still afford to keep up the necessary arms and armor and to support the number of attendants a heavy infantryman needed in battle. Cleomenes showed himself a skillful and courageous soldier and a clever strategist; by 227, he had at his back a core of seasoned mercenaries who had gone through many campaigns with him and would follow him anywhere.

That year, he marched north into Arcadia where he stationed the Spartan citizen-soldiers who were ignorant of his intentions, and then immediately returned home with his mercenaries. Catching the city completely unawares, he murdered four of the five Ephors, banished those Spartans who were most firmly against reform of any kind, and made himself sole master of Laconia without opposition. Immediately, he set to work to bring the state back in line with the old laws of Lycurgus—or at least so much of the laws of Lycurgus as he felt Sparta could afford. On a great field day of personal dedication, he and the rest of the propertied classes contributed all their wealth to the purpose of the state, all the land was redistributed, and a new citizen body of 4,000 Spartans enrolled. In addition, the old Spartan education and regimen were instituted again: children of seven once more began their barracks schooling, and the Spartan men returned to the old common mess. Personal wealth was abolished, and the ancient customs of simplicity and austerity once more became the fashion.

There can be no doubt that the great majority of Spartans were honestly inspired in their sudden conversion to the Lycurgan system, no matter how barren and depressing such a way of life may appear to us—or even to Greek contemporaries. The population won over by Cleomenes had been poor and oppressed, working as tenants on lands once theirs, now governed by the bailiffs of absentee landlords. Worse, they had to eke out their existence in the homeland of an army that had once struck terror into the hearts of Greeks from Sicily to Phoenicia. In recent years, Spartan soldiers had had to seek employment abroad, in the Greek cities of Italy, in Crete, or masterminding a Carthaginian victory over Romans on the sands of Africa; now they could stay home and help to rebuild the glories of past centuries.

As if to demonstrate the solidarity of all Spartans, Cleomenes at once marched out of Laconia, leaving it undefended, and began to attack the Achaean League wherever it had established a strongpoint, from

Argos to Elis. Everywhere the new-style Spartan army went, it was cheered on by local radicals who saw in Cleomenes a heroic social reformer who would remodel the social and political structure of their cities. Some of the Achaean leaders felt threatened by the resurgence of Sparta as a first-rate military power; others were appalled by the prospect of social and economic reform in their own backyards. Whatever their motives, they seized a moment when the power of their founder Aratus was at its lowest ebb and offered Cleomenes the presidency of the league on the condition that they be able to remain in power in their own states and that questions of social reform be tactfully shelved for the moment.

But fate now played the first of two cruel jokes on Cleomenes. On his way to a conference with the leading Achaeans, he was struck down by a crippling stomach ailment—probably a bleeding ulcer. He was forced to retire to Sparta to recuperate, and during his illness, the charismatic Aratus once more regained control of Achaean affairs. In desperation, this cunning statesman now took the only action he thought would both protect his own ascendancy and banish the specter of social revolution forever: he invited in the hated Macedonian army, giving King Antigonus of Macedon control of the citadel of Corinth in return for his military intervention against Sparta.

In spite of superior odds, Cleomenes performed miracles for several years. The Spartan army was likely to appear anywhere. Its superbly trained and disciplined men were able to make long forced marches at a rate not seen since the days of Alexander the Great. In 222, as he was gradually being forced back into the valley of the Eurotas, Cleomenes finally resolved to offer set battle to the combined Achaean and Macedonian forces, reckoning it worth the gamble of winning or losing all on one throw; he could not tolerate a slow deterioration of his country's strength. But once more fate was arranging an ironic denouement. As King Antigonus of Macedon was maneuvering his troops into position at Sellasia, north of Sparta, messengers were speeding through the eastern Peloponnesus with the news that a huge army of Illyrians had invaded Macedon and that the whole country would be overrun if the Macedon army did not return at once. Two hours after the Spartan army had been shattered in defeat on the battlefield of Sellasia—in fact, while Cleomenes and his friends were galloping down the road to the sea to take ship for bitter exile in Egypt—Antigonus received the news and immediately departed for home, leaving Aratus and the nervous Achaeans to settle Sparta's fate.

This they were able to do only temporarily. Rebellion broke out once more and appeals reached Cleomenes and his lieutenants, now waiting on the whims of Ptolemy III at the court in Alexandria. But it took time to get the ear of the ruler of the Nile Valley, caught up as he was by so many questions of diplomacy, of internal administration, of diversions and amusements. When Ptolemy finally seemed to be coming around to a decision to send Cleomenes home, it was too late: the aging king suddenly died and the throne passed to his son, Ptolemy IV, a chubby and frivolous voluptuary who left all matters of state to a sullen and suspicious vizier, while he himself threw his energies into every form of vice his clever and degenerate companions might invent.

The contrast must have been startling in those days when Cleomenes and fellow Spartans called vainly at court to ask for passage home. We can picture a crowd of perfumed exquisites in silks and jewelry suddenly falling silent or giggling nervously as the Spartans arrive—vast, bronzed men, sleek and vicious, wearing the simplest type of coarse tunic, jaws set grimly and looking around them with boredom and indifference, like caged animals.

Frustrated by devious chamberlains and revolted by the crowds of epicene courtiers, Cleomenes and his friends began spending more time out at the nearby barracks, where thousands of mercenary soldiers from the Peloponnesus and elsewhere in Greece were stationed. Here they felt at home, with rough, honest troops who had shared their sort of life for many years. But these visits made Ptolemy's advisors apprehensive of Cleomenes' growing popularity with the army; the royal exile was soon put under house arrest. Cleomenes' growing desperation now drove him to contemplate an insane and quixotic plan. Breaking out of his improvised prison one day at noon, he traversed the streets of Alexandria with twelve companions, proclaiming liberty to the people and calling upon them to revolt from their corrupt king. But the well-fed and blasé Alexandrians were quite content with their lot and would have nothing to do with stirring alarums set afoot by fierce Spartans. The exiles, finally realizing the hopelessness of their gesture, took the Spartan way out. They ran themselves through and expired on a main thoroughfare of Alexandria—a silent reproach to a population they considered craven and servile.

In many ways, Cleomenes was ahead of his times. Violent revolution was to break out again in the Greek world but was never remotely as successful as his well-thought-out program. But in another sense, he was a reactionary, an old-fashioned throwback to a vanished age. Like Spartans and many other Greeks of past centuries, he believed that his country's genius glowed brightest and burned most fiercely in the glorious crucible of war—the same sort of rubbish given maximum exposure during the last 100 years by romantic super-patriots, but of little appeal to the survivors of the late twentieth century who know only too well who gets hurt in wartime. Cleomenes had hoped to consummate his revolution by conquest. But the desperate reaction he aroused destroyed both him and his revolution.

The Bureaucrat: Tiberius of Smyrna

Early in the reign of the emperor Tiberius (A.D. 14–37), the emperor's slavemasters added to his staff a handsome boy from the Greek city of Smyrna, a large commercial center on the coast of Asia Minor. The youth was as quick-witted as he was good-looking. He learned Latin and swiftly mastered the various jobs assigned to him; as luck would have it, his duties brought him often into the presence of the emperor. Tiberius was normally bad-tempered, suspicious, and cruel, but he could appreciate a pleasantly competent and intelligent slave who got his jobs done—especially when he compared him to his usual company, which ran heavily to fawning senators asking favors and informers reporting treason and malfeasance on all sides. As the Greek slave grew older, he showed himself suitable for training in the secretarial duties of the imperial household. In these tasks too he proved reliable, hard-working, and discreet.

When a slave reached the age of thirty, Roman law permitted him to purchase his freedom with his master's consent. A measure of the favor in which the young Greek was held is shown by the fact that he was manumitted while yet in his twenties, and that his freedom was given him without charge. He then took the name of his master, as was customary, and his official appellation would have been Tiberius Julius Augusti libertus ———. Unfortunately, we do not know his *cognomen*, by which he would have been known informally. Six decades later, when he died, the Roman poet Statius addressed a consolation to his son Claudius Etruscus, a wealthy Roman knight and the poet's patron. Almost all we know about the lengthy career of this Greek freedman comes from Statius' poem.[1] But Statius never mentions the gentleman's *cognomen*, so we are forced either to call him Claudius Etruscus' father, or to use his acquired name, Tiberius.

Augustus had intended that the Roman Empire be ruled by the Senate in partnership with himself and the Roman knights, who ranked just below the Senate. But Augustus was also fanatic about preserving at least the forms of the old republic. He badly needed a class of civil servants to deal with the enormous and ever-growing mass of paperwork arising out of imperial business. He realized, however, that knights and senators, on one hand, would resent the subservient positions they would have to occupy, and on the other hand, would continually be looking out for their own interests rather than those of the empire. For these reasons, from the very beginning, Augustus and his successors after him entrusted some of the most vital and sensitive imperial business to slaves and freedmen. We are thus treated to the

---

[1] Statius *Silvae* 3. 3. There is a good treatment by P. R. C. Weaver, "The Father of Claudius Etruscus," *Classical Quarterly* 15 (1965), pp. 145–154.

paradox of Roman knights and senators cloaking themselves with high honors and empty titles, while the real work of the empire was carried forward day by day by an almost unseen class of Greeks and Hellenized Orientals, most of whom had begun their lives as slaves. These bureaucrats tended to be conscientious and hardworking, but to the emperors their greatest value was their loyalty, for they owed everything to the emperor personally, and they recognized that when his reign should end, their careers and even their lives might be in great jeopardy. The rewards of being an imperial freedman were attractive: besides generous stipends, the staff was entrusted with a great deal of information about imperial affairs, and they were not the first to discover that knowledge is power. More than one imperial freedman retired to live a quiet but luxurious life on broad estates after his days of active service were over. But it was always best to remain as invisible as possible. With the passing of an emperor, those privy to too many secrets or those who had acquired too much in the way of obvious wealth might suddenly disappear.

Evidently the young freedman from Smyrna learned how to avoid unwelcome attention. When the aged Tiberius died, the freedman went on to serve Caligula (37–41). He was on the unstable young emperor's staff, in some capacity, during the highly publicized "invasion" of Britain, which never came off. When the praetorian guard ended Caligula's erratic reign by murdering him, Tiberius' usefulness evidently outweighed the liability of his previous association with the mad ruler, for he went on to work for the emperor Claudius (41–54). Perhaps he had already become a financial specialist; no one with a sound grasp of Roman accounting procedures was lightly disposed of, particularly after Caligula had had his way with the imperial *fiscus* for four years.

The emperor Tiberius had spent the last years of his reign in seclusion; Caligula was hopelessly incompetent; Claudius must at least be considered eccentric. The lack of able and responsible leadership for over ten years meant that more and more work and decision making fell to the lot of the imperial freedmen. Under Claudius, this almost invisible, underground government finally received official recognition by formal organization into offices and departments, which would rate cabinet status in a modern state. The Greeks who occupied these ministries during the reign of Claudius actually surpassed the emperor in the powers they shared. Senators, generals, and foreign ambassadors competed for their favor.

Any request for action by the emperor passed through the office of Callistus, the secretary *a libellis*. Narcissus, the freedman *ab epistulis*, handled all official imperial correspondence and was really equivalent to a secretary of state. The imperial finances were managed by the secretary *a rationibus*, an office made famous by the notoriously wealthy Pallas, about whom the most information has survived. Al-

Portrait of a young boy from the
first century A.D. (*Courtesy, Museum of Fine Arts, Boston*)

though all incoming business was addressed to the emperor and all
actions signed by his name, only a tiny fraction ever came to his attention. They were taken care of by these lively and enterprising Greeks
who managed to rule an empire conscientiously while their own fortunes flourished accordingly. Tiberius occupied some position of middle rank, possibly under Pallas in the department *a rationibus,* until
the latter part of Claudius' reign when he was promoted to senior rank,
possibly as a financial procurator. It was also during this period that
he married a noble lady from a family of consular rank. Their two sons
later entered the order of knights and one of them, Claudius Etruscus,
was a well-known member of Roman society and a literary patron near
the end of the first century.

The emperor Claudius leaned heavily on his freedmen for advice
as well as routine business. During the crisis of the year 48, when the
infidelity of the empress Messalina assumed the proportions of a plot
to put her lover on the throne, the freedmen were in virtual control of
Rome for a few days. They revealed the plot to Claudius in the most
convincing manner, considering the delicacy of the affair, meanwhile
giving orders to the military concerning the various courtiers who were
to be arrested and held. Narcissus, on his own authority, gave the order
for Messalina to be executed without trial. Shortly afterward, when
Claudius decided to marry again, he called together Narcissus, Callistus,
and Pallas to advise him on the choice of a bride. The arguments of

The emperor Nero (54–68) so admired the Greeks that he declared them emancipated in 67—a policy hastily reversed after his death the next year. (*Hirmer Fotoarchiv*)

Pallas won the day for Agrippina, the emperor's own niece (who poisoned her husband a few years later and put her son Nero on the throne).

In the year 52, Claudius was indebted to Pallas for a bit of legal advice. He took the opportunity to deliver a speech to the Senate full of praise for his secretary *a rationibus*. The Senate responded by voting Pallas—who was claimed during the debate to be descended from Arcadian kings—full praetorian regalia and a gift of fifteen million sesterces. The artful Greek freedman, whose fortune already stood at over 300 million sesterces, accepted the honors but asked that he might be allowed to remain in his accustomed poverty! This was the gesture (described on p. 186) that so infuriated Pliny half a century later.

Power, fame, and wealth had their drawbacks. When Nero became emperor in 54, Pallas was the only member of the top secretariat who made the transition safely, and he was fired a year later. Tiberius, however, once more managed to remain invisible, although he seems to have spent most of Nero's fifteen-year reign out of Rome, probably as a procurator in the eastern provinces. Here, both his native Greek tongue and his financial experience could have been used to good effect. It may be that during his foreign service he met and impressed the general Vespasian, who was eventually to become emperor.

In June of the year 68, Nero was overthrown and succeeded on the imperial throne in quick succession by Galba, Otho, and Vitellius. A year later, Vespasian was acclaimed emperor by his legions and began his march from Judaea back to Italy, leaving his son Titus to quell the three-year-old Jewish revolt. From June 68 until December 69, there was a wild scramble among prudent men in government to avoid attention and any suspicion of belonging to the party of anyone who might possibly be marked down for future vengeance. It was a tricky time, particularly for an imperial freedman. Miraculously, Tiberius survived again, and in addition, he backed the right candidate. Vespasian officially became emperor in December 69, and the Greek financial

expert was named secretary *a rationibus,* now responsible for all imperial revenues and expenditures. His duties are described for us with
an almost comic effusiveness by Statius:

> In your sole charge are the riches all nations render and the vast
> world's tribute; the bullion that Hiberia casts up from her mines of
> gold, the glistening metal of Dalmatian hills; all that is swept in from
> African harvests, or ground on the threshing-floors of sultry Nile, or
> gathered by the diver in Eastern waters; the fatted flocks of Spartan
> Galaesus, transparent crystal, Massylian oak-wood and the stately
> Indian tusk. Sole steward, you are charged with and you direct what
> Boreas and fearsome Eurus and cloudy Auster waft into our coffers.
>
> Statius *Silvae* 3. 3. 85–97[2]

Statius goes on to describe Tiberius' duties, similar to those of a
director of the budget: he must calculate the expenditures of the Roman
army and fleet and the costs of such imperial construction projects as
bridges, harbors, and roads. He is also in charge of the mint and must
make sure that the year's revenue of precious ores is turned into imperial coinage.

Tiberius served as *a rationibus* for twelve years, no doubt amassing
a comfortable private fortune, for the Romans did not consider it a
conflict of interest for an official to use his position to assist himself
in private business. Pallas, in fact, had never been accused of outright
embezzlement. He had piled up his huge fortune by selling military
contracts, by collecting "finder's fees," and by simply accepting the
many gifts thrust upon him by entrepreneurs or politicians who were
either repaying favors or laying up a store of credit against which future
favors might be drawn. Although Tiberius had many of the same opportunities, he was no Pallas, and the good old corrupt days under
Claudius and Nero were no more. That the freedman found promotion
and honors under Vespasian meant that he must have been far more
scrupulous in his official conduct than Pallas, for Vespasian was a
hardheaded and practical businessman and found the treasury in a
shambles after fifteen years of Nero. Anyone who was to manage the
fiscus for Vespasian must have devoted long hours to restoring it. As
the poet Statius said: "You were seldom at peace; your heart was closed
to pleasure; your fare was meager, and never did draughts of wine dull
your industry."

Tiberius had been born about A.D. 3. Therefore, by the end of Vespasian's reign in 79, he was an old man. Nevertheless, when Vespasian
died and his son Titus took the throne, Tiberius continued as *a rationibus;* we must assume he had become a Roman institution by then, an

---

[2] A. M. Duff, *Freedmen in the Early Roman Empire* (Cambridge, England: W. Heffer &
Sons, 1958), p. 153. Reprinted by permission of W. Heffer & Sons.

The emperor Vespasian (A.D. 69–79) and his son the emperor Domitian (81–96), seen here on a relief with a personification of Rome, were only two of the ten rulers served by the father of Claudius Etruscus. (*Scala/Art Resource, N.Y.*)

elder statesman presumed to be indispensable to the imperial treasury. But Titus' unstable brother Domitian, smoldering in resentment over what he considered an insulting lack of honors given him by father and brother, hated all institutions connected with the rest of his illustrious family, and when Titus unexpectedly died of an illness in 82, the new emperor banished the old treasury secretary, indispensable or not.

The exile lasted for seven years. But Tiberius retained his vigor right until the end. The emperor Domitian relented in about 90, and Tiberius was allowed to return to Rome, in time to enjoy the opening of his son's opulent new baths. He died peacefully soon after. Over a span of ninety years, Tiberius of Smyrna had served ten emperors, six of whom had died violently. It is quite a record of survival when we consider that the age might have been one of general peace and prosperity for the common person, but one of continual mortal danger for anyone connected with the power structure. In an era when so many sought honors or wealth or high position, Tiberius kept his head down and avoided the scythe that periodically cut down anyone who had grown too mighty. In a period when a change of emperors usually meant that the old imperial staff was cleaned out like ripping out an old ledger page, Tiberius seems to have been the exception. He was always just a bit too useful, and never quite wealthy or ambitious enough to attract lightning. This was the remarkable career of a Roman minister of state, the sort of civil servant who kept the empire functioning amidst irresponsible senators and inept emperors, although he had been born a simple Greek slave.

The Imposter: Alexander of Abonuteichos

The rule of five wise and conscientious emperors between 96 and 181 brought the standard of living within the Roman Empire to a high point. This is the period the historian Edward Gibbon believed to have been the golden age of the human race because of almost uninterrupted peace and prosperity throughout the empire and a series of rulers "who delighted in the image of liberty and were pleased with considering themselves as the accountable ministers of the laws." But at the beginning of the reign of Marcus Aurelius (161–181), after a succession of plagues and disastrous earthquakes and with a growing threat of invasion by German tribes spreading fear and confusion along the Danube frontier, a pervading sense of anxiety led to a revival of superstition among all classes from the most ignorant to the gloomy and suspicious emperor himself. As usual, a climate of uneasiness furnished a stimulus to the schemes of quacks and rogues; the king of them all was Alexander, the prophet of Abonuteichos.

The region of Paphlagonia, of which Abonuteichos was a major seaport, was legendary in antiquity for the coarseness, vulgarity, and general stupidity of its inhabitants. At the same time, the general prosperity of the empire had penetrated to these southern shores of the Black Sea so that gullibility and wealth were to be found in conjunction. In this town, sometime early in the second century A.D., was born a youth of extraordinary qualities named Alexander. His face and form were beautiful, his voice was charming and hypnotic in tone, his very physical presence was electrifying, and if this were not enough, he was endowed with superb intelligence. Nor were such talents to be encumbered by the slightest trace of conscience or moral scruple.

As a handsome boy, Alexander entered the most immediately rewarding career for one of his looks—the profession of male prostitute.

One of his patrons turned out to be a highly successful rogue, a self-professed sorcerer who dealt in charms, curses, love potions, and the like. He made Alexander his protégé and taught him the basic rules for fleecing the gullible, together with a great deal of very real medical knowledge, for every confidence game requires a certain amount of authentic training in some field. When the old man died, Alexander went into partnership with another swindler and spent quite a few years practicing frauds and deceptions of various kinds all over the Greek world, until they managed to extract a sizable lump of capital from a rich and lonely old Macedonian woman.

In Macedon, Alexander had purchased an enormous tame snake, and now the idea struck him: with such a prop and with his own medical knowledge, why not found an oracle of Asclepius, the son of Apollo and the god of medicine? All that was required was a little audacity, suitable preparation, and a naturally slow-witted population. Audacity, Alexander had in sufficient quantity. Some mysterious bronze tablets were hidden in Chalcedon, and when they were found, they predicted the rebirth of the God Asclepius and his father Apollo at Abonuteichos, which Alexander knew full well was inhabited by just the sort of rich simpleton he needed. In fact, when informed of the prophecies, the city immediately voted to build a temple for Asclepius so it would be ready when he chose to make his reappearance on earth. This did not take long. Alexander returned to his home town claiming

Alexander's version of Asclepius was famed far and wide. This human-headed snake and coin were found in the Athenian agora. The coin bears the legend "Ionopolitans: Glycon." (Courtesy, the American School of Classical Studies at Athens)

descent from Asclepius, and although everyone knew perfectly well that his whole family was baseborn, his appearance in an impressive costume was accompanied by the discovery of a number of contrived oracles designed to make him seem a figure of destiny. This impression Alexander furthered by swooning regularly, foaming at the mouth, and feigning madness from time to time.

When he felt the populace had been sufficiently cultivated, he took an empty goose egg, put a newborn snake in it, sealed it up again with clay, and hid it in the footings of the new temple. The next day he appeared in public clad only in a golden loincloth and told the admiring throng in the marketplace to make ready to receive their god. Then, running in a frenzy to the temple, he dug up the hidden egg, broke it open and revealed the tiny snake—an animal everyone knew was the favorite guise of Asclepius. The simple and pious burghers were thunderstruck with amazement. For several days, Alexander stayed in seclusion allowing the excitement to develop, and crowds from all over Bithynia and Paphlagonia descended on Abonuteichos. Then he allowed the mob to file through his house, where he was discovered sitting on a throne with the huge snake looped around his body. Its head, however, was hidden under his robe, and a cunningly made human head hovered to the left of Alexander's beard, its mouth worked by hidden horsehair pulleys, and looked exactly as if it were really part of the snake. As predicted, the throng went mad with joy and awe. Just to think that Asclepius and Apollo should have chosen *their* town to stage a revival!

As soon as possible, Alexander began the oracle business in earnest, emphasizing—as was natural—Asclepius' talents for medical diagnosis and therapy, but also promising to answer any kind of question. To emphasize the dignity of his oracle, he charged 1⅓ drachmas for each oracle—an amount equivalent to two days' wages for a common laborer and quite a bit higher than the price charged at competing shrines. Questions were given to him sealed with wax. These he would accept and answer the next day without ever seeming to have opened the package. In reality, he spent evenings lifting the seals off carefully with a hot needle, or making an impression of the seal and then copying it perfectly. Questions such as "How can I cure my stomachache?" he could answer easily enough by prescribing some common palliative; other queries of a more delicate nature he would answer in vague and archaic verses, after the fashion of Delphi, leaving it to the true believers (and there were thousands) to discover that at least some part of the response would fit any eventuality. At any rate, his success was so instantaneous that a handful of cynics or those disillusioned by absurd responses scarcely mattered.

The establishment of Alexander grew larger and larger as he hired secretaries and assistants and a full priestly apparatus to staff the temple. Then he began to send his people to the big cities of Asia and Greece, some as public relations men to spread word of the fantastic new oracle, and others as secret agents to find out in advance what sort of answers ought to be given to whom. He modestly promised to be able to find runaway slaves, detect burglars and brigands, dig up hidden treasures, heal the sick, and even do his best to raise the dead.

The greatest people in the eastern provinces began to visit Alexander, and for a truly generous fee, he treated them to responses given by the snake Asclepius himself (with the human head wagging and a confederate in the next room speaking through a cleverly disguised tube attached to the snake's "head"). Severianus, the Roman governor of Cappadocia, asked if he ought to fight the Parthian invaders of Armenia, and the snake replied:

> Having humbled Parthians and Armenians under your nimble spear,
> You shall return to Rome and the glorious Tiber water. . . .

When Severianus' entire force was surrounded by the Parthians and wiped out, Alexander hastily changed the recorded oracle to read:

> Better for you not to lead a force against Armenians,
> Lest some man in flowing robes launching grim death
> Against you from his bow cut off the light of life.

Lucian *Alexander* 27

Alexander's agility in such instances actually increased the reverence in which he was held, so word began to reach Rome of this great new cult and oracle in far off Paphlagonia.

P. Mummius Sisenna Rutilianus had had a brilliant senatorial career at Rome, serving as consul in about 155 and governor of one of the European provinces a few years later. Nevertheless, it was well known that this otherwise astute Roman politician was a religious neurotic, eagerly seeking out every new cult or shrine with a feverish desire for personal communication with some deity or other. When he sent servants all the way to Abonuteichos to find out about the reborn Asclepius, their enthusiastic reports spurred him to instant action. He began to subject every aspect of his life to the approval of the oracle. Some responses were not so lucky. When he asked who should teach his son, the god replied, Pythagoras and Homer. A few days later the boy died, and for once Alexander was speechless. But Rutilianus himself came to his defense, saying that his boy, having left this world, was undoubtedly enjoying instruction in the next one from the two sages at that very moment. The old man had outlived previous wives, so in order to make their relationship permanent, Alexander had the god instruct Rutilianus to marry Alexander's daughter, who was said to have been begotten of Selene the goddess of the moon when she had been attracted to Alexander's sleeping form one night.

Despite the most incredible rubbish of this sort, the cult of Asclepius at Abonuteichos became the fashion for the Roman elite. Through friends in government, Alexander was able to have his name legally changed to Glycon, the town of Abonuteichos changed to Ionopolis, and he was even granted permission to issue coinage. Perhaps the crowning moment for the oracle was when the emperor Marcus Aurelius himself asked whether he should cross the Danube to fight the wild Marcomanni, a German tribe currently creating much mischief on the frontier. The god promised victory if two live lions and a quantity of herbs and flowers were hurled into the river first. The ceremonies were duly observed, the animals swam to the German bank, where they were quickly dispatched by the curiously watching barbarians, who were otherwise quite unimpressed and gave the Romans a sound thrashing, killing over 20,000, and eventually penetrating as far as northern Italy. The embarrassed Alexander could only protest that the god had only predicted victory—he had not predicted whose victory it would be.

The career of Alexander is hilariously and savagely portrayed for us by Lucian of Samosata, one of the funniest writers of antiquity. Lucian was by persuasion an Epicurean, a philosophy that denied any sort of divine influence on the lives of human beings. Lucian was himself a personal enemy of Alexander, and he tells us how the Epicureans and Christians of Paphlagonia—normally bitter foes—joined together in an attempt to expose and humiliate Alexander. But the popularity of the cult was far too great; in fact, it was dangerous to criticize it, for the oracle could easily unleash a mob of religious fanatics against any impious attacker. Moreover, as Lucian found out when he attempted to proceed legally against the shrine, it was protected by eminent Romans like the befuddled Rutilianus. Even Alexander's custom of having pretty choir boys sent to him to debauch was overlooked by the faithful; in fact, men boasted that their wives had been seduced by the handsome prophet.

It is a bit disconcerting to think that people normally as clever as the Greeks and as astute as the Romans should be taken in by such an obvious fraud. Sheer audacity combined with novelty and a promise of easy answers during an age of anxiety seem to have assured Alexander of his success. In addition, Alexander was a true professional: he prepared well and labored long hours to create his cult. With his looks, his presence, his quick wits and capacity for endless scheming, he might even have become emperor or something very close to it, if he had been aimed in a different direction at the right time. As it was, he was able to influence emperors, to make imperial policy, to amass riches, and to keep life around him interesting at all times, if not particularly savory.

The Philosopher: Hypatia of Alexandria

The emperor Constantine gave Christianity a favored status throughout the empire. Once it could compete on an equal basis, various attractions of the religion drew throngs of new worshipers and helped it outdistance its closest rivals. In 361, the emperor Julian—by education and inclination a Greek humanist and pagan—sought to reverse the trend by a number of laws designed to make Christianity difficult, if not completely illegal. There is no way to tell how successful this policy might have been if it had been continued for a generation. But Julian was killed fighting the Persians, and his successors reconfirmed the semiofficial position of Christianity as the state religion. The emperor Theodosius I (378–395), a violently devout man, did everything in his power to impose orthodoxy upon his subjects, going so far as to close down the two greatest Panhellenic pagan institutions, the Olympic Games and the oracle of Apollo at Delphi. Apollo, in fact, had himself predicted the end of his worship thirty years previously, sending to the emperor Julian this sad message from his Delphic priestess:

> Fallen lies the well wrought hall.
> Phoebus has no longer a chamber, nor laurel of prophecy,
> Nor murmuring spring; the water of speech is halted.
>
> Philostorgius *Historia Ecclesiastica* 7. 77

Despite the triumph of Christianity, paganism flourished in many parts of the empire—particularly large urban centers with a long history of culture and intellectual pursuits. An intellectual elite all the more ardently espoused pagan philosophies in Athens, Antioch, and Alexandria, and the Platonic Academy flourished until it was closed by decree in the year 529. Most of the major philosophical schools survived by contributing to the synthesis known as Neoplatonism, an eclectic system of ethical rationalism taught most influentially by Plotinus (205–270), who spent most of his life at Rome as the center of a circle of important and powerful individuals.

By its very vagueness, its tolerance, and its appeal to reason, Neoplatonism was doomed when faced by the crusading zeal (and violent intolerance) of early Christianity. In a troubled world, it offered little in the way of concrete answers or even ideals, and the writings of Plotinus somehow lacked the passion and zest of the Gospels:

> The Good is not at all in want of intellectual perception. For there is not any thing else beside itself which is the good of it; since when that also which is different from the Good intellectually perceives it, it does this in consequence of being boniform, and possessing a similitude to the good. It likewise intellectually perceives that which it sees, as good and desirable to itself; and in consequence of receiving as it were the imagination of good.   Plotinus *Enneads* 5. 6

Such profundities were hardly designed to set souls aflame and make people thirst after righteousness.

Alexandria had always resisted control by outside powers, feeling itself almost a sovereign state, at least in the cultural sense, and this situation persisted even when the state began officially to frown on paganism. In late-fourth-century Alexandria, pagan philosophy and learning still flourished as they had in the days of the Ptolemies, so that an inhabitant of this sprawling city of millions on the Egyptian coast might never have guessed that elsewhere in the empire cities lay dying, famine and decay were to be seen everywhere, and barbarians were spilling across every mountain pass and ford. In Alexandria, the emphasis remained on style and learning; one of the most learned of the Alexandrian aristocracy was the mathematician Theon. About 370, a daughter was born to Theon and his wife, and they realized very soon that their girl was possessed of an extravagant intelligence, even by Alexandrian standards.

Hypatia began her scholarly career as a mathematician, like her father, writing commentaries on astronomy and on conic sections. But her mind refused to be limited by one or two narrow fields, and like so many Greek thinkers before her, she took all philosophy as her province. By the time she was twenty-five, she was famous throughout the eastern Mediterranean and was attracting students from everywhere who flocked to her lectures and surrounded her wherever she went. She could commonly be seen in the streets of Alexandria, a woman of great beauty and charm but dressed in a simple philosopher's cloak, with a great entourage of students or fellow scholars, discoursing on some thorny problem from the works of Plato, Aristotle, Pythagoras, or the more recent Plotinus. Despite her beauty, she resolutely rejected suitors, and a rather vulgar anecdote graphically demonstrates her revulsion for the physical aspects of love.[3] But she had many devoted male friends: students, scholars, statesmen, and fellow philosophers. When deep in the excitement of learned conversation, in that exercise of the intellect so many Greeks regarded as the highest form of human activity, sexual distractions were forgotten in an even more passionate communion of minds.

One of her dearest friends was Synesius of Cyrene, who came from a city 500 miles to the west on the Libyan coast. As a young man, Synesius was drawn to Neoplatonism by the lectures of Hypatia, and their relationship ripened into a warm and tender friendship that persisted even when he married a Christian girl, was himself gradually converted, and eventually became bishop of Ptolemais at home in Libya. Synesius is a fascinating character—an example of the best sort of Greek intellect hanging on in a world where all culture and all civilized

---

[3] *Suda* s.v. "Hypatia."

institutions seemed to be dying. The light still burned in Alexandria, and Hypatia could pursue her career almost oblivious to political crises and the encroachment of savage tribes, but just a few score miles outside the Egyptian capital barbarism was beginning to close in. In Libya, the thoughtless economies of an incompetent bureaucracy had withdrawn needed militia; the letters of Synesius are full of horror stories about the wild Libyan tribes, which had begun a systematic assault on the civilized centers on the coast. Starting as a private citizen from an old aristocratic family and then more actively as churchman and bishop, Synesius was a model of statesmanship, seeing his civic duty and performing it without fear in the tradition of Solon or Socrates. Many of his letters to the court at Constantinople plead for military assistance, or even just weapons. Later on, as bishop, he did not hesitate to excommunicate a psychopathically cruel local magistrate.

Synesius' hymns foreshadow one of the great art forms of the Middle Ages—the Christian liturgy. But in his later years, nearly insane with grief over the death of his last surviving child, it was to the pagan Hypatia he wrote: "mother, sister, and teacher," he calls her in a sad and touching letter that symbolizes the despair many Greeks must have felt as the shadows lengthened across the classical landscape (*Letter 16*). Whether Hypatia could understand this despair amidst the almost unchanged pace of Alexandrian life we do not know, but her life too was shortly to end, not in quiet resignation, like Synesius, but in hideous violence—so completely foreign to her whole existence and to everything she stood for.

In 412, when Hypatia had become a distinguished maiden lady of middle age and was still the most sought-after pagan philosopher of the city, the bishop Cyril succeeded his uncle as Patriarch of Alexandria, a position in the Christian hierarchy second only to the treasured See of Constantinople. By nature, Cyril was arrogant, intolerant, and capable of vicious hatred. As a youth, he had spent five years as a devotee of the monks of Nitria, a debased commune of fanatics in the western desert who were little better than brigands with an excess of pious self-righteousness. Even while in the desert, Cyril feverishly pursued his studies of Christian doctrine. In the words of the eighteenth-century historian Edward Gibbon, "He extended round his cell the cobwebs of scholastic theology, and meditated the works of allegory and metaphysics, whose remains, in seven verbose folios, now peaceably slumber by the side of their rivals."[4]

When he became patriarch, Cyril swiftly embroiled himself in the potentially most incendiary issues of the city. First of all, he deprived a harmless Christian sect of their place of worship and their other

---

[4] E. Gibbon, *Decline and Fall of the Roman Empire*, Everyman's Library Edition, vol. 5 (New York: E. P. Dutton & Co.), p. 12.

paraphernalia on the grounds of heresy. But he was just warming up for a major coup. One morning he led a carefully collected mob in destroying the houses and businesses of the Alexandrian Jewish community, whose rights and interests had been legally recognized by 700 years of Ptolemaic and Roman statutes. The prefect of Egypt, a friend and disciple of Hypatia named Orestes, now remonstrated with the intemperate patriarch, whose response was to appeal to the friends of his youth: 500 wild Nitrian monks came in off the desert to provide an unofficial army for Cyril. One day they actually assaulted Orestes as he was riding through the city. One of their number was captured and executed—Cyril gave him the splendid funeral ceremonies usually reserved for martyrs.

Lost in her studies, Hypatia was totally uninvolved in the three-year quarrel between Cyril and the prefect Orestes, who often visited her for conversation despite the fact that he was a devout Christian himself. But now Cyril spread the rumor that the prefect was being corrupted by his friendship with an unclean pagan woman, who dared to mock the Lord by her preoccupation with heretical pagan philosophy. One day, competely unaware of her danger, Hypatia rode into a mob of monks who were waiting along her usual route. She was dragged from her chariot, stripped naked, and carried into a nearby church where she was torn to pieces with pottery sherds. In such a savage manner died a perfectly innocent victim of a complex power struggle, in a denouement as bloody as any devised by classical Greek tragedy. "With her the Greece that is a spirit expired—the Greece that tried to discover truth and create beauty and that had created Alexandria."[5]

SUGGESTIONS FOR FURTHER READING

For Cleomenes see Plutarch, *Agis and Cleomenes*, based in part on Polybius, in part on the lost history of Phylarchus. See also T. W. Africa, *Phylarchus and the Spartan Revolution* (Berkeley and Los Angeles: University of California Press, 1961). For Tiberius see as indicated in the notes and see also A. M. Duff, *Freedmen in the Early Roman Empire* (New York: Barnes and Noble, 1958), p. 153 f., pp. 173 ff. Alexander's career is known entirely from Lucian, *Alexander, or the False Prophet*. For Hypatia, what little we know comes from an article in the *Suda*, an eleventh-century Byzantine lexicon, and from many letters written to her by Synesius. Charles Kingsley's nineteenth-century novel *Hypatia* is not without interest.

---

[5] E. M. Forster, *Alexandria* (New York: Doubleday Anchor Books, 1961), p. 56.

Epilogue

.Let Death come down to slavish souls and craven heads
With his sharp scythe and barren bones, but let him come
To this lone man like a great lord to knock with shame
On his five famous castle doors, and with great awe
Plunder whatever dregs that in his sturdy body still
Have not found time, in its great fight, to turn from flesh
And bone into pure spirit, lightning, joy and deeds.
The archer has fooled you, Death, he's squandered all your goods,
Melted down all the rusts and rots of his foul flesh
Till they escaped you in pure spirit, and when you come,
You'll find but trampled fires, embers, ash and fleshy dross.[1]

FIFTEEN CENTURIES separate Hypatia and the giant of modern Greek literature quoted above, whose latter-day Odysseus hurled such defiance at approaching death. It seems a long time for anything characteristically Greek to have survived, particularly when we consider the number of disasters that overtook the land and people of Greece during this time. The very monks who murdered Hypatia were not an isolated phenomenon, nor was her death merely a cruel accident. This event was typical of a long-delayed movement that was eventually to eliminate nine centuries of Greek cultural domination of the eastern Mediterranean. This movement was nationalism—in both Egypt and Syris—and was surprising only because it was so long in coming. The Nitrian monks were Coptic Christians (the word *Copt* is derived from the Greek *Aigýptios*) and in this sense Egyptian nationalists as well. It is paradoxical that a religion as universal as Christianity should have furnished the first vehicle through which nationalism could express itself, but there is no disputing that this took place, both in Egypt and in Syria, where a parallel movement was under way. Because of the intense theological differences that arose with Constantinople, it was with some relief that these regions quietly slipped beneath the tide of Arab conquest in the seventh century.

The loss of much of the Near East meant that the Greek world was pushed back to Asia Minor and the Aegean basin at the very time this

---

[1] Lines 27–38 of Book 23 of Nikos Kazantzakis, *The Odyssey: A Modern Sequel*, trans. by Kimon Friar. (Copyright © 1958, 1986 by Simon & Schuster, Inc.) Reprinted by permission of Simon & Schuster, Inc.

part of the world was undergoing severe attack from a number of invading tribes. The Goths of the fourth and fifth centuries were followed in the sixth and seventh by waves of Slavic peoples who came in much larger numbers and who became a significant element in the population of the southern Balkans. Minor incursions by Arabs and crusading Europeans marked the next few hundred years. From about 1100 on, the specter of the Turks rose in the East, and Greece became a land under siege. The Fourth Crusade never reached the Holy Land, turning aside to besiege and eventually sack Constantinople in 1204. For more than a century, much of mainland Greece was ruled by barons from western Europe while the Aegean Islands and Crete became the domains of Venetian and Genoese adventurers for as much as 400 years more. By bizarre misadventure, Athens fell under the domination of a wandering group of Spanish mercenaries, the memory of whose rule from 1311 to 1380 is reflected in the modern reproach, "not even a Catalan would do that!" The final Turkish conquest in mid-fifteenth century cut off the Aegean basin from intercourse with Western Europe on the eve of the European Renaissance. Almost immediately, the Ottoman Empire began to be manipulated by a number of smart Greeks in the employ of the Sultan, but for almost four centuries, the great mass of the population was treated with a combination of casual brutality and neglect. In some instances, the Turks wrought massive demographic changes, bringing whole populations of Albanians down into the Peloponnesus and onto the Aegean Islands.

The Greek War of Independence (1821–1829) attracted the attention of all Europe, as well as eventual military assistance from the great powers. In subsequent decades, an increasing swarm of professing philhellenes from Europe and America visited the land of classical heroes following the example of Lord Byron, who had come during the war to help the descendants of Leonidas and Themistocles and who died during the siege of Mesolonghi. "For Greeks a blush—for Greece a tear," Byron had said in disillusioned wonder, and in general, the initial reaction of the early travelers was disappointment. They ventured into a land glorified by poets and philosophers—a land whose ancient artists and sculptors had depicted a godlike race of marble heroes and beauties—and found dirt, squalor, brutality, and ignorance on every hand. Crippled beggars crowded the steps of the Parthenon, and in the sordid alleys of Sparta and Thebes, flies crawled on the faces of children. Part of this dismal picture could be blamed on the degradation of the Turkish occupation, but as time went on, it seemed to European observers, no matter how sympathetic, that the land of wit, light, and philosophy had somehow become peopled with an apathetic, incompetent race composed equally of simpletons and brigands.

As early as 1830 a young German scholar had looked to Slavic and Albanian population movements for the explanation. According to Jacob Fallmerayer:

> The Hellenic race in Europe has been exterminated. . . . Not one drop of pure, unmixed Hellenic blood flows in the veins of the Christian population of Greece today. A storm has flooded the entire Peloponnesus with a new race, related to the great tribe of the Slavs. And a second, perhaps no less important revolution caused by the migration of the Albanians into Greece has completed the destruction. Scythian Slavs, Illyrian Arnauts, children of midnight lands, blood relatives of the Serbs, Bulgars, Dalmatians, and Muscovites—these are the people whom we call Hellenes today and whose ancestry, to their own astonishment, we trace back to Perikles and Philopoimen.[2]

The fallacies inherent in his line of reasoning are obvious. First of all, what in the world might "pure, unmixed Hellenic blood" be? It is impossible to guess at the ethnic mix of the first Greek culture that arose during the second millennium B.C. During the next thousand years Greeks continued to intermarry with neighboring peoples, themselves products of intermarriage. All through the archaic and classical periods, Greek men had children by foreign slave women; the laws of most cities accepted these children as pure Greeks. No matter what learned scholars might require of them, the ancient Greeks refused to be racists. As the Athenian philosopher and orator Isocrates said in his Panegyric oration, "The name Hellene has come to mean an outlook rather than ancestry and we call those Hellenes who share our culture rather than our common origin."

During the subsequent Hellenistic period, whatever pure Hellenic race there might ever have been was entirely diluted by mixture with people who had grown up speaking various Semitic languages in the Near East. Yet Lucian, who was Syrian by birth, was as Hellenic as Plato because he was a product of a Hellenic culture.

Later scholars have shown that Fallmerayer had both his facts and his interpretations wrong. Much of the depressing external appearance of Greece in the early nineteenth century was due to abysmal poverty, which it has taken more than a century to alleviate. But characteristic Hellenic traits were there to be seen by anyone not blinded by an idyllic picture-book concept of what Greece ought to be. To cite just one example, on the eve of their struggle for independence, Greeks probably had the highest literacy rate of any people in Europe. When Turkish

---

[2] Translated from *Geschichte der Halbinsel Morea während des Mittelalters I* (Stuttgart: Tübingen, 1830), iii–v.

governors ordered church schools shut down, children crept at night to underground schoolrooms dug out under the foundations of deserted buildings to learn their letters.

A modern world that rejects prejudice and racism of any kind often enjoins us to deny the existence of national character as a barrier to international understanding. But this sort of attitude, with its well-intentioned simplemindedness, is the greatest barrier to understanding. The visitor who expects Greeks to act, or react, like Americans, or Germans, or anyone but Greeks is doomed to perpetual frustration, if not anger. Modern Greeks have an incredible range of attitudes and behavior patterns, which are all their own and which are readily apparent to anyone who dips (even in translation) into one of the richest literatures of the twentieth century or who follows, in an informed way, the various essays and articles perceptive historians and travelers have written about Greece.

Greeks usually know themselves best: in the summer of 1968, an editorial writer for the Athenian newspaper *Estia* had this to say about the driving habits of his compatriots: "These incorrigible modern Greeks let loose all their racial shortcomings as soon as they get behind the wheel of a car: a love of being first, a gross misapprehension based on false pride, obstinacy, careless self-confidence, extreme selfishness, jubilation at breaking rules and regulations, contempt for the rights of others."

One's views of the typical ancient Greek are too often shaped by memories of the wisdom of Socrates, or of the unflappable Pericles, or of the noble serenity and calm on the faces of innumerable marble statues. The Greeks loved the ideal of moderation in all things, we are told, but as a sage observer noted, if this were an easy or simple thing to accomplish, they would never have bothered to inscribe it above the entrance of the temple of Apollo at Delphi. We could certainly imagine Archilochus driving a car much as just described. We can also see these characteristics in the people of Aristophanes' comedies and in the peevish, childish quarrel between Achilles and Agamemnon in the *Iliad*. St. Paul observed that "all the Athenians and strangers which were there, spent their time in nothing else, but either to tell, or to hear some new thing." Although Paul was critical, this was the spirit that kept literacy alive and that makes Greece today one of the most passionate newspaper-consuming nations in Europe.

Everyone who knows the Greeks can supply their own list of characteristics: good humor, volubility, love of noise and excitement, stubbornness, pride sometimes carried to silly extremes, and courage too—one can go on indefinitely. The point is that there must be something in the Greek character that clings tenaciously to the stony Greek countryside, that is maintained despite the invasion of multitudes or occupation by barbarians. In my opinion, it is irrelevant to deal with the question of racial or ethnic purity. For the Greek character is not only tenacious but infectious: over the centuries, Slavic, Arab, Frankish, Turkish, and Albanian chromosomes have been forced to tumble along in the Greek wake. The Greek spirit conquered mighty Rome with minimal difficulty. Through the course of subsequent centuries of deprivation, invasion, brutalization, and reduction to political insignificance, it has been tough enough not only to survive, but to captivate and overturn the unwary ethos of whatever tribe should wander down the spine of the Balkans to gaze with wonder on a wine-dark sea.

SUGGESTIONS FOR FURTHER READING

A good summary of modern Greek history with a useful introductory background is John Campbell and Philip Sherrard, *Modern Greece* (London: Ernest Benn, 1968).

Index